Build your own LEGO Knights Realm

THE BIG UNOFFICIAL LEGO® BUILDER'S BOOK

HEEL

Acknowledgement

Thanks to some pioneers and revolutionaries, some of whom we know in person and admire:

2LegoOrNot2Lego	- Derfel Cadarn -	Karwik	McBricker	T.Oechsner
Arvo Brothers	Digger1221	Lazer Blade	Mijasper	Taz-Maniac
ArzLan	Eastpole77	lego_nabii	Misterzumbi	ted @ndes
Bart Willen,	Fianat	Legohaulic	Nannan Z	TheBrickAvenger
Brian Corredor	Fraslund	LEGOLAS	NENN	Théolego
Bricksonwheels	Fredoichi	Legonardo Davidy	Ochre Jelly	tnickolaus
Brickthing	Gabe Umland	Legopard	„Orion Pax"	Toltomeja
Bricktrix	Gambort	Legotrucks	Paul Vermeesch	x_Speed
Bruceywan	gearcs	_lichtblau_	Pepa Quin	Xenomurphy
captainsmog	Henrik Hoexbroe	‚LL'	RoccoB	
Cole Blaq	Homa	Mark of Falworth	Sir Nadroj	
Cuahchic	Joe Meno	markus19840420	Sirens-Of-Titan	
DecoJim	Jojo	marshal banana	Spencer_R	

A special thanks goes to Christian Treczoks, who supported us with his tremendous castle ruin, amazing trees and other greens for our photo sets.

HEEL Verlag GmbH
Gut Pottscheidt
53639 Königswinter
Tel.: 02223 9230-0
Fax: 02223 9230-13
E-Mail: info@heel-verlag.de
www.heel-verlag.de

© 2014 HEEL Verlag GmbH

Authors: Joachim Klang, Tim Bischoff, Philipp Honvehlmann, Lutz Uhlmann
Layout, Design and Illustration: Odenthal Illustration, www.odenthal-illustration.de
Photography: Thomas Schultze, www.thomas-schultze.de
Translation: Andrew Brown in association with First Edition Translations Ltd, Cambridge, UK
Editor: Ulrike Reihn-Hamburger

Printed in Slovakia

ISBN 978-3-86852-925-8

Content

The authors

Joachim Klang. Also known as "derjoe" or just "Joe." As usual, he's your guide through the book. He never gets tired of hatching new ideas – and, yet again, he's not the only one.

Lutz „El-Lutzo" Uhlmann. He takes our models apart. When he puts them back together again, he often cuts down on the number of bricks needed in the instruction manual. Awesome!

Tim Bischoff. This twenty-year-old is by now a real fixture on the team. With his fresh new ideas he even manages to improve on the models the rest of us have created. You can see straightaway what teamwork can do.

Philipp Honvehlmann. Known as "Maydayartist" online. Full of new ideas and already totally part of our team. Historical buildings are one of his passions.

Christian Treczoks. He might also be called "Lord of the Trees," even though he wouldn't like to be restricted to this area. Some of his other works can be seen in this book.

Foreword

We've been thinking about the things we used to love when we were playing at home as kids. And we realized that we all at some point owned a knights' castle. And that even now, tales of the age of chivalry, of magic and fantasy, still have a very special allure. Now, the LEGO® company has already produced a host of models on this very subject. So we set ourselves the task of creating something new. We were aware that not every child or LEGO® collector has the same amount of material at home, so we quickly designed a modular system for a knight's castle with walls, towers, and a drawbridge. This means that you can just use as many LEGO® bricks as you have available. And the individual modules can always be recombined in different ways, so that each castle can be given its own special shape – with more towers, perhaps, or with longer or angled walls.

In volume 4 of our LEGO® series, we've stayed true to our motto and have produced building materials in three different scales. So in this book you'll again find several Midi- or small-scale models, as well as one Brick Head. But this time, the vast majority of the designs have been built on the usual scale of LEGO® figures.

Even now, however, our main focus is on providing ideas and inspiration, and using the settings we create as a stimulus for people's imagination. We've already come across many original interpretations of models from our earlier designs on the Internet, and we'll be pleased if, yet again, we can allow your creativity to take wing.

By way of introduction, we begin in the traditional way with our 'Tips and Tricks' section. But this time, we start off with some ideas for all sorts of kitchenware and food, on the usual LEGO® figure scale, using small pieces that you can use, for instance, to decorate the table for a banquet in your throne room.

I hope you have a whole load of fun as you travel back in time!

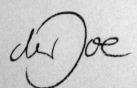

Tips, Tricks and Building Techniques

LEGO®-Geometry

In order to find one's way in the world of LEGO® bricks, essential terms and the LEGO® geometry need to be explained first. For those of you who know our first book „Build your own City", the following pages will be familiar.

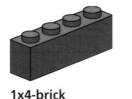

1x4-brick

Generally, there is a difference between bricks, plates, and tiles. Bricks and plates have studs; the surface of tiles is smooth.

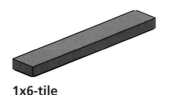

1x6-tile

Brick   **Plate**   **Tile**

The underside of almost all components shows the tubes. They are offset from the studs so that the holes and studs can gear into each other and hence allow for the building with bigger bricks than was possible with the hollow bricks from the beginning of LEGO®. Exceptions are the 1x1 elements that do not need a tube. An element always has one tube less than studs per row.

In order to properly identify bricks, plates, and tiles, you count the rows of studs (with tiles, it's the rows that a plate of the same size would have). Usually, the smaller number is listed first as the width and the larger number comes second as the length. Hence the bricks shown here are:

The geometry of the LEGO® bricks is easy to understand. There are two standard heights: flat elements (tiles and plates) and high elements (bricks). Plates and tiles are always 1/3 of a brick in height. Stacking 3 plates or 2 plates and 1 tile will result in the height of a brick.

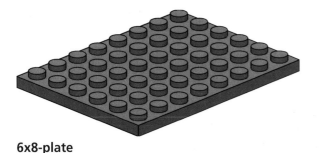

6x8-plate

LEGO® bricks are constructed in a ratio of 5:6. If you want to build a cube, you would have to use a 2x2 brick, a 2x2 plate and a 2x2 tile or four 2x2 plates and a 2x2 tile.

6

LEGO®-colors

To this day, the original colors of LEGO® bricks form the basic framework: yellow, red, blue, white, and black. Green, gray, and transparent followed quite quickly. Recently, numerous colors (by now 120, including specialties like chrome, milky or metallic) have been added to the sets; these colors occur with varying frequency or are rather rare.

Even today, LEGO® builders are repeatedly faced with the problem of not having enough bricks in a certain color to give their model a uniform appearance – particularly in cases of rare colors. That demands creativity. One possible solution is to build the model in the available color. Another one is to reduce the scale in order to get by with the available bricks in the chosen color. Certain elements could be differentiated in other colors to create optical units. Of course, you could also systematically buy bricks in a specific color and implement your idea.

Abbreviations

Several abbreviations and names circulate in the LEGO® fan base:

ABS (Acrylnitril Butadien Styrol) – LEGO® bricks are manufactured primarily from this material nowadays

AFOL (Adult Fan of LEGO®)

MOC (My own creation)

TLG (The LEGO® Group) – Abbreviation for the company itself

BURP (Big Ugly Rock Piece) – fantastic rocky landscapes can be built with these bricks

LURP (Little Ugly Rock Piece) – the small version

POOP (Pieces that can or should be made of other Lego pieces)

LUG (LEGO® User Group) – LEGO® fan base

TLC (LEGO® Train Club) – a LEGO® fan base that focuses specifically on building trains

JUMPER – make one out of two: this is a 1x2 plate that has only one stud in the middle.

SNOT (Studs not on top) – this abbreviation refers to a building technique where, using small tricks, for example, an underside can be attached to an underside or the construction direction can be turned 90 degrees. Some examples follow on the next pages.

Cheese Slopes – sloped bricks
These can be found as
$1x1x^{2}/_{3}$ and $1x2x^{2}/_{3}$ bricks

Food

We've mulled over the question of what tasty food can best be depicted in LEGO® form. You may have seen a few of these ideas knocking around already, but for the sake of completeness we'll show everything together with our other ideas.

Shortly before our photo session, LEGO® released the Ecto-1, with its exquisite cheese grater to go with our celebrated cheese slopes. Then there are the small round 1 x 1 plates in dark red with holes, for the lobster or spit roast.

In the Middle Ages, beer was thought to be suitable for children as, thanks to the brewing process, the wort was to a large extent germ-free, unlike drinking water.

The Exo Force hairstyle can be used as a head of lettuce, the round tile as beetroot, the croissants as chilies – LEGO® can provide you with more vegetables than you think.

The 1x2 door-rail plate isn't easy to find, but here fits perfectly into the curves of the pumpkin.

The tray is an original piece of LEGO®, of course – it comes from the Scala series.

The hands of mini-figures also work as lobster claws.

Scoops of ice cream can always be put to new uses – here as garlic.

Fishes' fins go well with grid tiles.

The recently released LEGO® set Ecto-1 includes an exquisite cheese grater.

These very simple tartlets look really tasty.

… everyone is bound to know this delicacy, and so a jar of hazelnut spread won't stay full for long.

The plate comes from the Friends series with yellow croissants and a round tile – and your helping of fries with mayonnaise is soon ready!

It's not easy to find a transparent red head, but you can also pour in some juice.

In the set of shelves there's a 1x3 bar to connect the radar dishes.

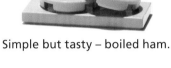

Simple but tasty – boiled ham.

The round 1x1 tile can be used for all purposes – mayonnaise or egg yolk.

Turn transparent 1x1 tiles and panels upside down to make elegant cut glassware.

A golden mini-figure head can be used as a pineapple.

Meanwhile there are enough panels with a hole in, for e.g. spit roasts.

Mustard or ketchup?

A gear level fastened onto the base from below – I always found this looked like mushrooms.

We know: knights didn't have electricity…

Gandalf

I n J. R. R. Tolkien's works, we encounter an ancient world that is mysteriously familiar and encourages us to dream up new fantasies. For our brick heads, we've chosen one of the main characters, in which the design principle can clearly be illustrated.

With a few changes, you can follow the instructions and easily create your own LEGO® heroes.

N

1

1x

1x

2x

2

2x

1x   2x

3

2x

2x

1x   2x

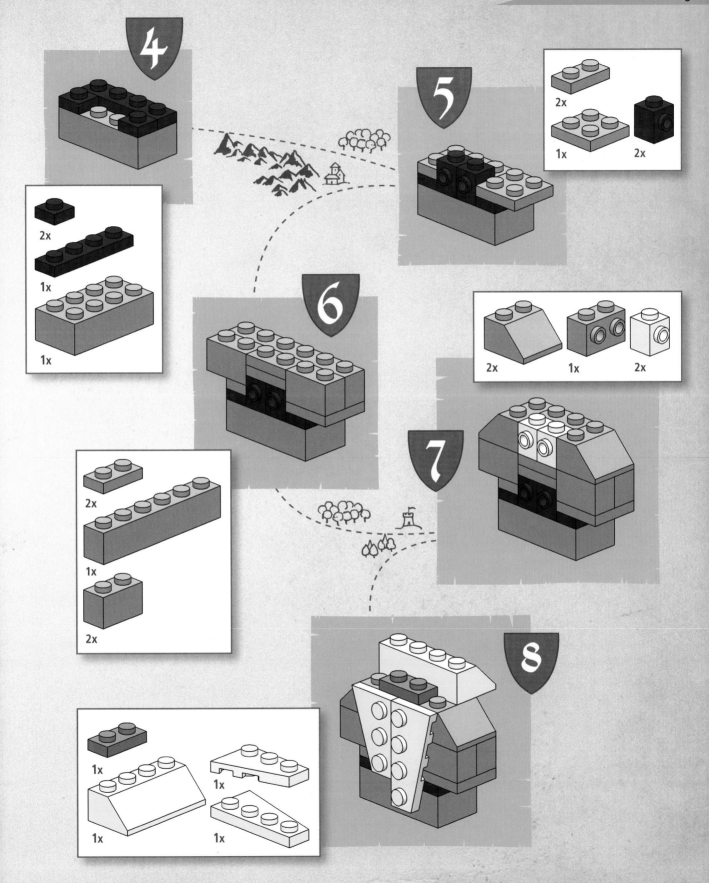

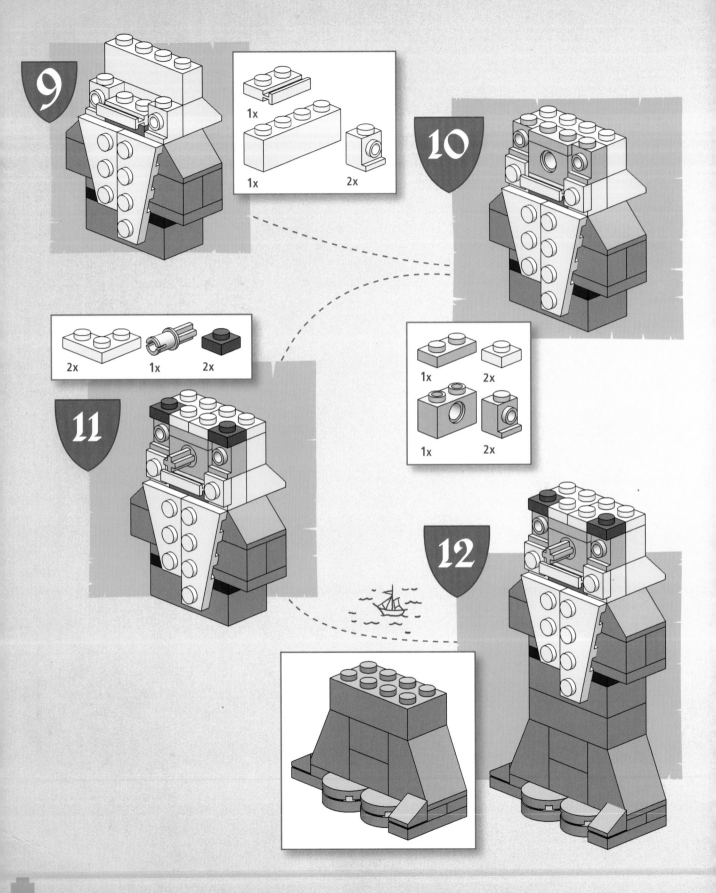

13

1x 1x

1x 1x

1x

1x

2x 1x

15

14

16

17

1x 1x

1x 1x

1x 1x

18

1x 1x

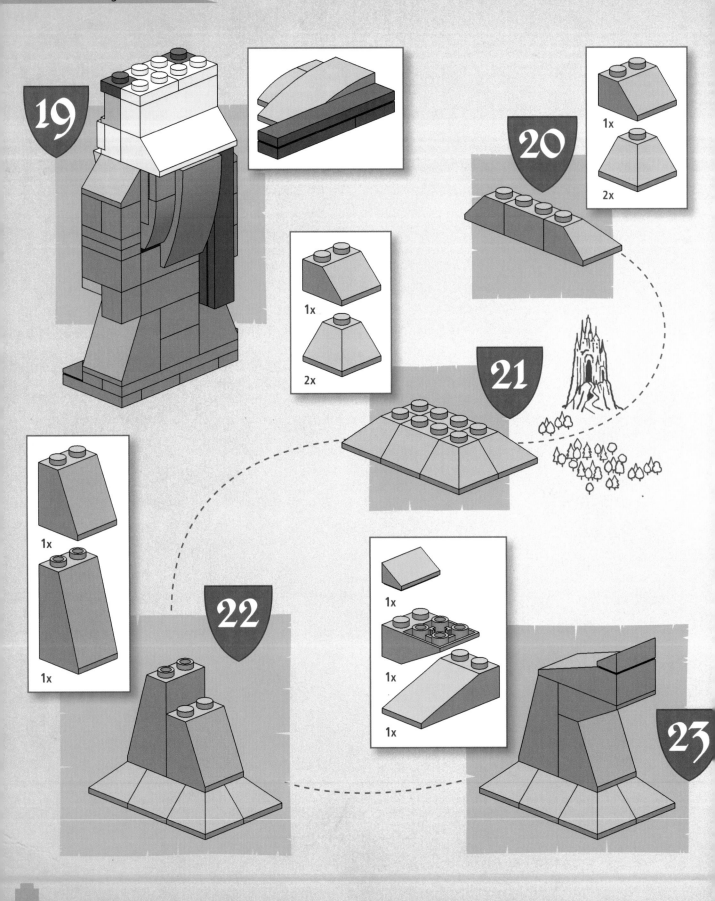

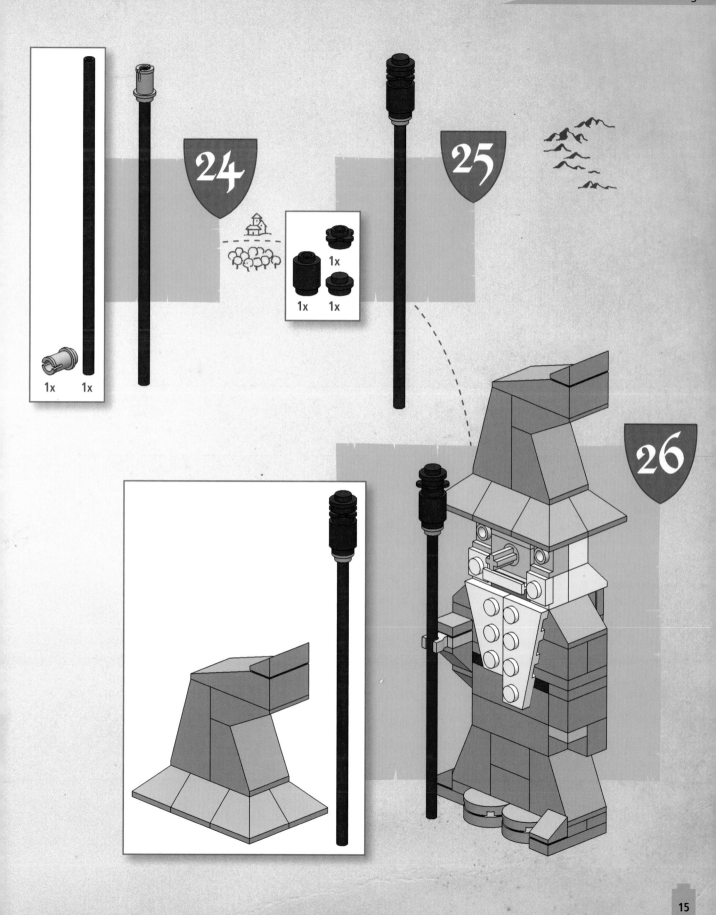

Parts List

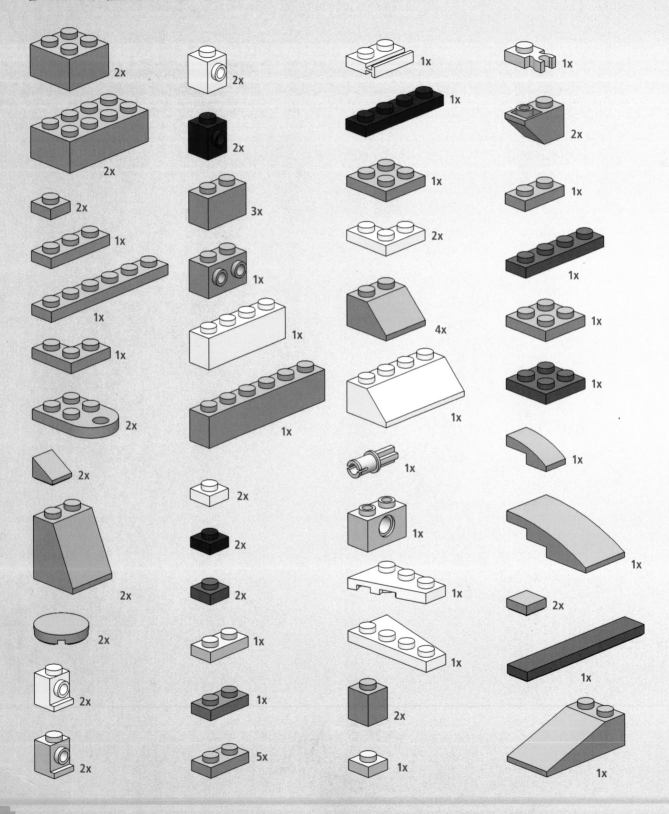

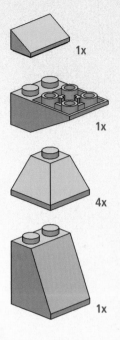

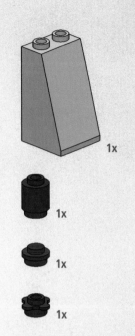

Quantity	Color		Element	Element Name
2		Light Bluish Gray	3003	Brick 2 x 2
2		Light Bluish Gray	3001	Brick 2 x 4
2		Light Bluish Gray	3024	Plate 1 x 1
1		Light Bluish Gray	3623	Plate 1 x 3
1		Light Bluish Gray	3666	Plate 1 x 6
1		Light Bluish Gray	2420	Plate 2 x 2 Corner
2		Light Bluish Gray	3176	Plate 3 x 2 with Hole
2		Light Bluish Gray	54200	Slope Brick 31 1 x 1 x 2/3
2		Light Bluish Gray	3678b	Slope Brick 65 2 x 2 x 2 with Centre Tube
2		Light Bluish Gray	4150	Tile 2 x 2 Round with Cross Underside Stud
2		White	4070	Brick 1 x 1 with Headlight
2		Tan	4070	Brick 1 x 1 with Headlight
2		White	87087	Brick 1 x 1 with Stud on 1 Side
2		Reddish Brown	87087	Brick 1 x 1 with Stud on 1 Side
2		Light Bluish Gray	3004	Brick 1 x 2
1		Light Bluish Gray	11211	Brick 1 x 2 with Two Studs on One Side

Quantity		Color	Element	Element Name
1		White	3010	Brick 1 x 4
1		Light Bluish Gray	3009	Brick 1 x 6
2		White	3024	Plate 1 x 1
2		Reddish Brown	3024	Plate 1 x 1
2		Dark Bluish Gray	3024	Plate 1 x 1
1		Tan	3023	Plate 1 x 2
1		Dark Tan	3023	Plate 1 x 2
5		Light Bluish Gray	3023	Plate 1 x 2
1		White	32028	Plate 1 x 2 with Door Rail
1		Reddish Brown	3710	Plate 1 x 4
1		Light Bluish Gray	3022	Plate 2 x 2
2		White	2420	Plate 2 x 2 Corner
4		Light Bluish Gray	3039	Slope Brick 45 2 x 2
1		White	3037	Slope Brick 45 2 x 4
1		Tan	3749	Technic Axle Pin
1		Tan	3700	Technic Brick 1 x 2 with Hole
1		White	43722	Wing 2 x 3 Right
1		White	41770	Wing 2 x 4 Left
2		Light Bluish Gray	3005	Brick 1 x 1
1		Tan	3024	Plate 1 x 1
1		Tan	4085c	Plate 1 x 1 with Clip Vertical Type 3
2		Light Bluish Gray	3665	Slope Brick 45 2 x 1 Inverted
1		Light Bluish Gray	3023	Plate 1 x 2
1		Dark Bluish Gray	3710	Plate 1 x 4
1		Light Bluish Gray	3022	Plate 2 x 2
1		Dark Bluish Gray	3022	Plate 2 x 2
1		Light Bluish Gray	11477	Slope Brick Curved 2 x 1
1		Light Bluish Gray	93606	Slope Brick Curved 4 x 2
2		Light Bluish Gray	3070b	Tile 1 x 1 with Groove
1		Dark Bluish Gray	6636	Tile 1 x 6
1		Light Bluish Gray	30363	Slope Brick 18 4 x 2
1		Light Bluish Gray	85984	Slope Brick 31 1 x 2 x 0.667
1		Light Bluish Gray	3747b	Slope Brick 33 3 x 2 Inverted with Ribs between Studs
4		Light Bluish Gray	3045	Slope Brick 45 2 x 2 Double Convex
1		Light Bluish Gray	3678b	Slope Brick 65 2 x 2 x 2 with Centre Tube
1		Light Bluish Gray	3684	Slope Brick 75 2 x 2 x 3
1		Reddish Brown	3062b	Brick 1 x 1 Round with Hollow Stud
1		Reddish Brown	4073	Plate 1 x 1 Round
1		Reddish Brown	33291	Plate 1 x 1 Round with Tabs
1		Reddish Brown	71175	Technic Flex-System Hose 12L (240LDU)
1		Light Bluish Gray	4274	Technic Pin 1/2

Orthanc

aruman's Tower in Isengard is shown as the example of an architectural model. Its black color is excellent for creating a replica in LEGO®, as black should be available in everyone's collection of bricks.

We've constructed a platform for our model so that it can more easily be displayed on a desk or shelf, or in a cabinet.

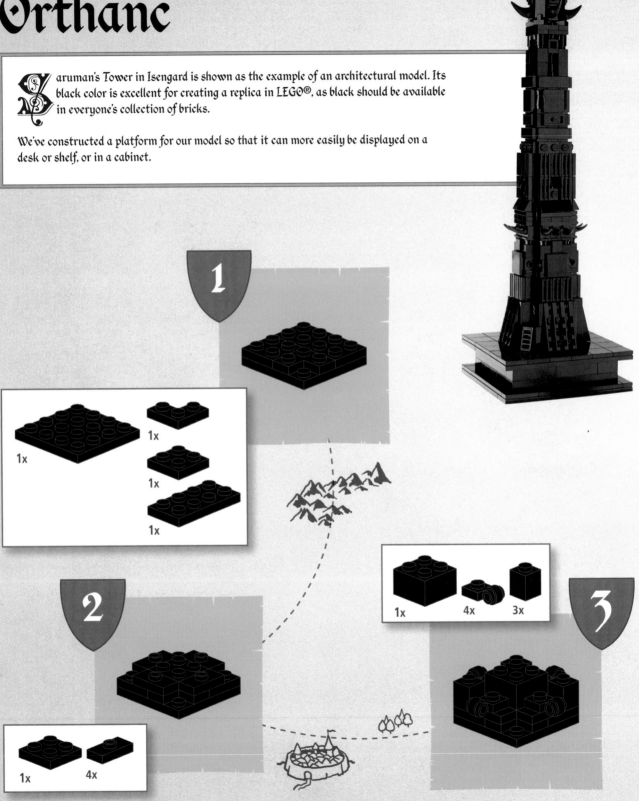

1

1x

1x

1x

1x

2

1x   4x

3

1x   4x   3x

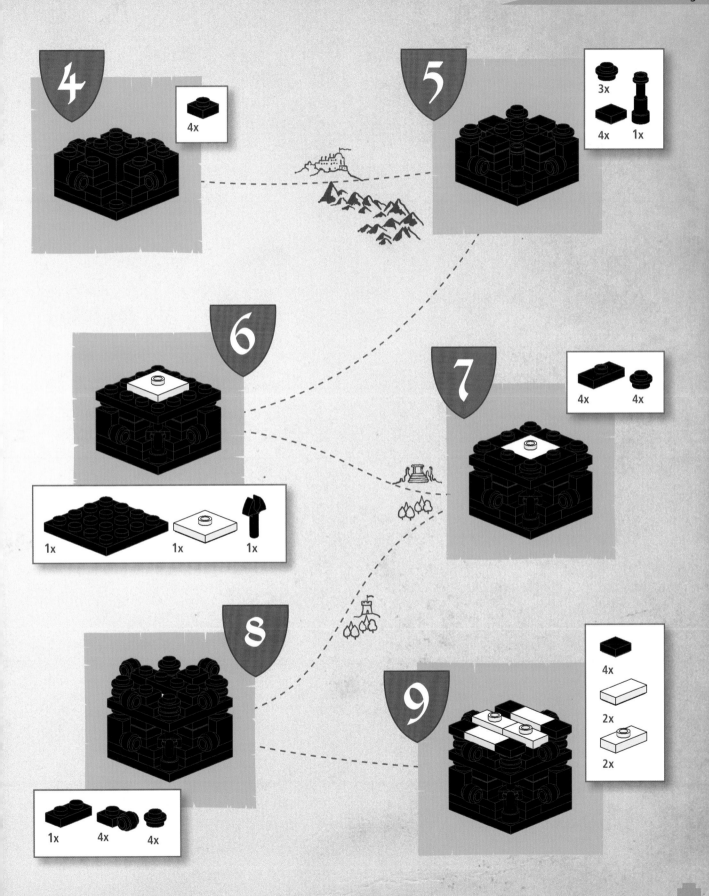

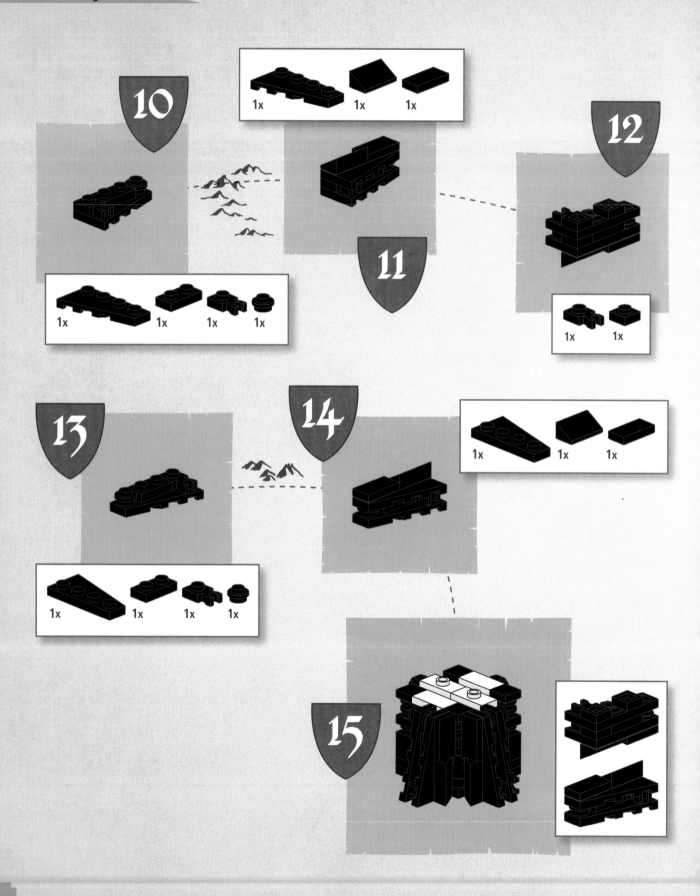

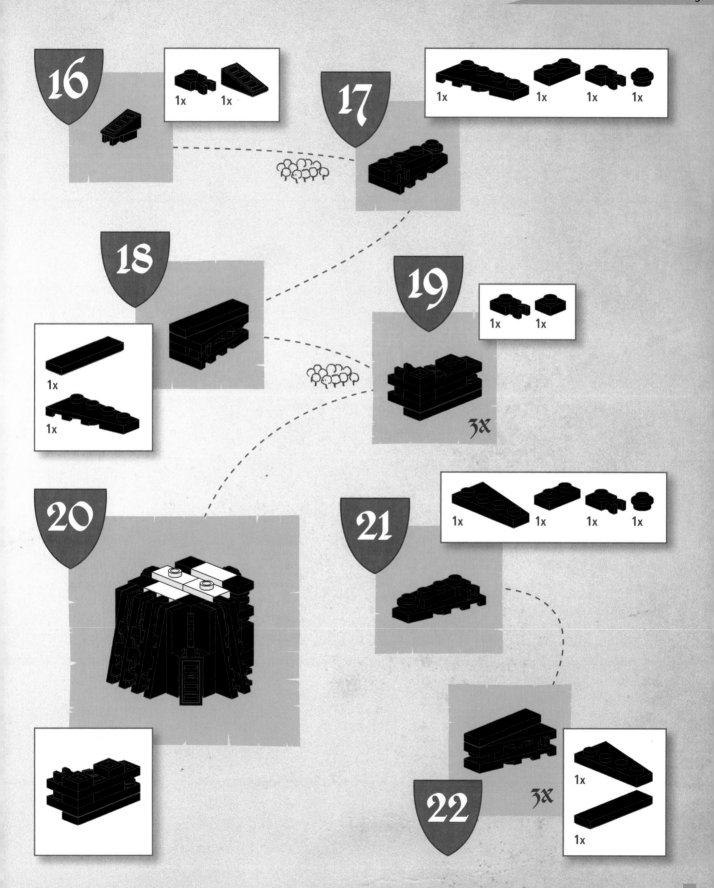

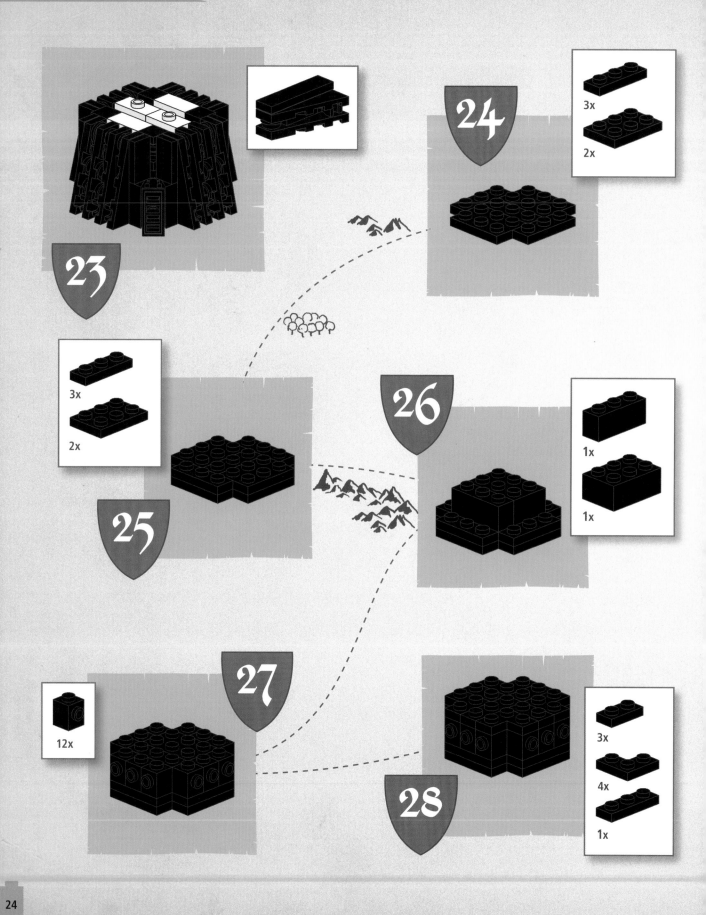

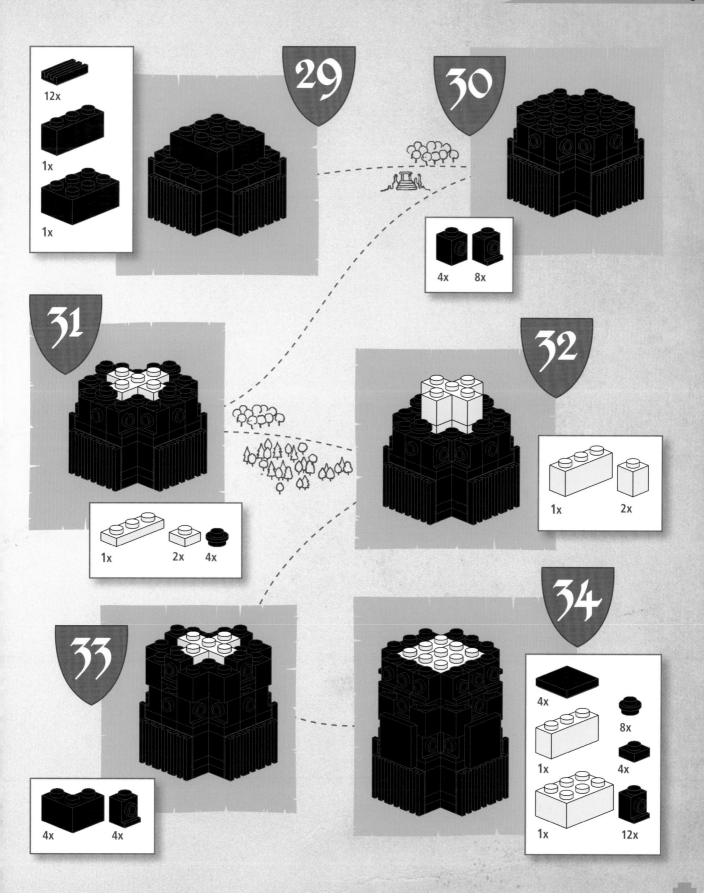

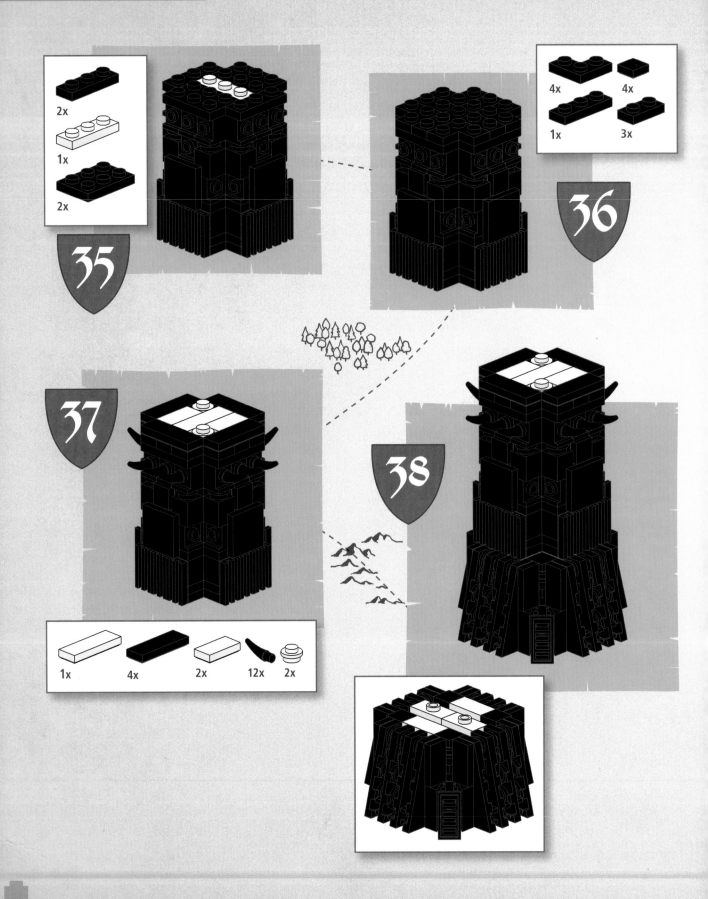

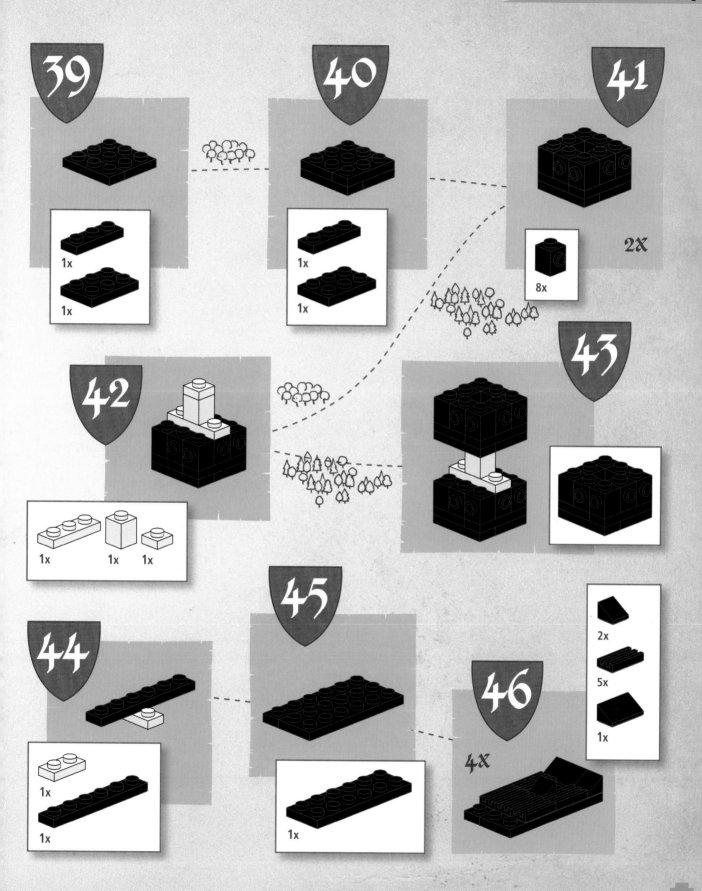

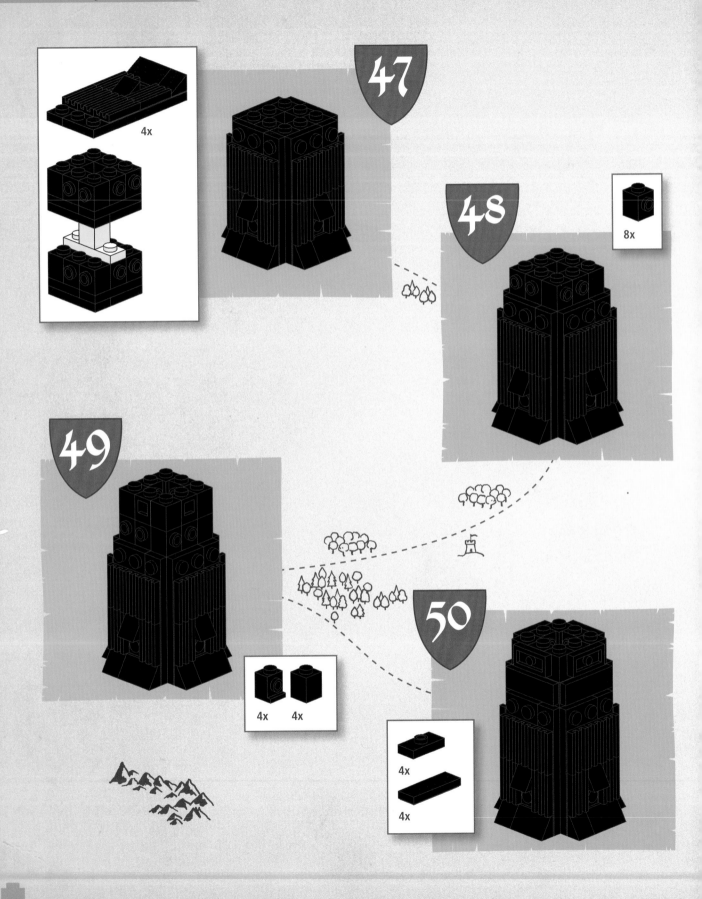

47

48

8x

49

4x   4x

50

4x

4x

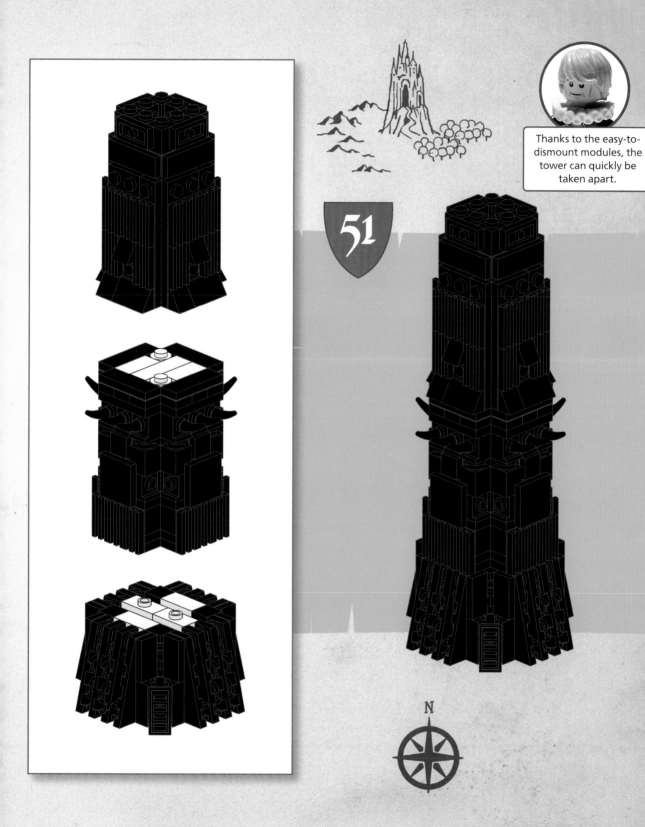

Thanks to the easy-to-dismount modules, the tower can quickly be taken apart.

N

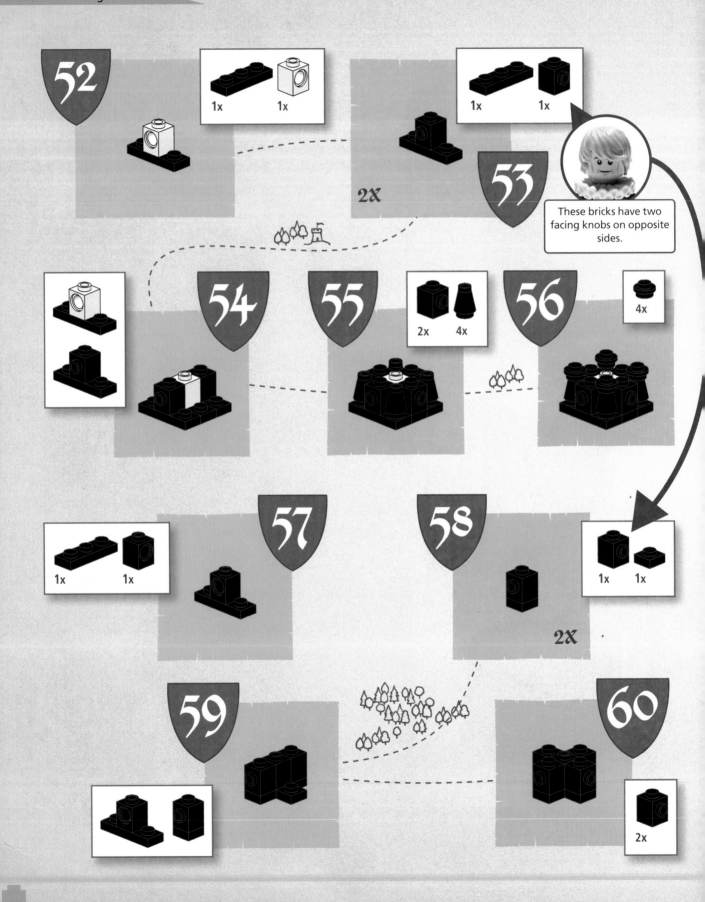

These bricks have two facing knobs on opposite sides.

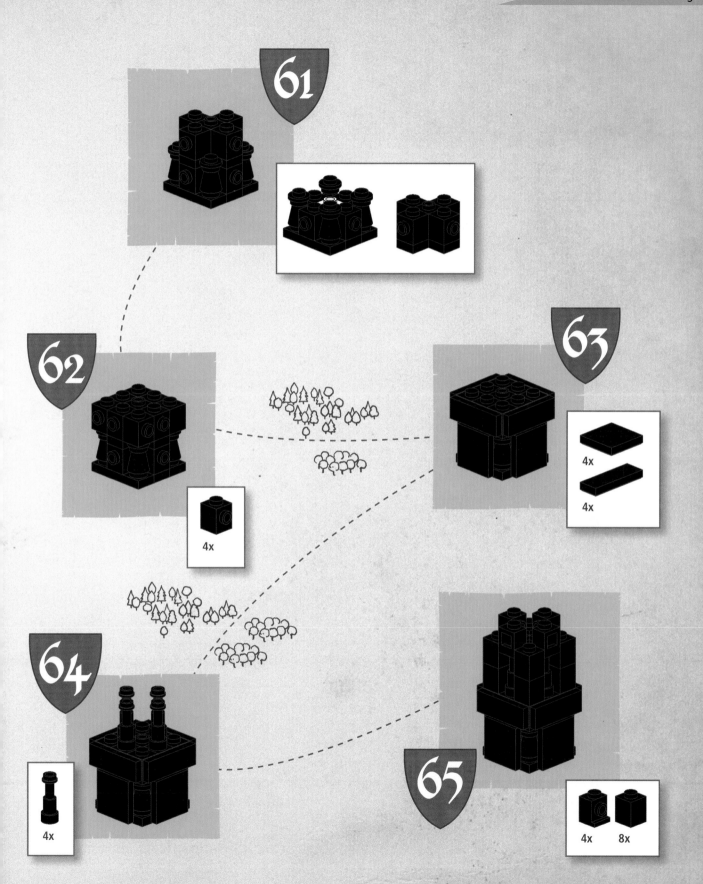

61

62

63

4x

4x

4x

64

4x

65

4x   8x

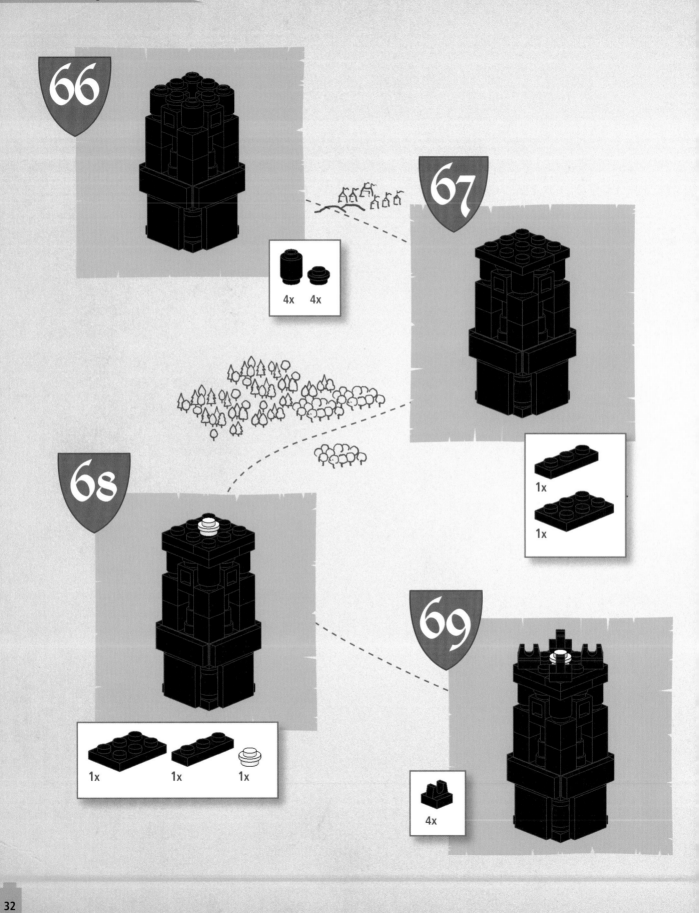

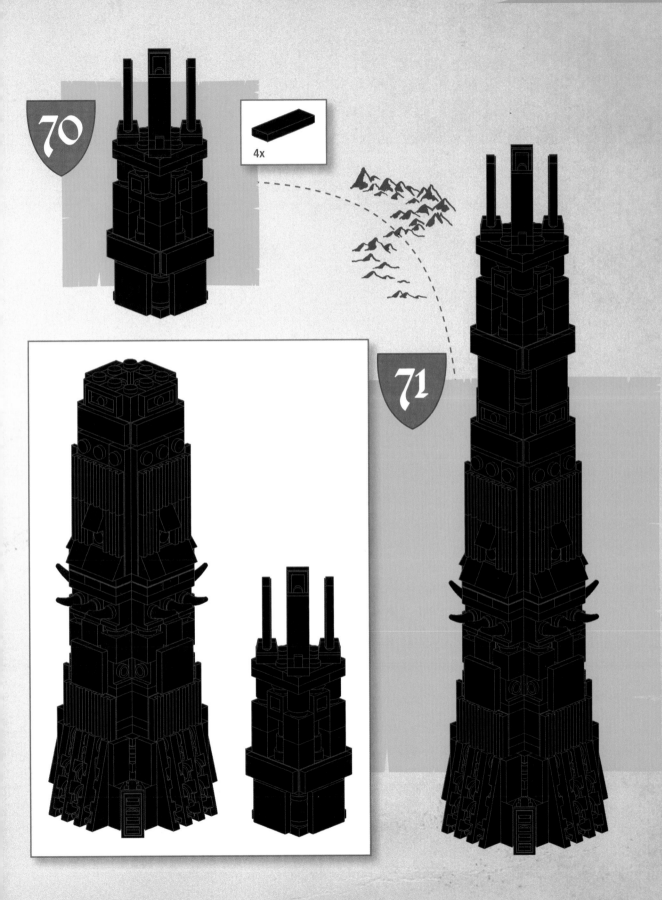

70

4x

71

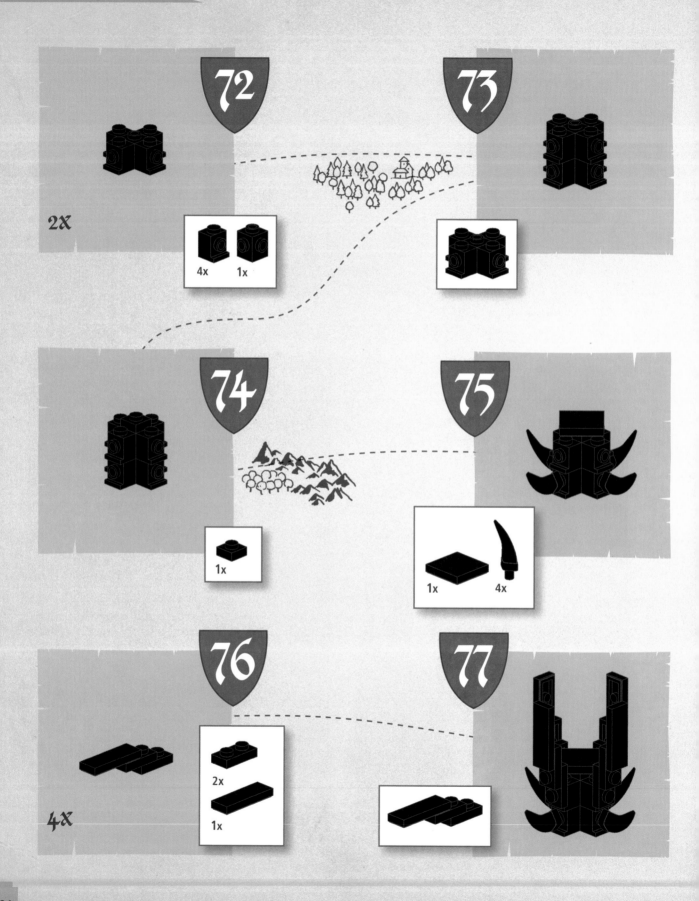

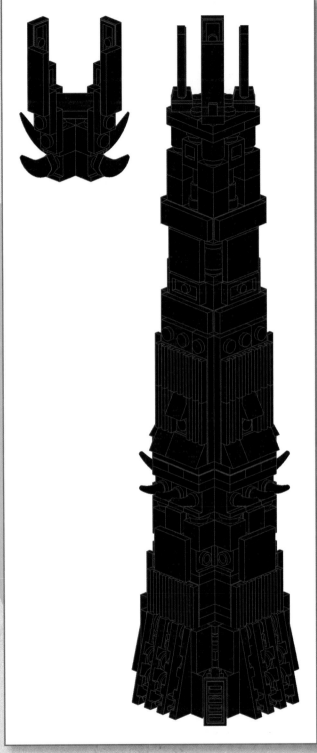

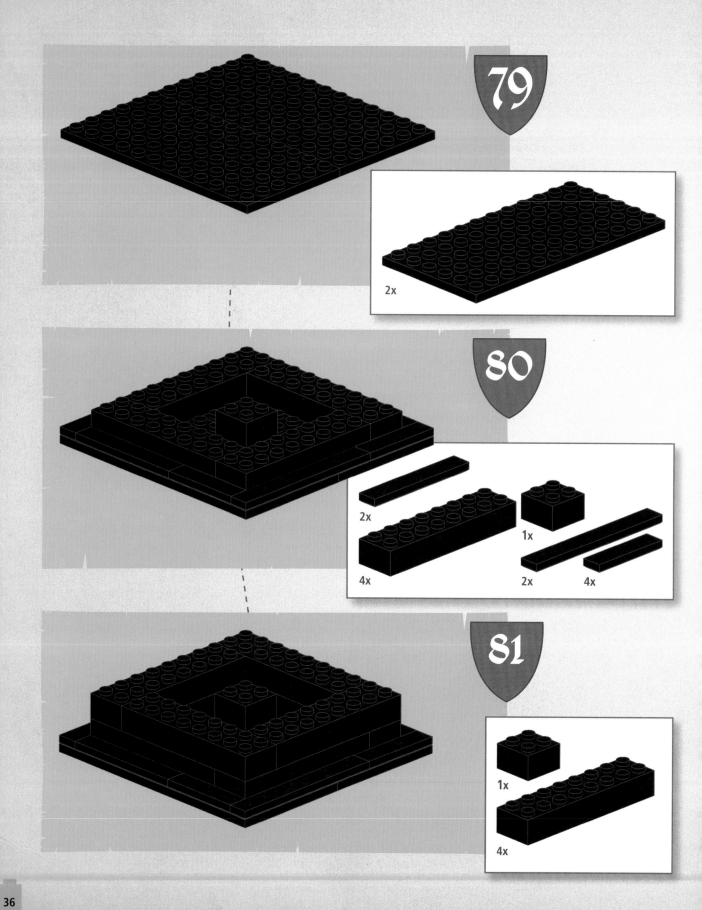

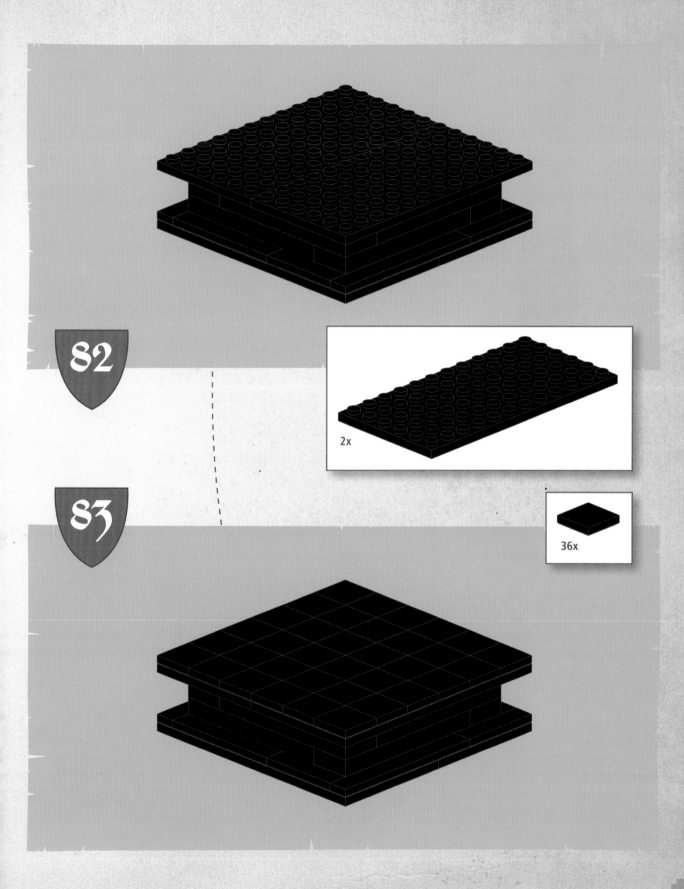

82

2x

83

36x

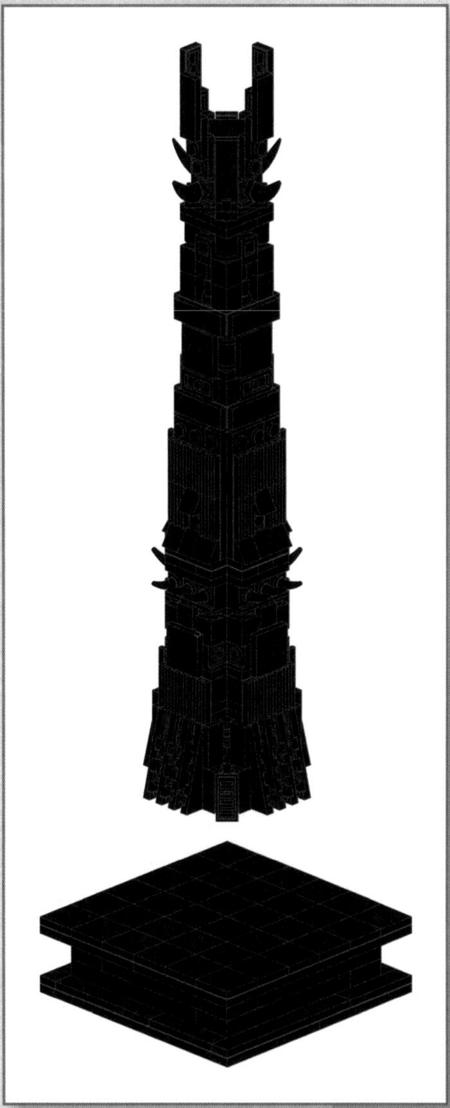

84

Ideal for the display cabinet or the desk.

Parts List

These bricks have two facing knobs on opposite sides.

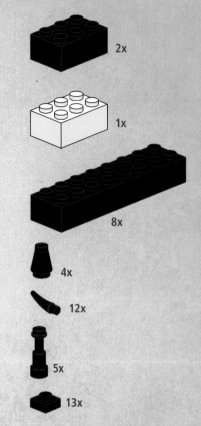

Quantity	Color		Element	Element Name
4		Black	87747	Bar 0.5L with Curved Blade 2L
1		Black	48729	Bar 1.5L with Clip
15		Black	3005	Brick 1 x 1
3		White	3005	Brick 1 x 1
4		Black	3062b	Brick 1 x 1 Round with Hollow Stud
40		Black	4070	Brick 1 x 1 with Headlight
48		Black	87087	Brick 1 x 1 with Stud on 1 Side
2		Black	4733	Brick 1 x 1 with Studs on Four Sides
4		Black	47905	Brick 1 x 1 with Studs on Two Opposite Sides
2		Black	3622	Brick 1 x 3
2		White	3622	Brick 1 x 3
3		Black	3003	Brick 2 x 2
4		Black	2357	Brick 2 x 2 Corner
2		Black	3002	Brick 2 x 3
1		White	3002	Brick 2 x 3
8		Black	3007	Brick 2 x 8
4		Black	4589	Cone 1 x 1
12		Black	88513	Minifig Helmet Viking Horn
5		Black	64644	Minifig Telescope
13		Black	3024	Plate 1 x 1

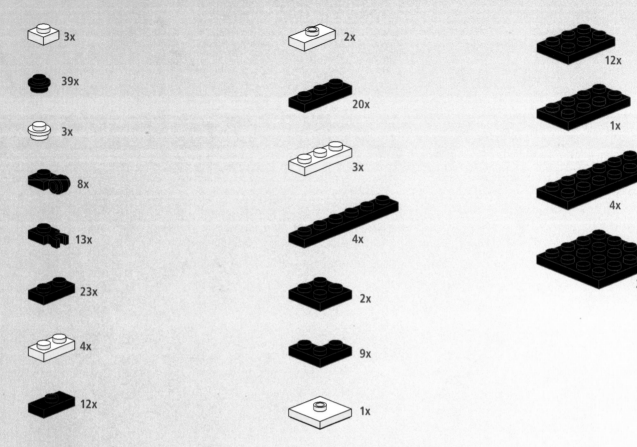

Quantity		Color	Element	Element Name
3		White	3024	Plate 1 x 1
39		Black	4073	Plate 1 x 1 Round
3		White	4073	Plate 1 x 1 Round
8		Black	4081b	Plate 1 x 1 with Clip Light Type 2
13		Black	4085c	Plate 1 x 1 with Clip Vertical Type 3
23		Black	3023	Plate 1 x 2
4		White	3023	Plate 1 x 2
12		Black	3794a	Plate 1 x 2 without Groove with 1 Centre Stud
2		White	3794a	Plate 1 x 2 without Groove with 1 Centre Stud
20		Black	3623	Plate 1 x 3
3		White	3623	Plate 1 x 3
4		Black	3666	Plate 1 x 6
2		Black	3022	Plate 2 x 2
9		Black	2420	Plate 2 x 2 Corner
1		White	87580	Plate 2 x 2 with Groove with 1 Center Stud
12		Black	3021	Plate 2 x 3
1		Black	3020	Plate 2 x 4
4		Black	3795	Plate 2 x 6
2		Black	3031	Plate 4 x 4

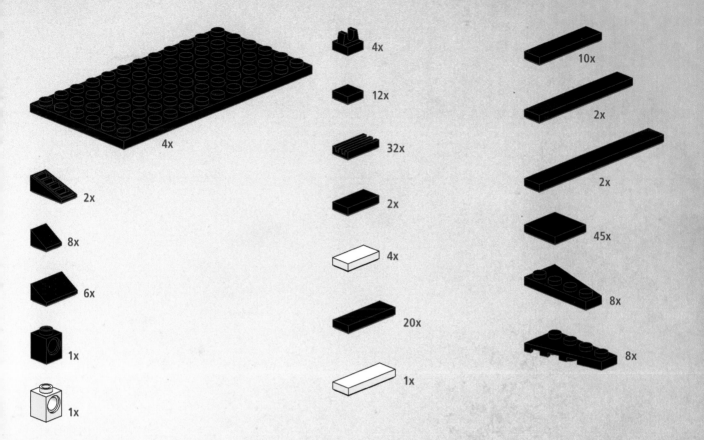

Quantity		Color	Element	Element Name
4	■	Black	3028	Plate 6 x 12
2	■	Black	61409	Slope Brick 18 2 x 1 x 2/3 Grille
8	■	Black	54200	Slope Brick 31 1 x 1 x 2/3
6	■	Black	85984	Slope Brick 31 1 x 2 x 2/3
1	■	Black	6541	Technic Brick 1 x 1 with Hole
1	□	White	6541	Technic Brick 1 x 1 with Hole
4	■	Black	2555	Tile 1 x 1 with Clip
12	■	Black	3070b	Tile 1 x 1 with Groove
32	■	Black	2412b	Tile 1 x 2 Grille with Groove
2	■	Black	3069b	Tile 1 x 2 with Groove
4	□	White	3069b	Tile 1 x 2 with Groove
20	■	Black	63864	Tile 1 x 3 with Groove
1	□	White	63864	Tile 1 x 3 with Groove
10	■	Black	2431	Tile 1 x 4 with Groove
2	■	Black	6636	Tile 1 x 6
2	■	Black	4162	Tile 1 x 8
45	■	Black	3068b	Tile 2 x 2 with Groove
8	■	Black	41770	Wing 2 x 4 Left
8	■	Black	41769	Wing 2 x 4 Right

Jousting knight

You can see from our jousting scene how much we enjoy working on this scale. The size of the board game figures is, in general, very attractive. With just a few pieces you can soon build up bigger scenes.

However, it took us several goes before we were satisfied with the show horse. In contrast to the version described in the manual, you'll also find in the panoramic depiction an equestrian version with a constructed head.

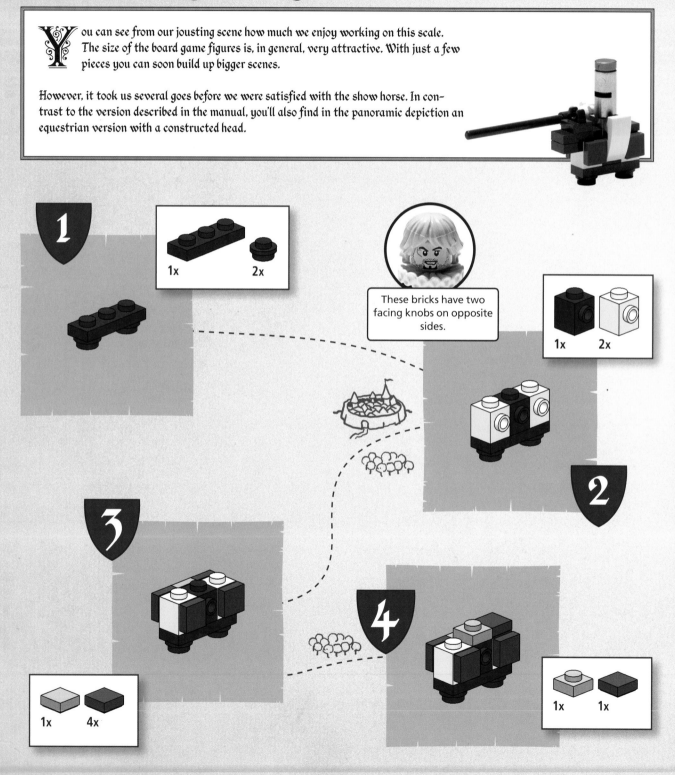

1 1x 2x

These bricks have two facing knobs on opposite sides.

1x 2x

2

3

1x 4x

4

1x 1x

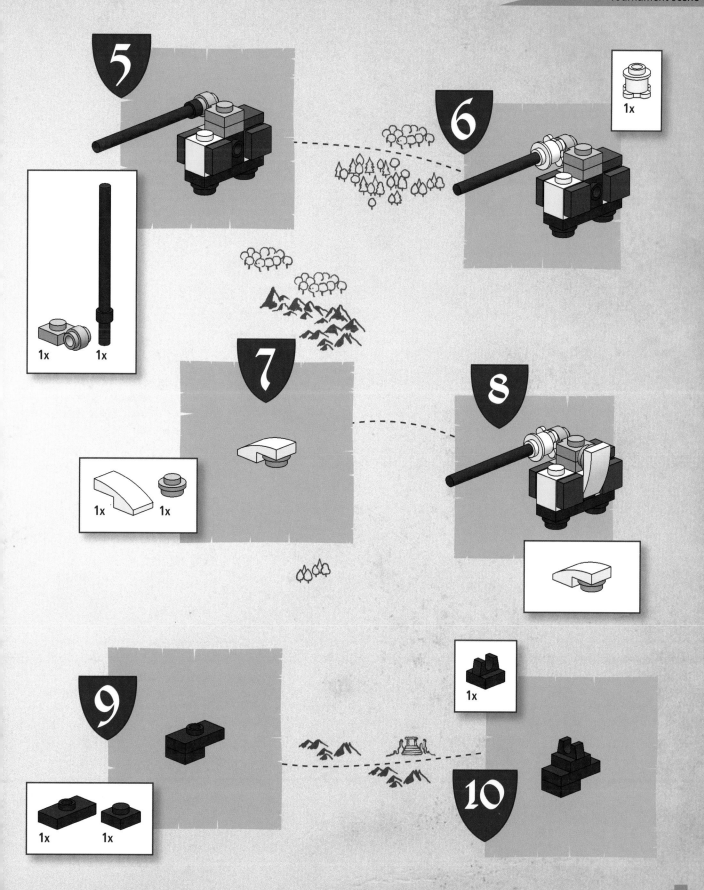

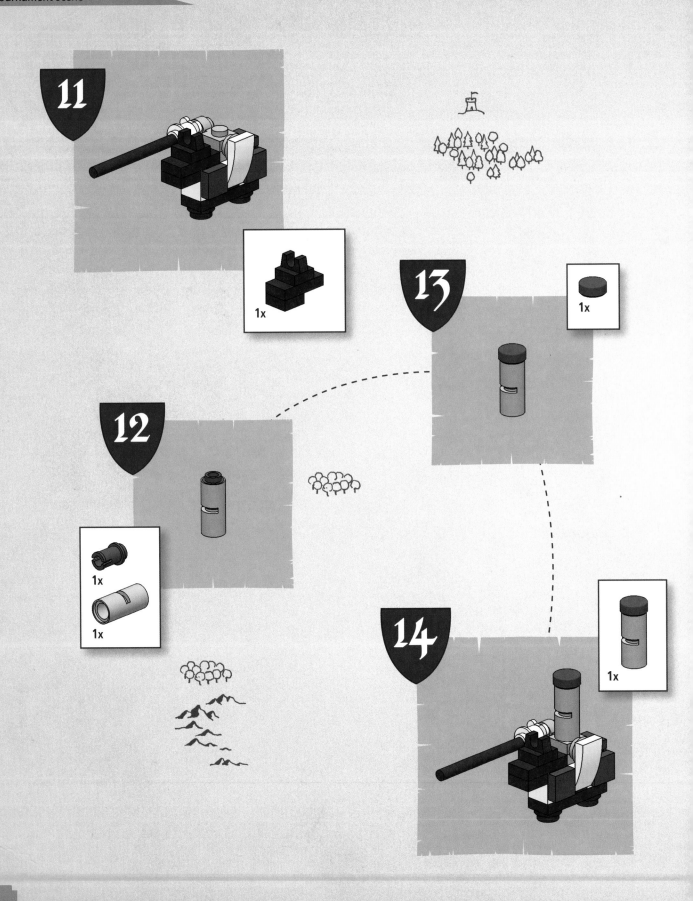

Parts List

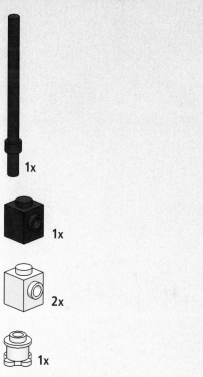

Quantity	Color		Element	Element Name
1		Reddish Brown	63965	Bar 6L with Thick Stop
1		Reddish Brown	47905	Brick 1 x 1 with Studs on Two Opposite Sides
2		White	47905	Brick 1 x 1 with Studs on Two Opposite Sides
1		White	33286	Brick 1 x 1 x 2/3 Round with Scala Base
1		Metallic Silver	3024	Plate 1 x 1
1		Reddish Brown	3024	Plate 1 x 1
1		Light Bluish Gray	4073	Plate 1 x 1 Round
2		Reddish Brown	4073	Plate 1 x 1 Round
1		Light Bluish Gray	4081b	Plate 1 x 1 with Clip Light Type 2
1		Reddish Brown	3794a	Plate 1 x 2 without Groove with 1 Centre Stud
1		Reddish Brown	3623	Plate 1 x 3
1		White	11477	Slope Brick Curved 2 x 1
1		Blue	4274	Technic Pin 1/2
1		Metallic Silver	62462	Technic Pin Joiner Round with Slot
1		Pearl Dark Gray	98138	Tile 1 x 1 Round with Groove
1		Reddish Brown	2555	Tile 1 x 1 with Clip
5		Blue	3070b	Tile 1 x 1 with Groove
1		Light Bluish Gray	3070b	Tile 1 x 1 with Groove

Small tents

ven our smallest knights, of course, need a tent in which they can prepare for their turn in the joust. We've shown a two-color version with awning and flag.

But you can of course build the tents in other shades – in the colors of your knight, for example.

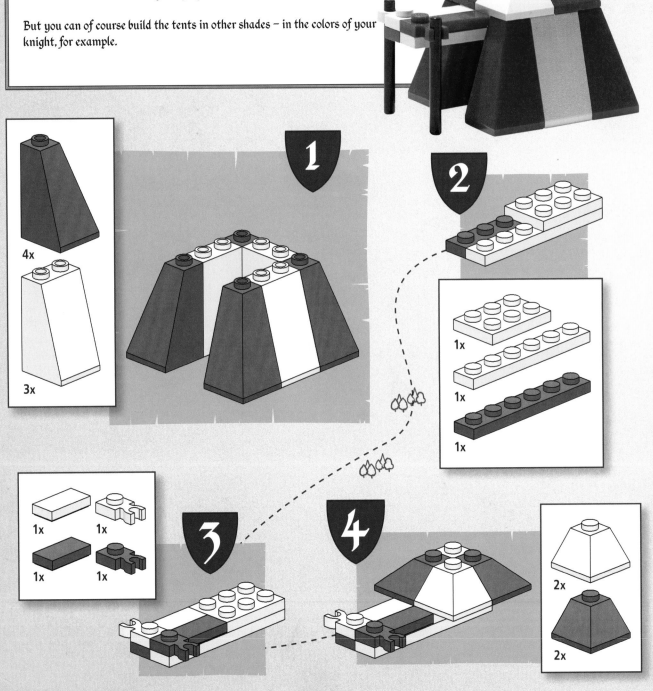

4x

3x

1

2

1x

1x

1x

3

1x   1x

1x   1x

4

2x

2x

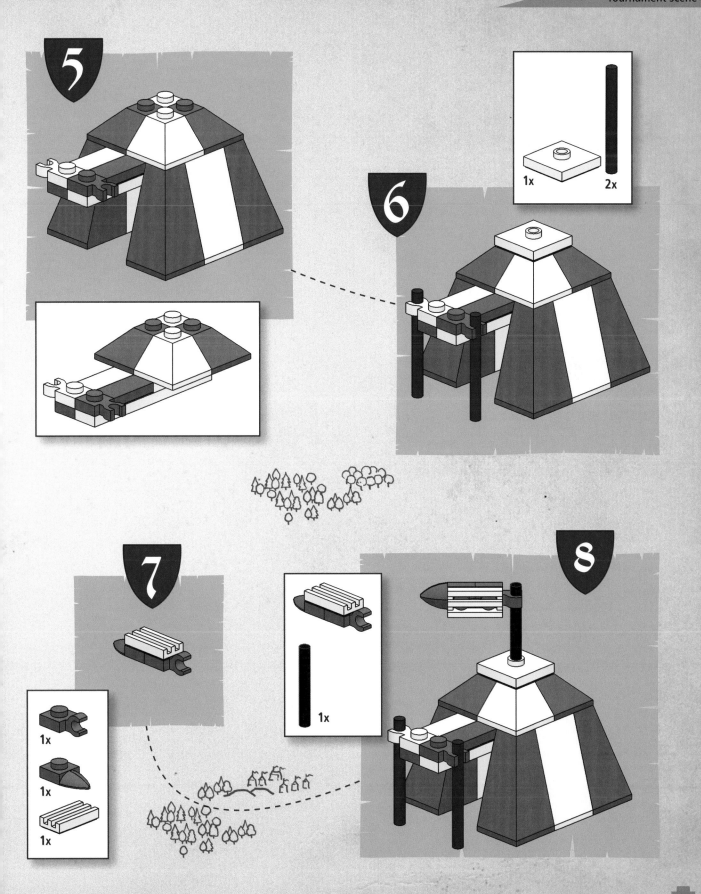

Parts List

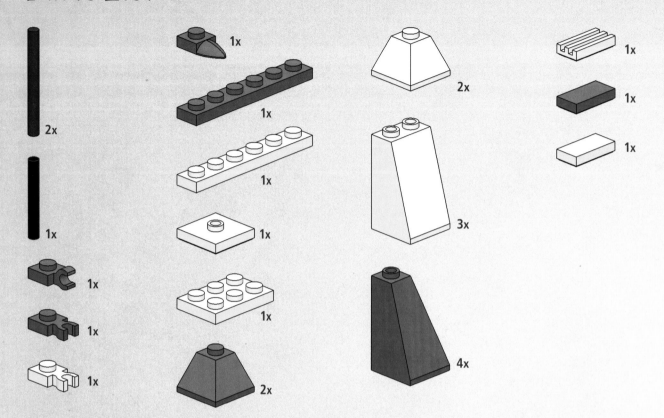

Quantity	Color		Element	Element Name
2		Reddish Brown	30374	Bar 4L Light Sabre Blade
1		Black	87994	Bar 3L
1		Red	61252	Plate 1 x 1 with Clip Horizontal (Open O-Clip)
1		Red	4085c	Plate 1 x 1 with Clip Vertical Type 3
1		White	4085c	Plate 1 x 1 with Clip Vertical Type 3
1		Red	49673	Plate 1 x 1 with Tooth
1		Red	3666	Plate 1 x 6
1		White	3666	Plate 1 x 6
1		White	87580	Plate 2 x 2 with Groove with 1 Center Stud
1		White	3021	Plate 2 x 3
2		Red	3045	Slope Brick 45 2 x 2 Double Convex
2		White	3045	Slope Brick 45 2 x 2 Double Convex
3		White	3684	Slope Brick 75 2 x 2 x 3
4		Red	3685	Slope Brick 75 2 x 2 x 3 Double Convex
1		White	2412b	Tile 1 x 2 Grille with Groove
1		Red	3069b	Tile 1 x 2 with Groove
1		White	3069b	Tile 1 x 2 with Groove

Leafy tree

L eafy trees can have a completely different effect depending on the color and the landscape. A bright green tone clearly indicates a tree in spring, while brown and red hues symbolize fall.

Some of you will recognize these designs from our first book (Build your own city). But as the leafy tree is an excellent conclusion to our jousting scene, we're showing it here again.

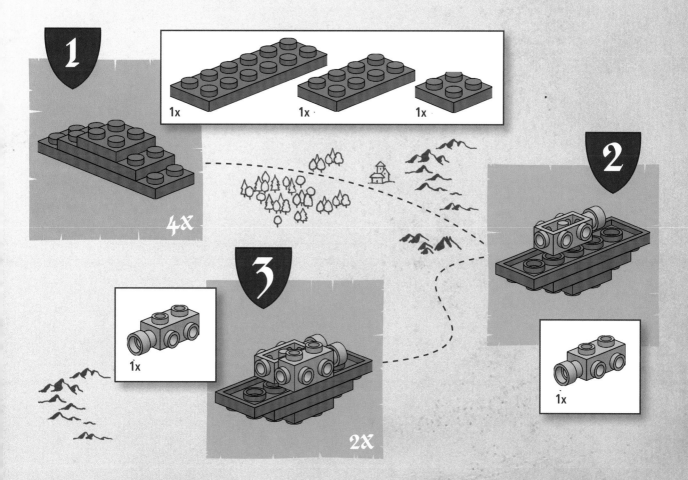

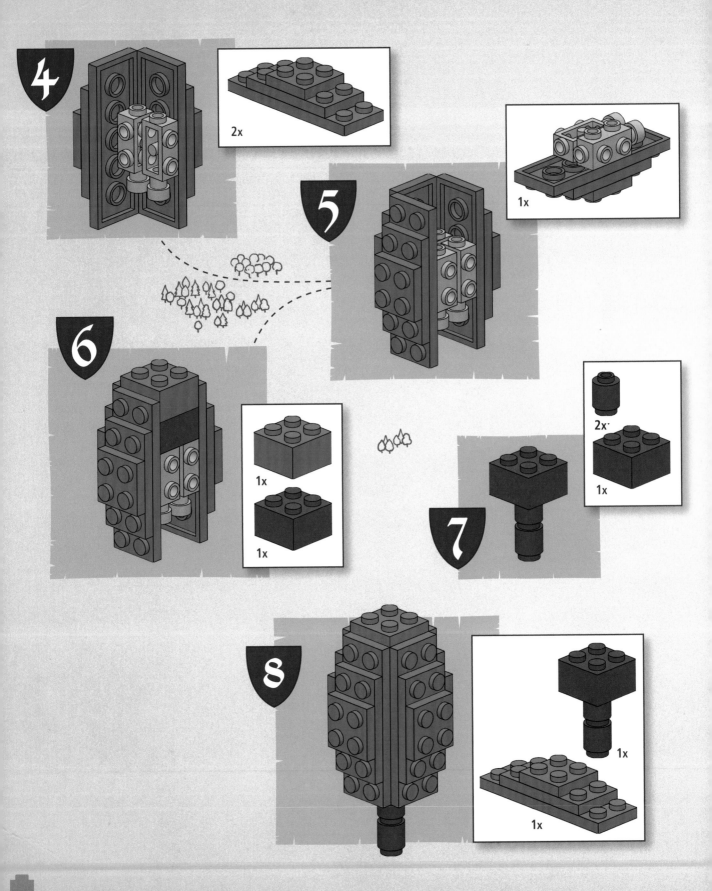

4

2x

1x

5

6

1x

1x

2x·

1x

7

1x

8

1x

1x

Parts List

 2x

 4x

 4x

 4x

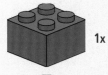 2x

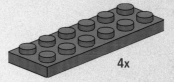 4x

 1x

With bigger tiles, e.g. 2x16, larger trees such as poplars etc. can be built.

Quantity		Color	Element	Element Name
2		Brown	3062b	Brick 1 x 1 Round with Hollow Stud
4		Light Gray	4595	Brick 1 x 2 x 2/3 with Studs on Sides
2		Brown	3003	Brick 2 x 2
1		Green	3003	Brick 2 x 2
4		Green	3022	Plate 2 x 2
4		Green	3020	Plate 2 x 4
4		Green	3795	Plate 2 x 6

Weirwood tree

This highly flamboyant tree with a face carved into its trunk was just crying out to be depicted in LEGO® pieces. We chose the quite special tree on the other side of the wall, in white and dark red, as a template.

But of course any other typical tree colors are just as suitable. If you leave out the face, it's a bit easier.

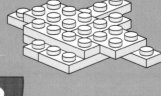

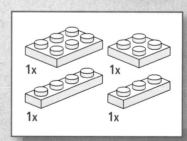

1

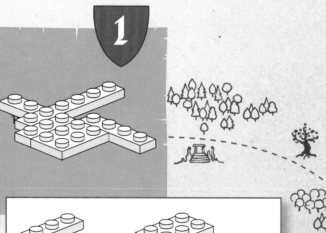

1x   1x

1x   1x   1x

2

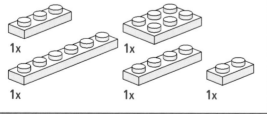

1x   1x

1x   1x

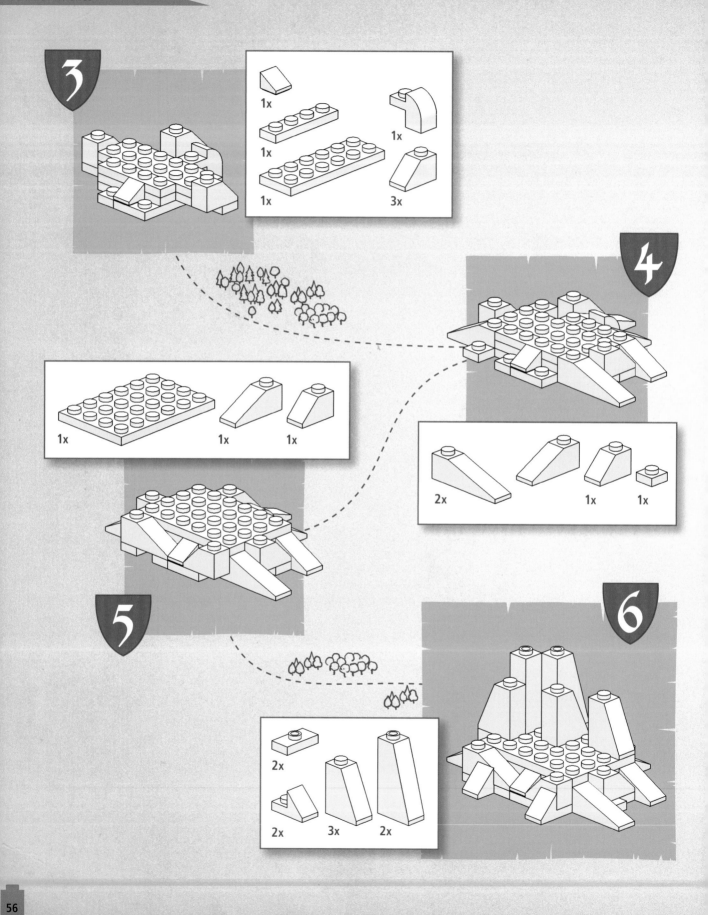

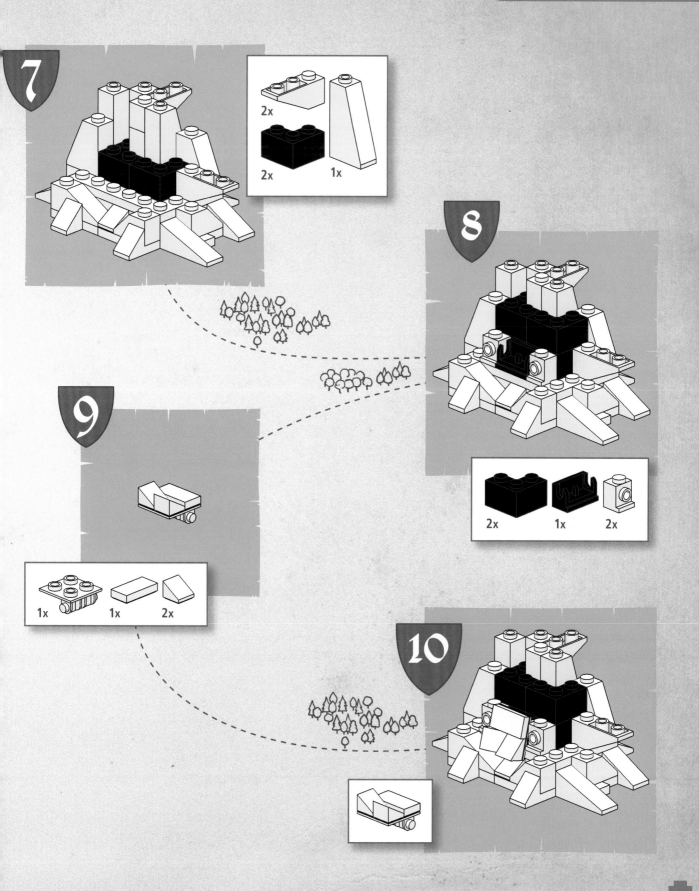

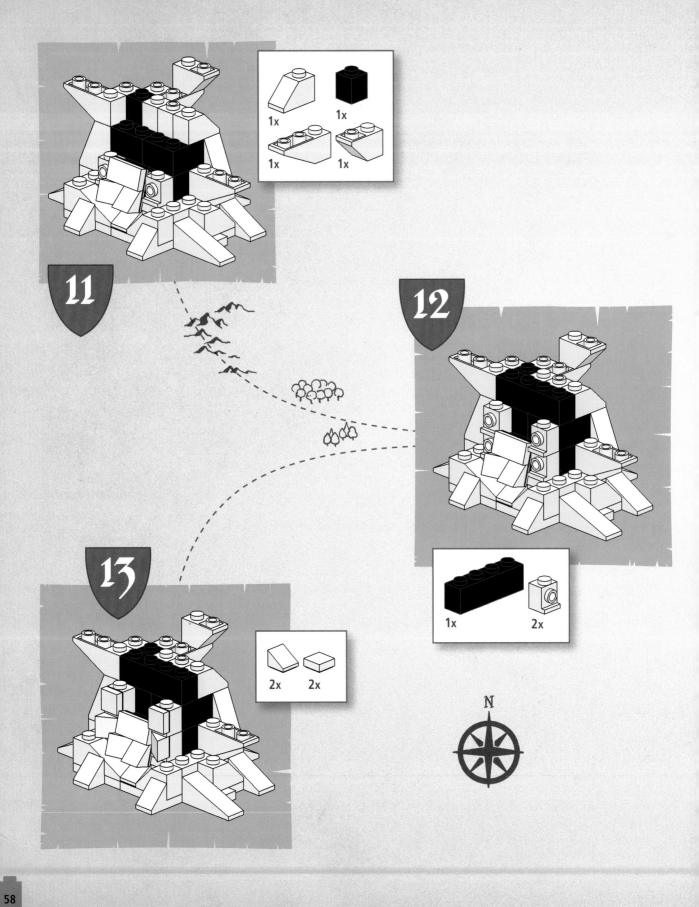

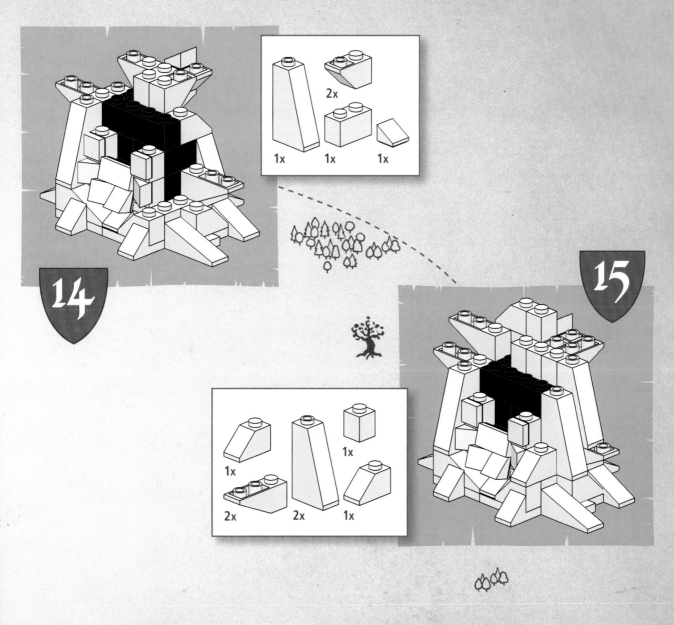

14

15

16

The tree looks good in brown, too.

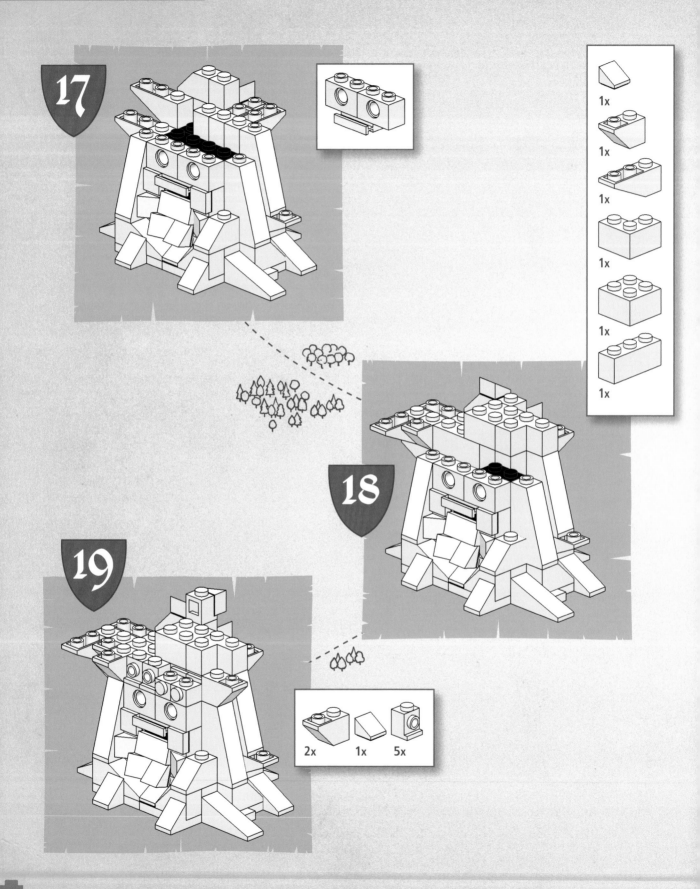

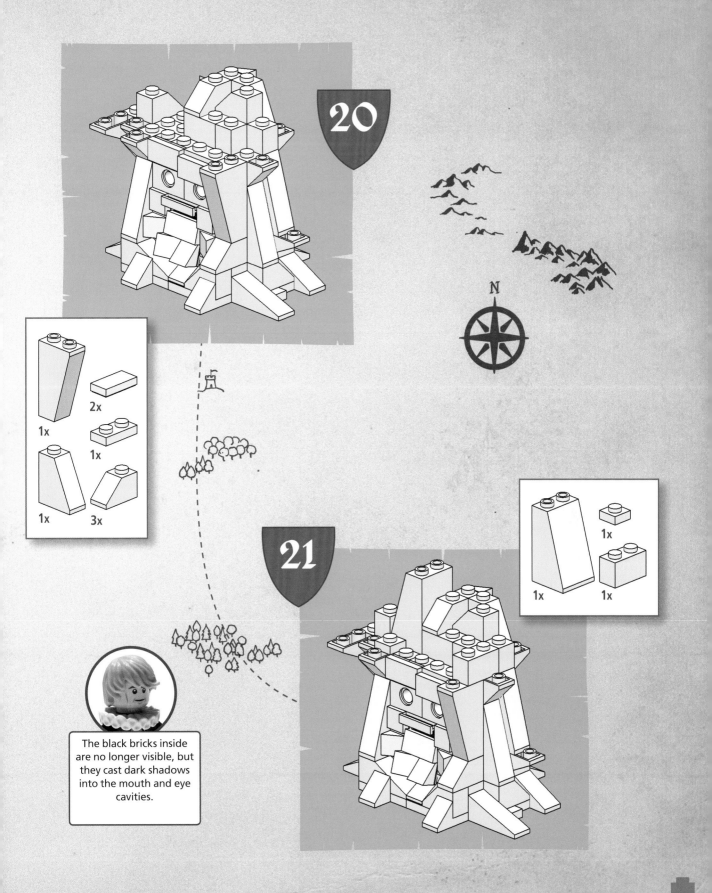

20

2x

1x

1x

1x

3x

21

1x

1x

1x

1x

The black bricks inside are no longer visible, but they cast dark shadows into the mouth and eye cavities.

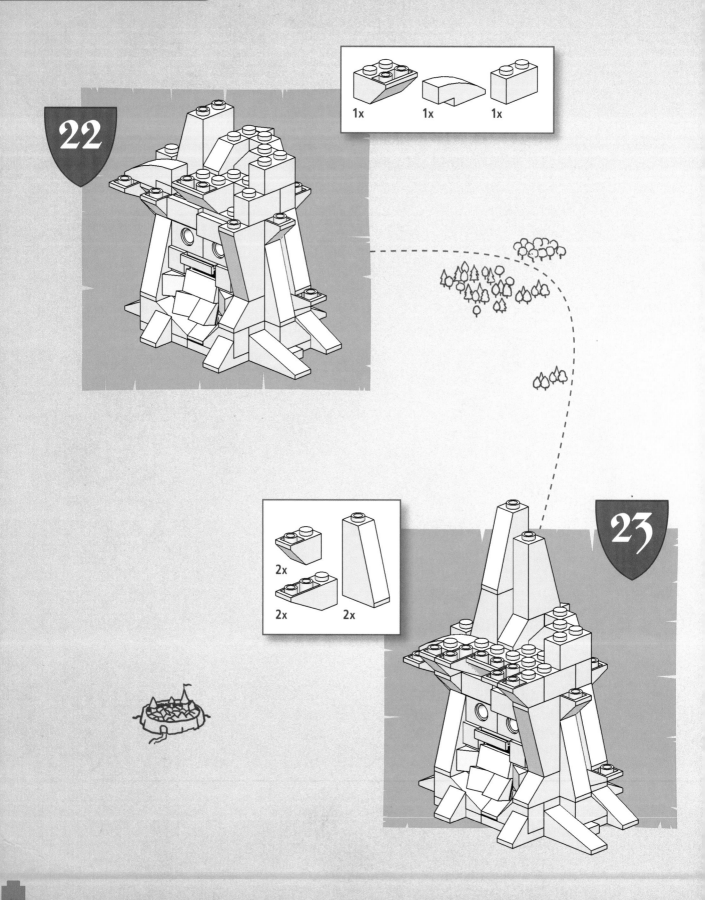

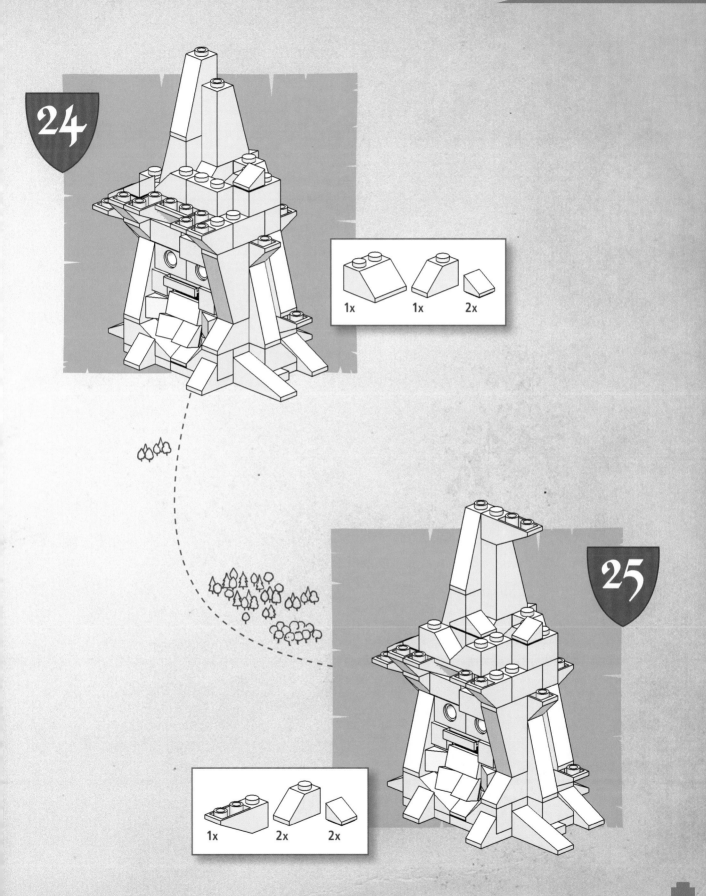

2x   2x   1x   1x

26

27

2x   2x   2x

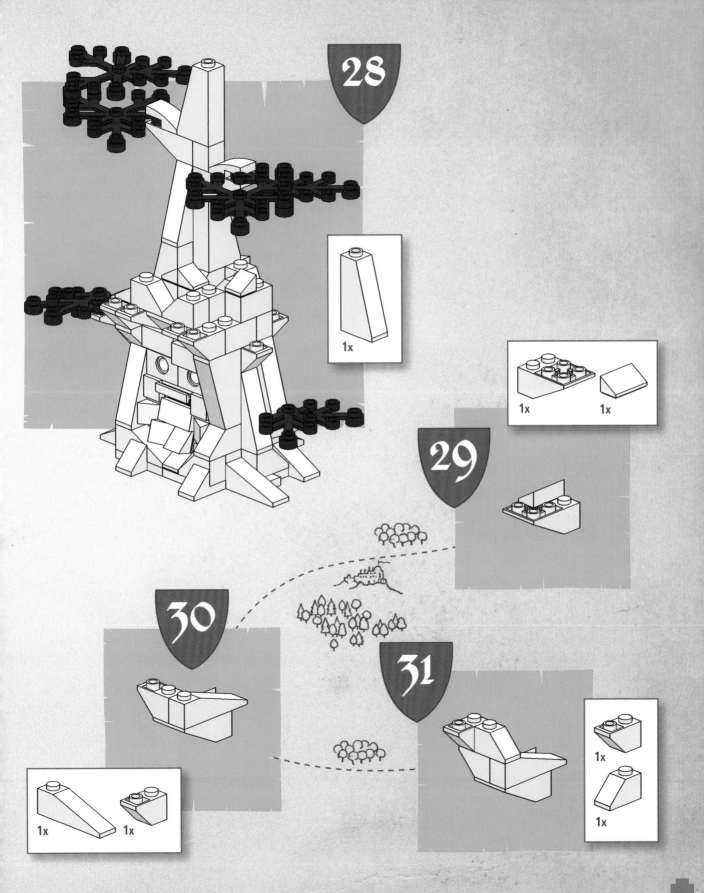

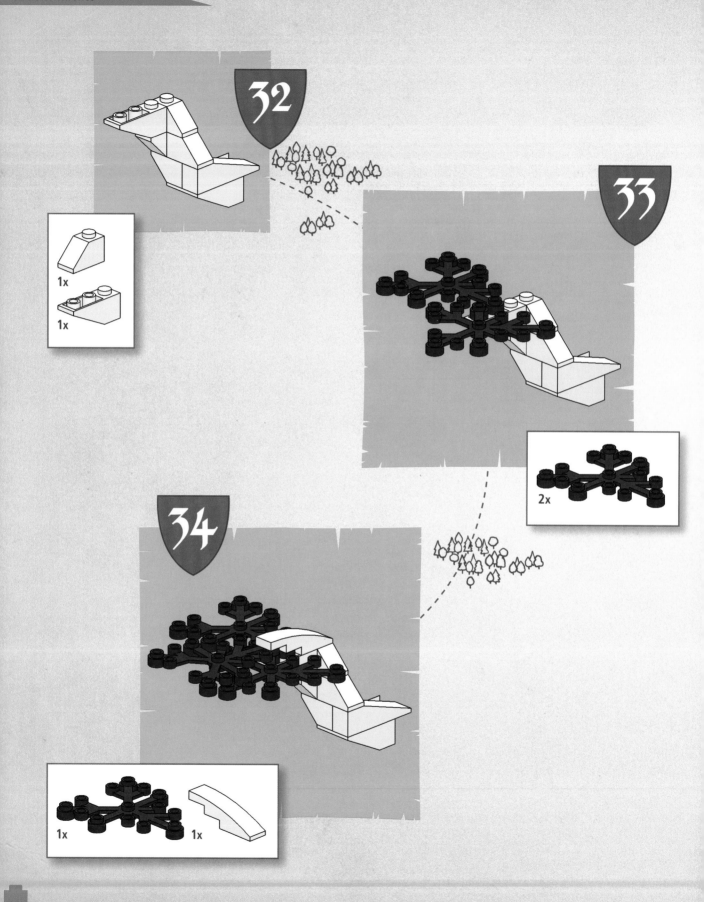

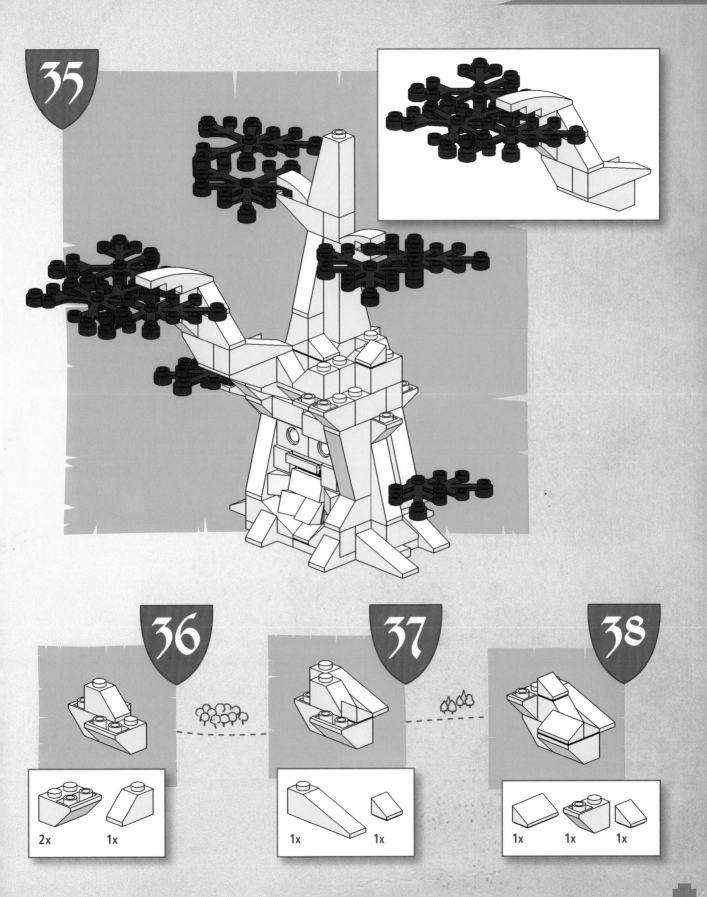

35

36 2x 1x

37 1x 1x

38 1x 1x 1x

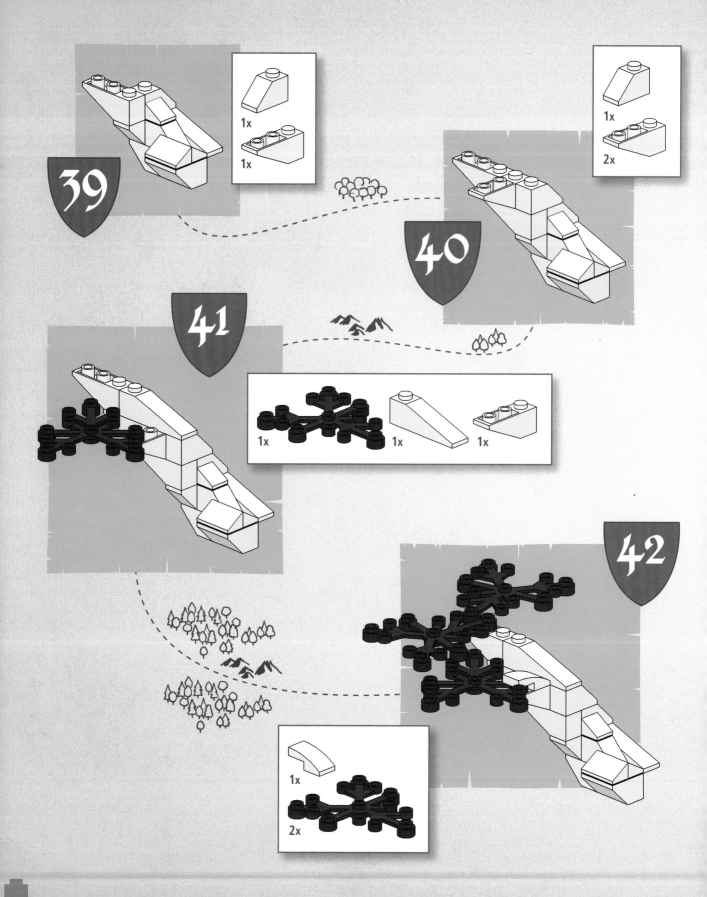

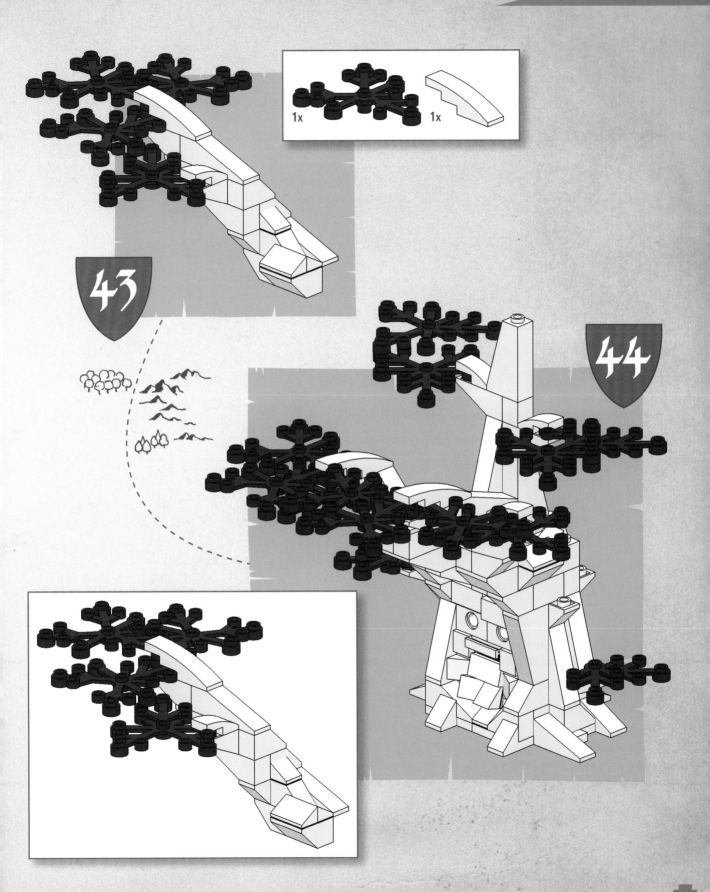

43

44

1x   1x

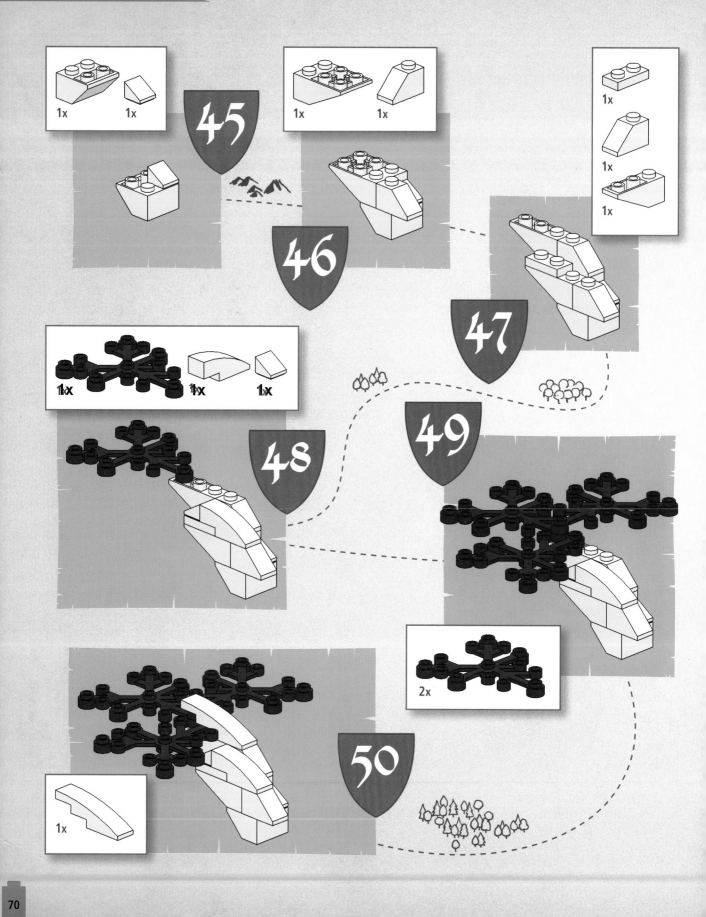

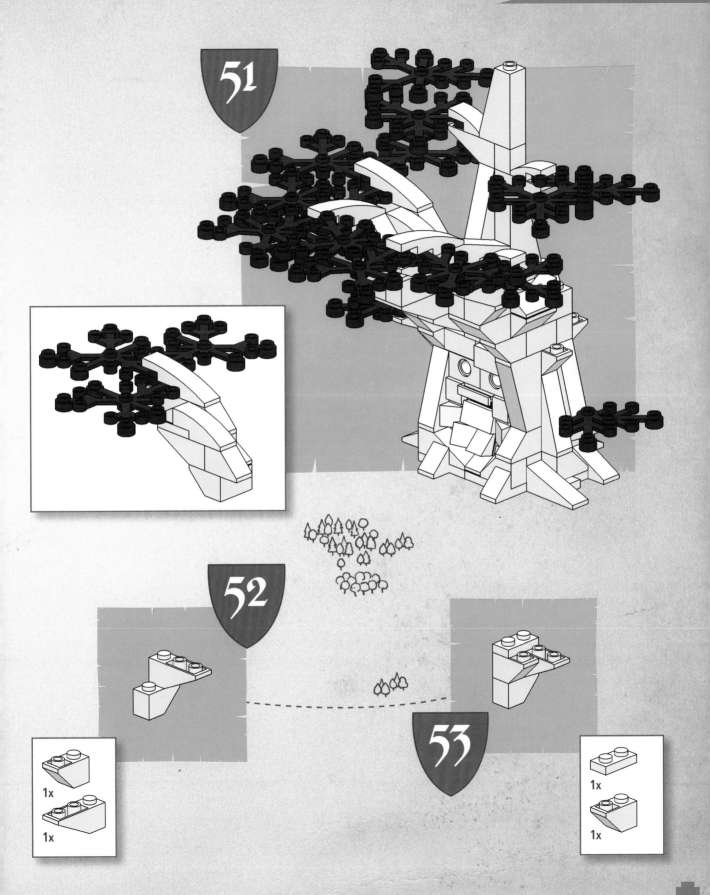

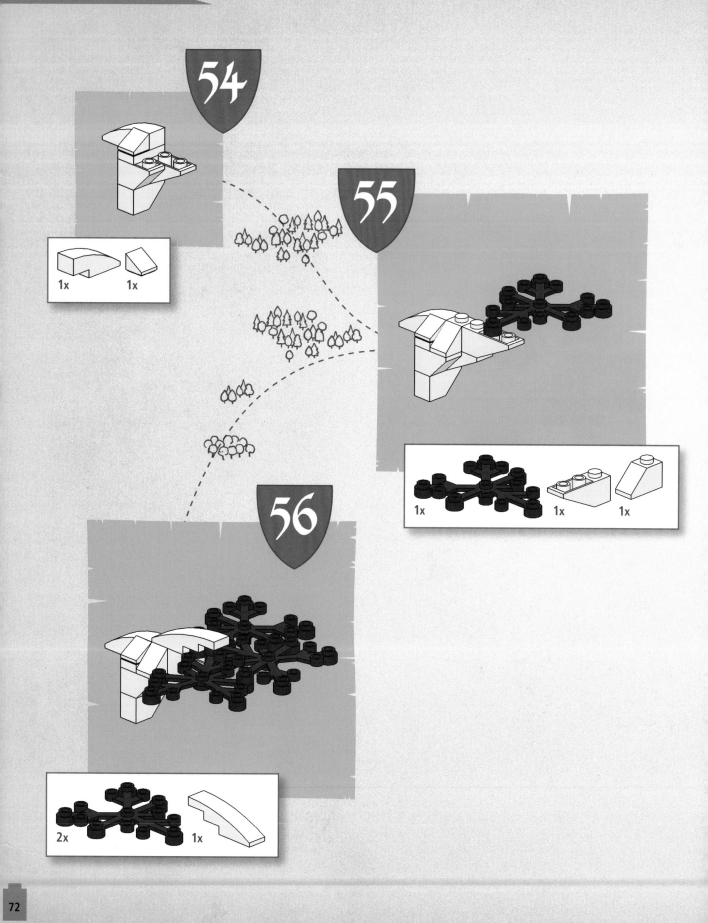

57

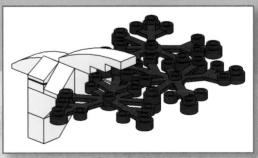

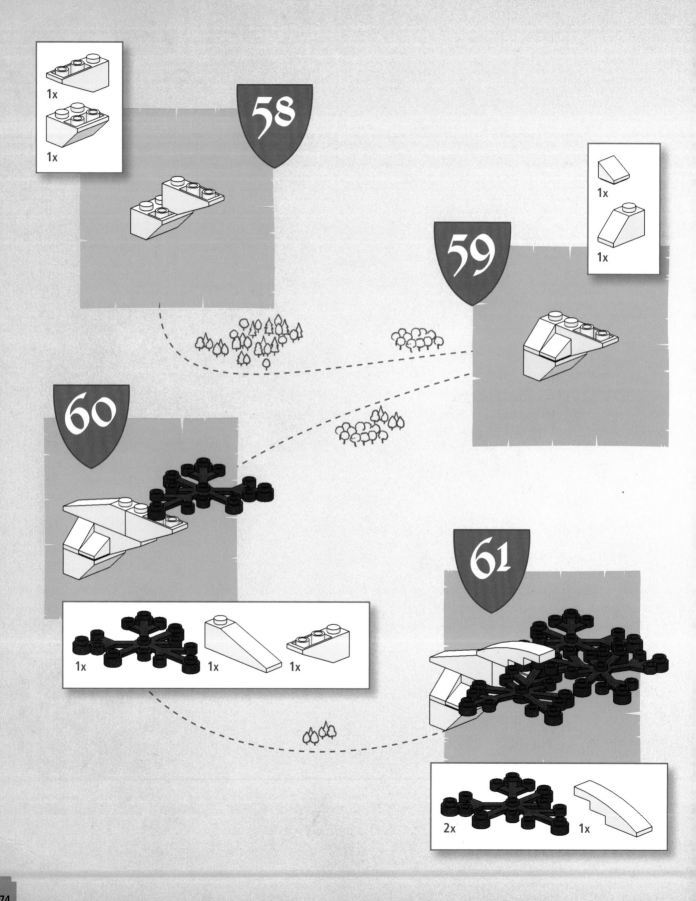

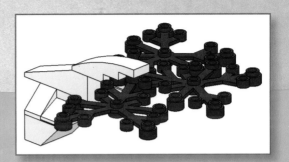

63

2x   1x

64

1x

65

1x

1x

66

Parts List

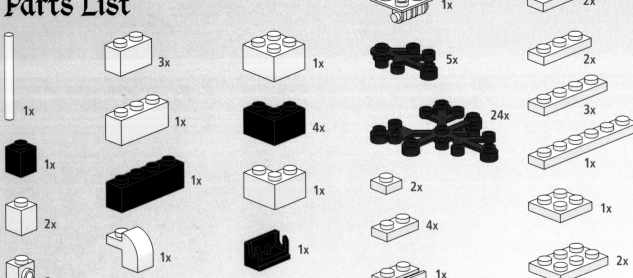

Quantity	Color		Element	Element Name
1		White	30374	Bar 4L Light Sabre Blade
1	■	Black	3005	Brick 1 x 1
2		White	3005	Brick 1 x 1
9		White	4070	Brick 1 x 1 with Headlight
3		White	3004	Brick 1 x 2
1		White	3622	Brick 1 x 3
1	■	Black	3010	Brick 1 x 4
1		White	6091	Brick 2 x 1 x 1 & 1/3 with Curved Top
1		White	3003	Brick 2 x 2
4	■	Black	2357	Brick 2 x 2 Corner
1		White	2357	Brick 2 x 2 Corner
1	■	Black	3937	Hinge 1 x 2 Base
1		White	6134	Hinge 2 x 2 Top
5	■	Dark Red	2423	Plant Leaves 4 x 3
24	■	Dark Red	2417	Plant Leaves 6 x 5
2		White	3024	Plate 1 x 1
4		White	3023	Plate 1 x 2
1		White	32028	Plate 1 x 2 with Door Rail
2		White	3794a	Plate 1 x 2 without Groove with 1 Centre Stud
2		White	3623	Plate 1 x 3
3		White	3710	Plate 1 x 4
1		White	3666	Plate 1 x 6
1		White	3022	Plate 2 x 2
2		White	3021	Plate 2 x 3

Quantity	Color		Element	Element Name
1		White	3795	Plate 2 x 6
1		White	3032	Plate 4 x 6
6		White	60477	Slope Brick 18 4 x 1
18		White	54200	Slope Brick 31 1 x 1 x 2/3
2		White	85984	Slope Brick 31 1 x 2 x 2/3
4		White	4286	Slope Brick 33 3 x 1
20		White	4287	Slope Brick 33 3 x 1 Inverted
2		White	3747b	Slope Brick 33 3 x 2 Inverted with Ribs between Studs
23		White	3040	Slope Brick 45 2 x 1
13		White	3665	Slope Brick 45 2 x 1 Inverted
1		White	3039	Slope Brick 45 2 x 2
5		White	3660	Slope Brick 45 2 x 2 Inverted
4		White	60481	Slope Brick 65 2 x 1 x 2
9		White	4460	Slope Brick 75 2 x 1 x 3
1		White	2449	Slope Brick 75 2 x 1 x 3 Inverted
1		White	3684	Slope Brick 75 2 x 2 x 3
3		White	11477	Slope Brick Curved 2 x 1
3		White	50950	Slope Brick Curved 3 x 1
5		White	61678	Slope Brick Curved 4 x 1
2		White	92946	Slope Plate 45 2 x 1
2		White	3700	Technic Brick 1 x 2 with Hole
2		White	3070b	Tile 1 x 1 with Groove
3		White	3069b	Tile 1 x 2 with Groove

Dragon

e were a little wary of trying out our ideas on this model, as there are already quite a few artists out there who've created fantastic dragons. But then we got itchy fingers and we thought we'd have a go ourselves. We decided to make a type of dragon in which the arms are also the wings. Fans of the series will immediately see that the dragon ought actually to be black, but if you follow our instructions you can build him yourselves.

But in that case, we recommend that you replace the beige-colored parts with dark grey parts. You could also build a green or dark green version, the wings are available in green too.

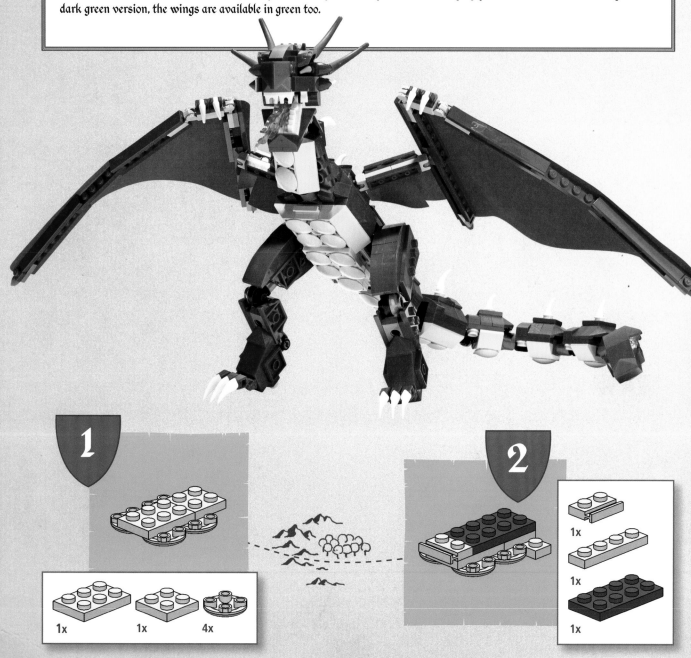

1

1x   1x   4x

2

1x

1x

1x

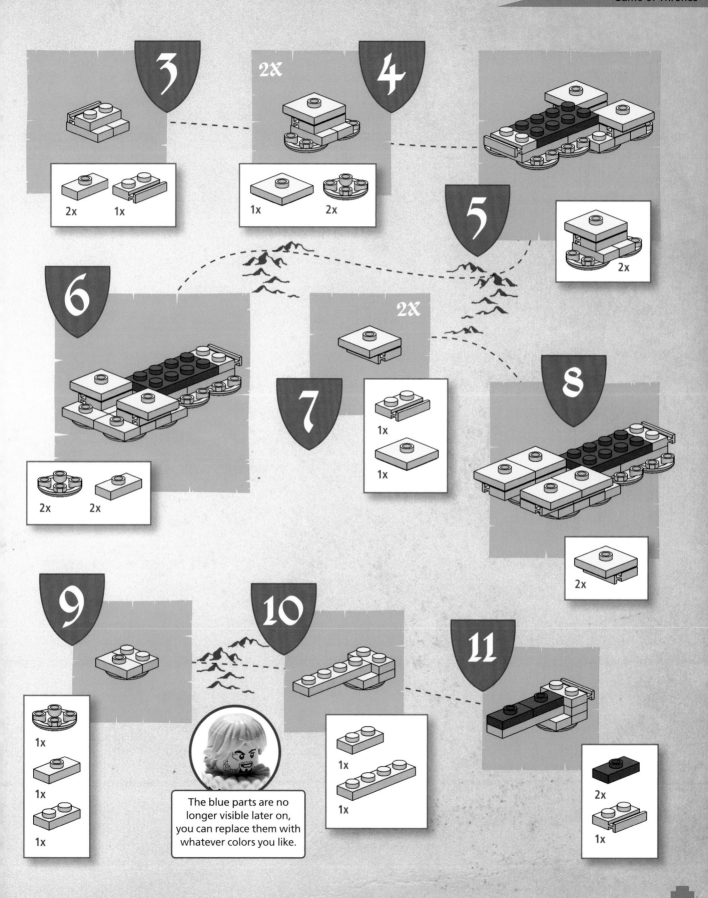

3

2x

4

5

2x

6

7

2x

8

9

10

11

The blue parts are no longer visible later on, you can replace them with whatever colors you like.

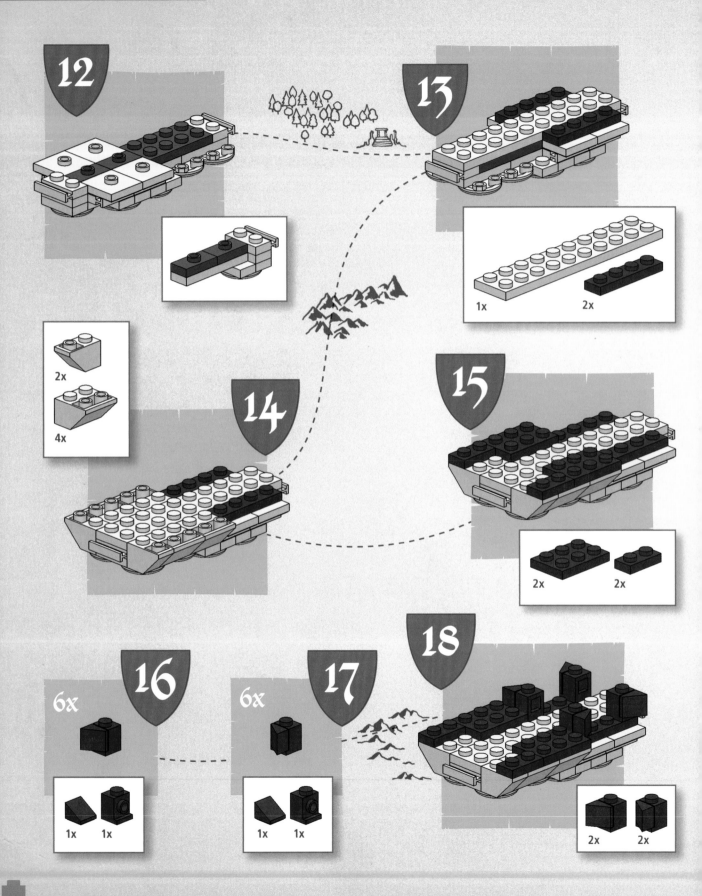

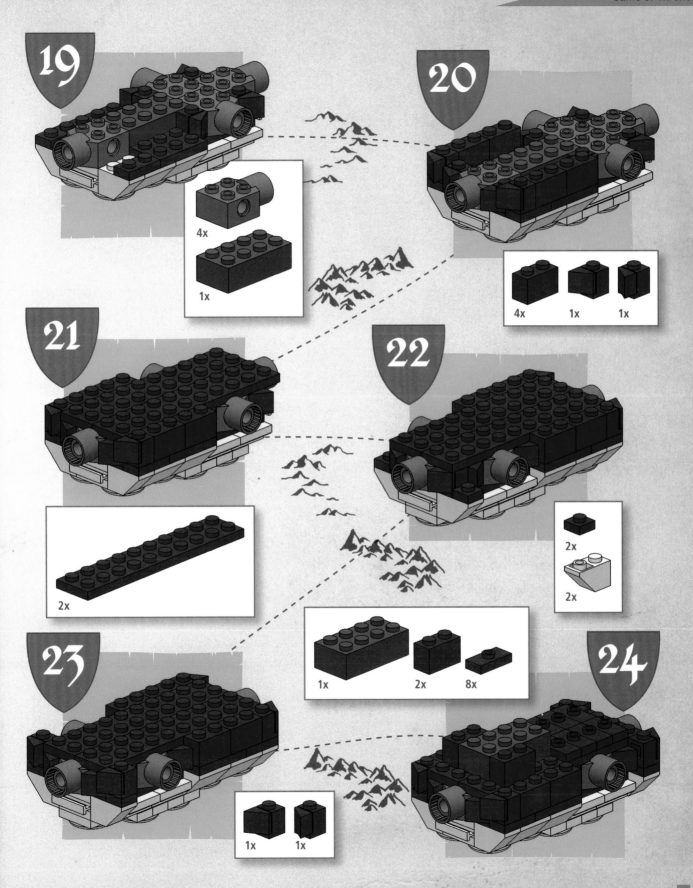

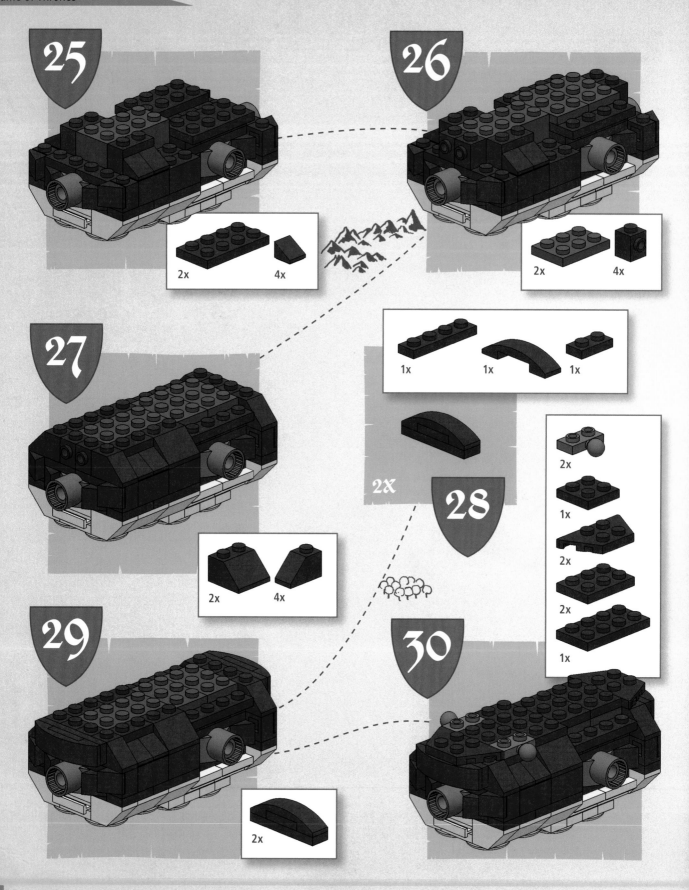

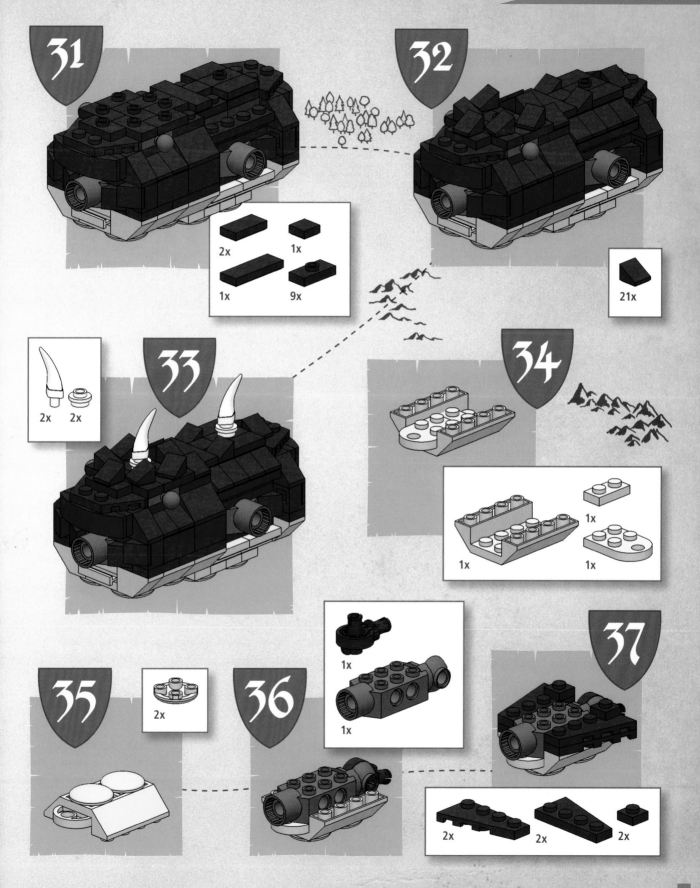

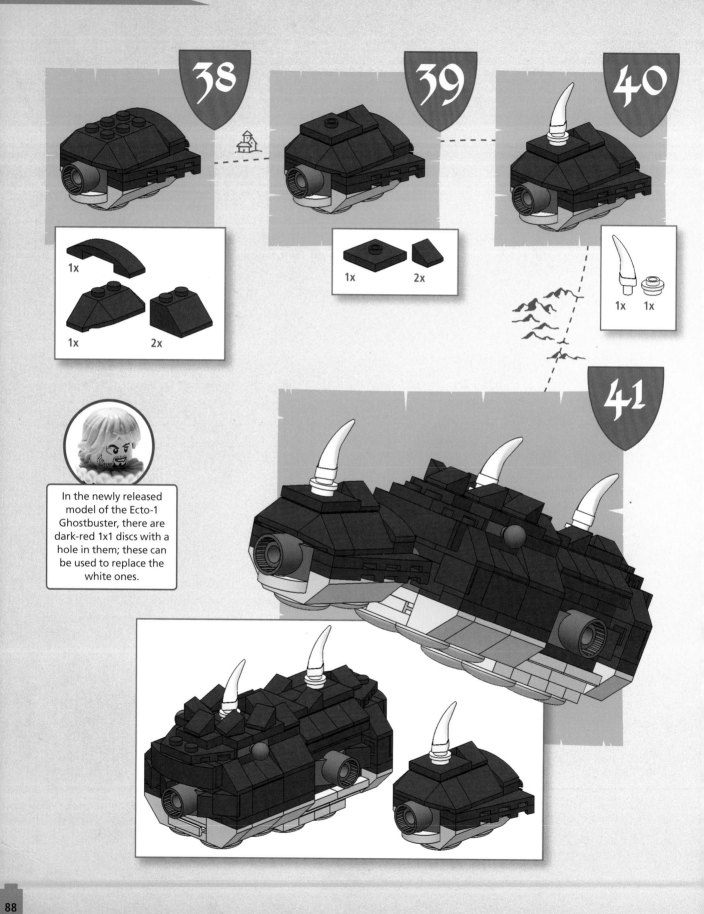

38

1x

1x   2x

39

1x   2x

40

1x   1x

41

In the newly released model of the Ecto-1 Ghostbuster, there are dark-red 1x1 discs with a hole in them; these can be used to replace the white ones.

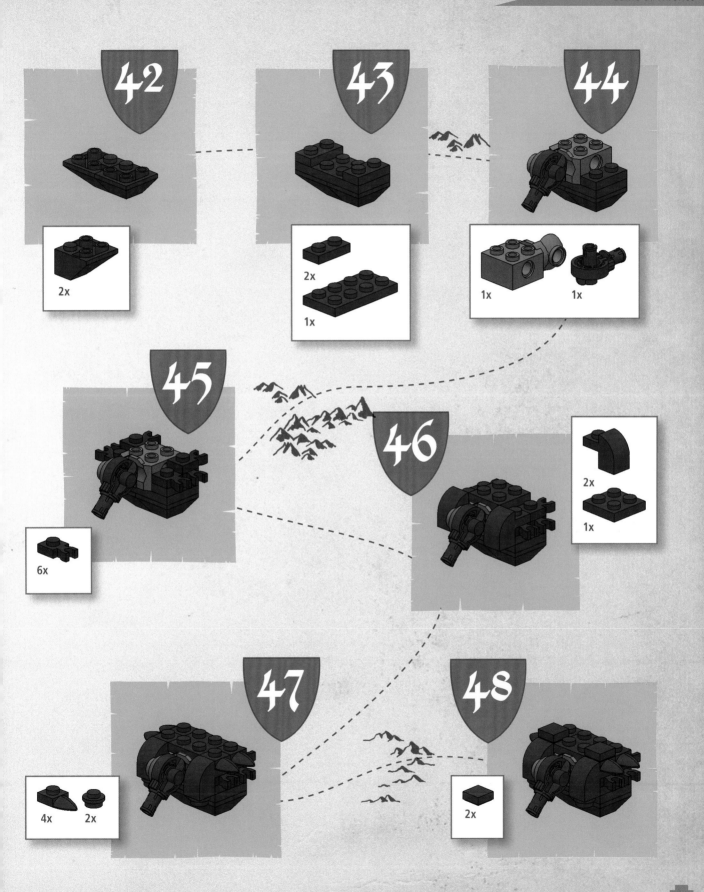

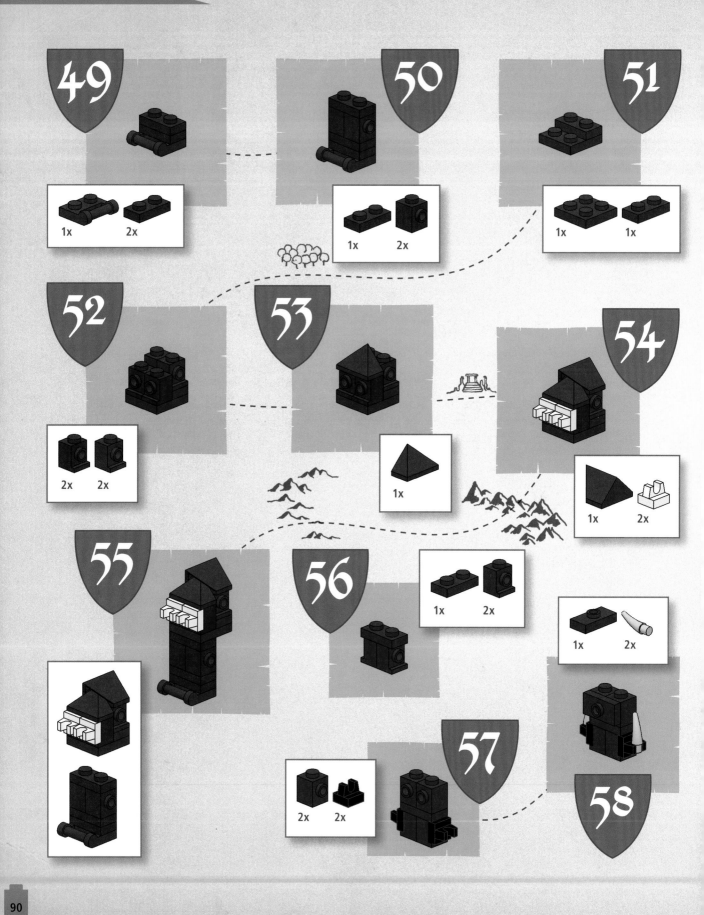

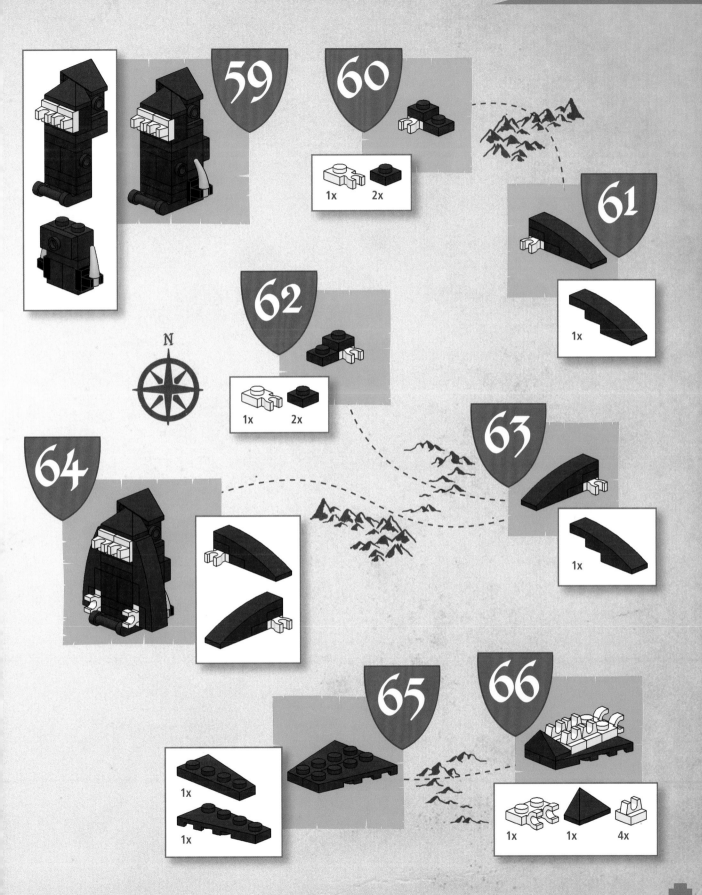

59

60

1x   2x

61

1x

62

1x   2x

63

1x

64

65

1x

1x

66

1x   1x   4x

N

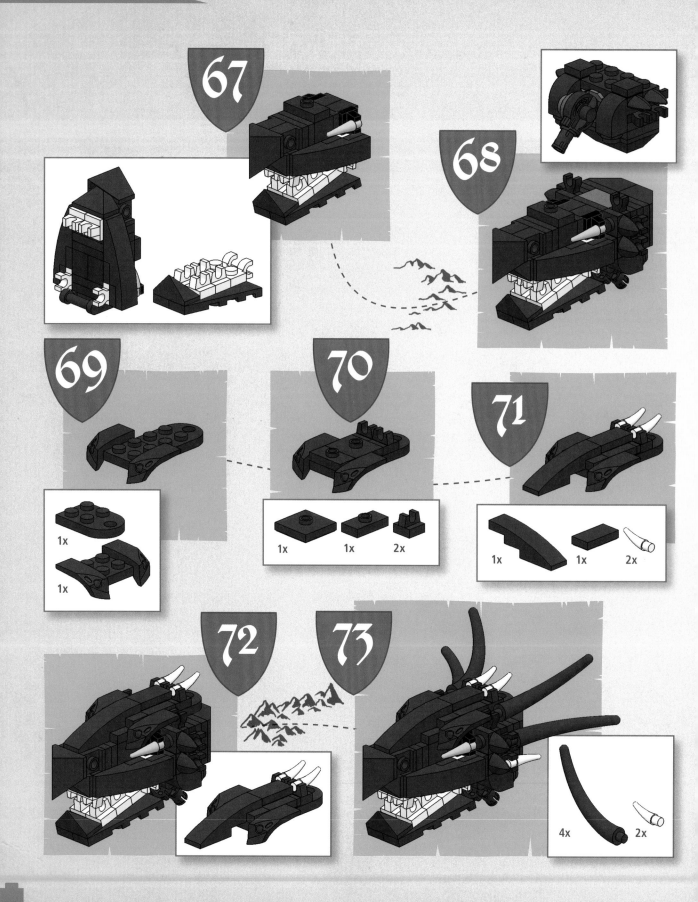

67

68

69

70

71

1x 1x

1x 1x 2x

1x 1x 2x

72 73

4x 2x

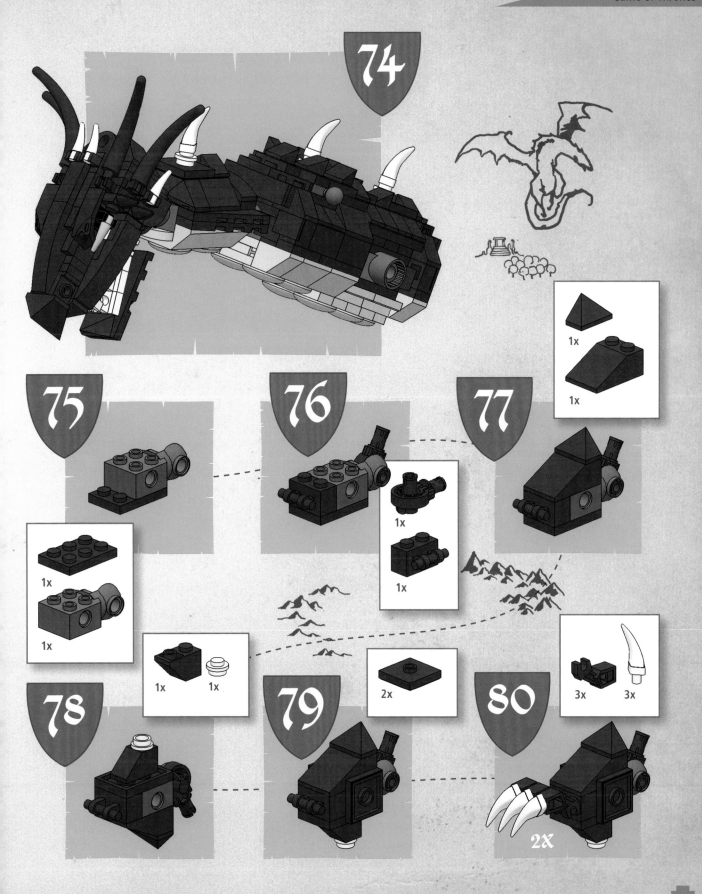

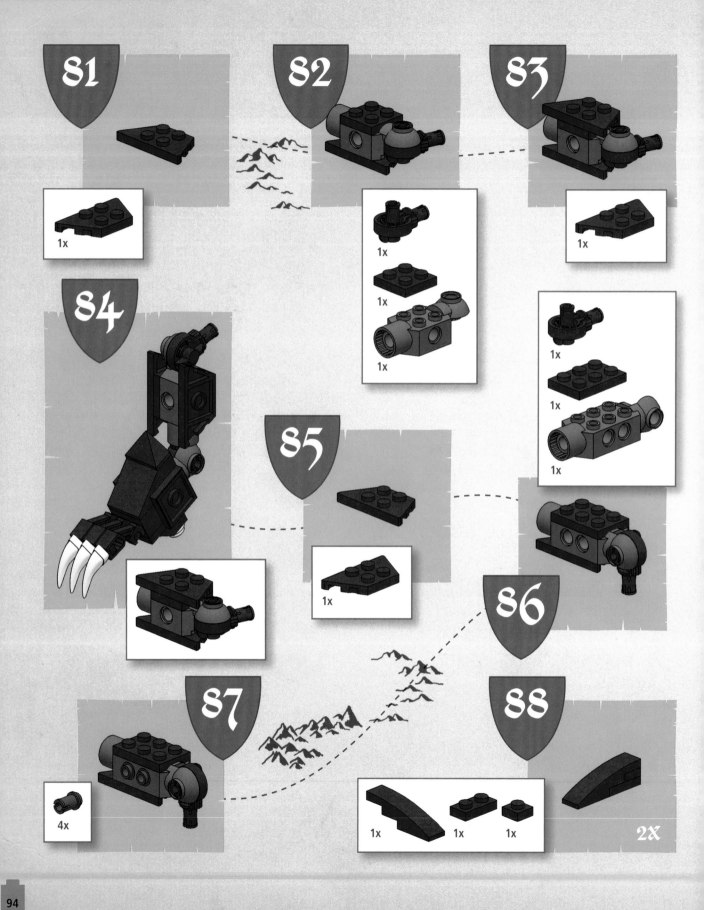

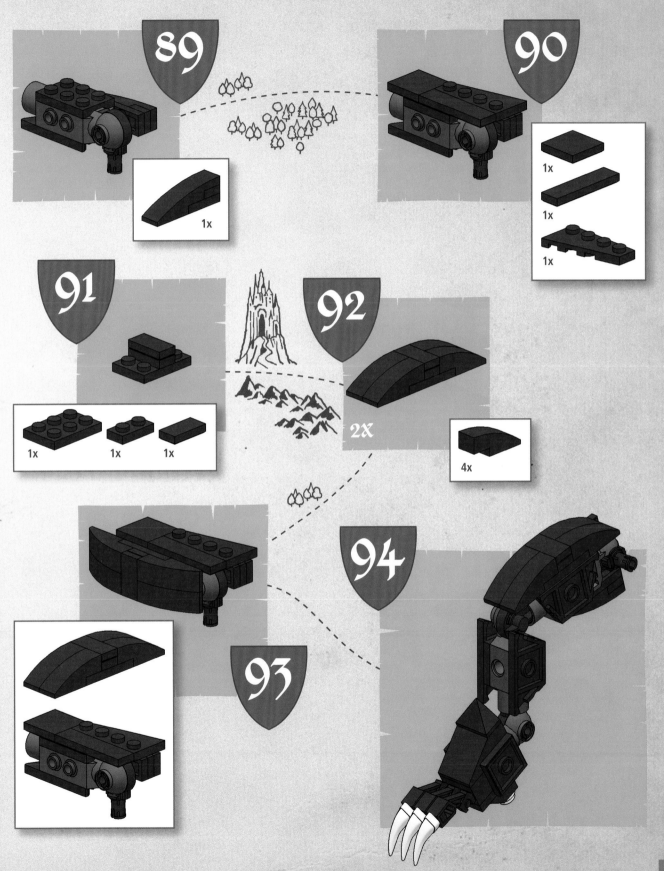

89

1x

90

1x

1x

1x

91

1x 1x 1x

92

2x

4x

93

94

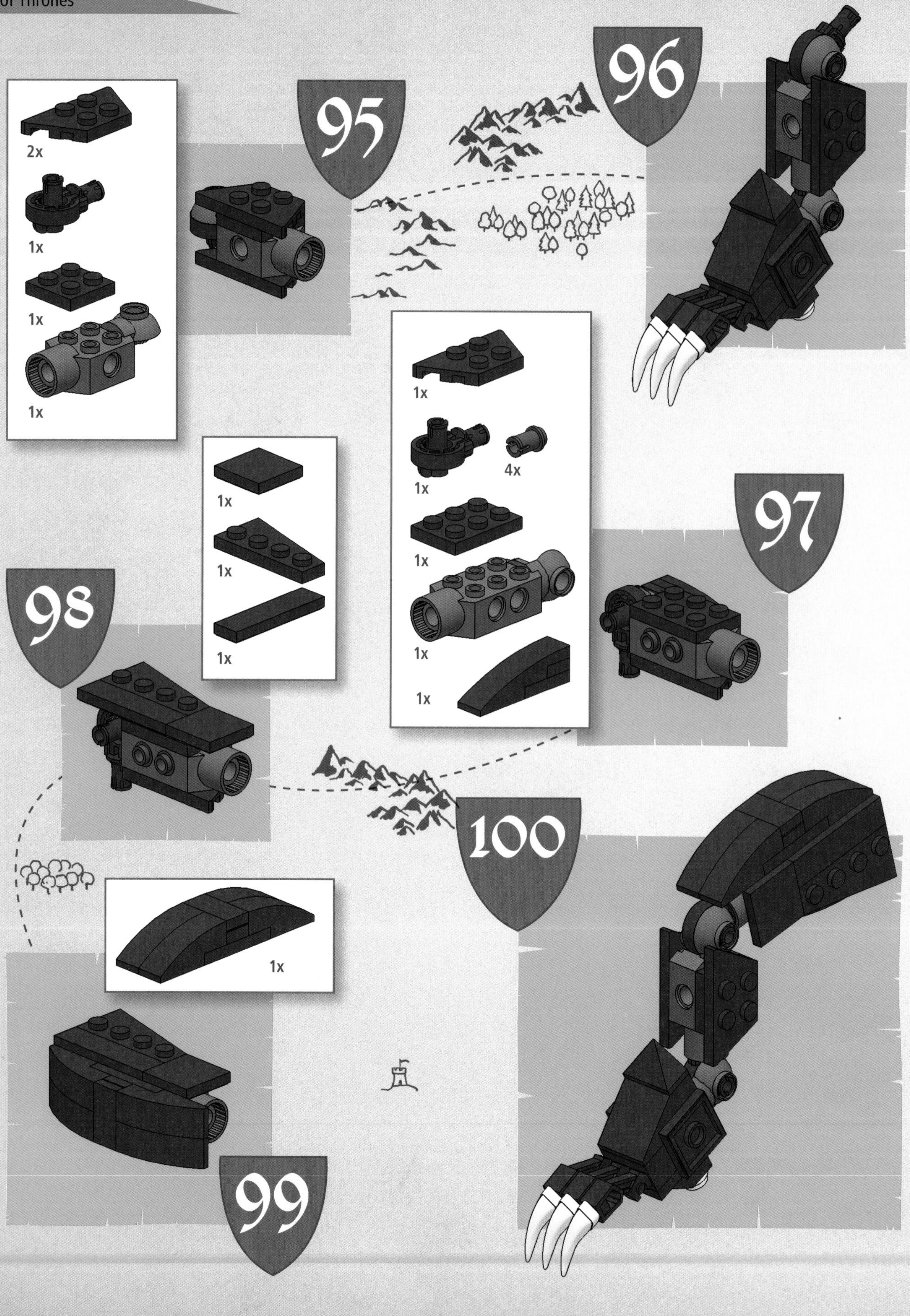
2x
1x
1x
1x
95
96
1x
1x
4x
1x
1x
1x
97
1x
1x
1x
98
100
1x
99

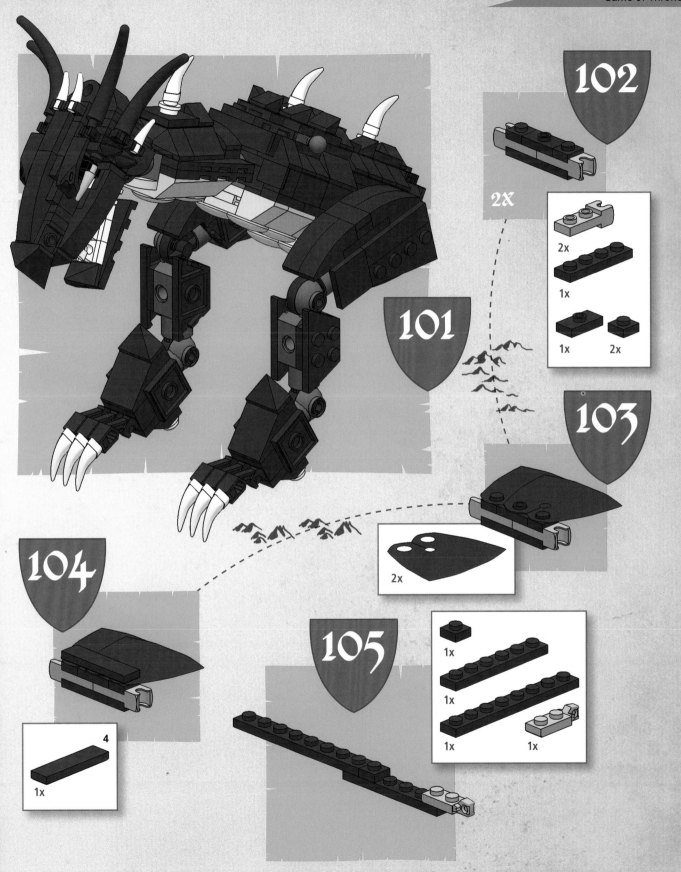

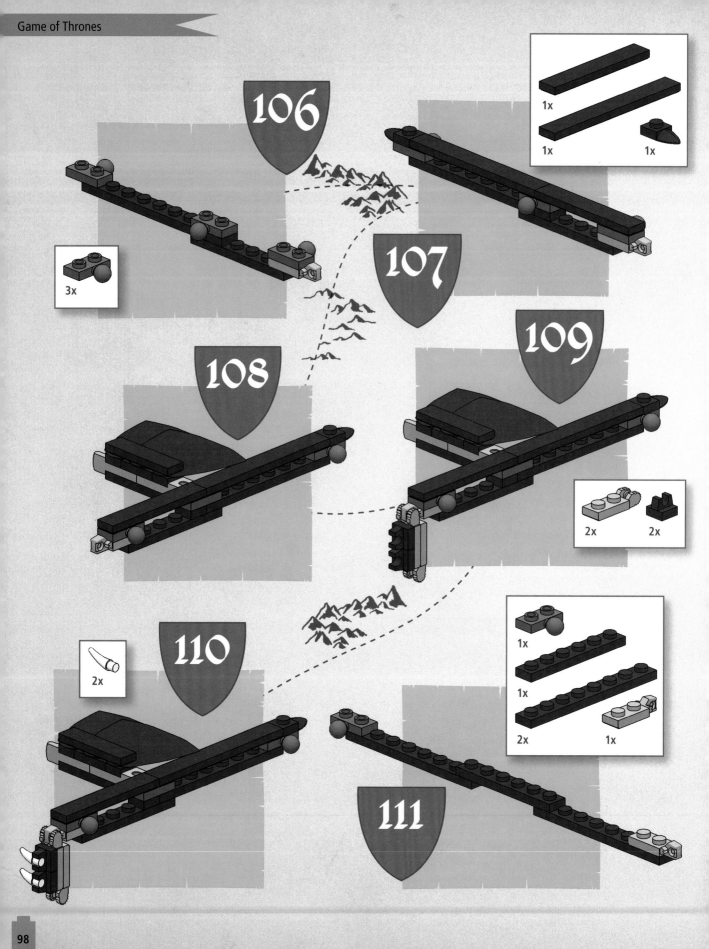

106

107

108

109

110

111

1x

1x

1x

3x

2x

2x

2x

1x

1x

2x

1x

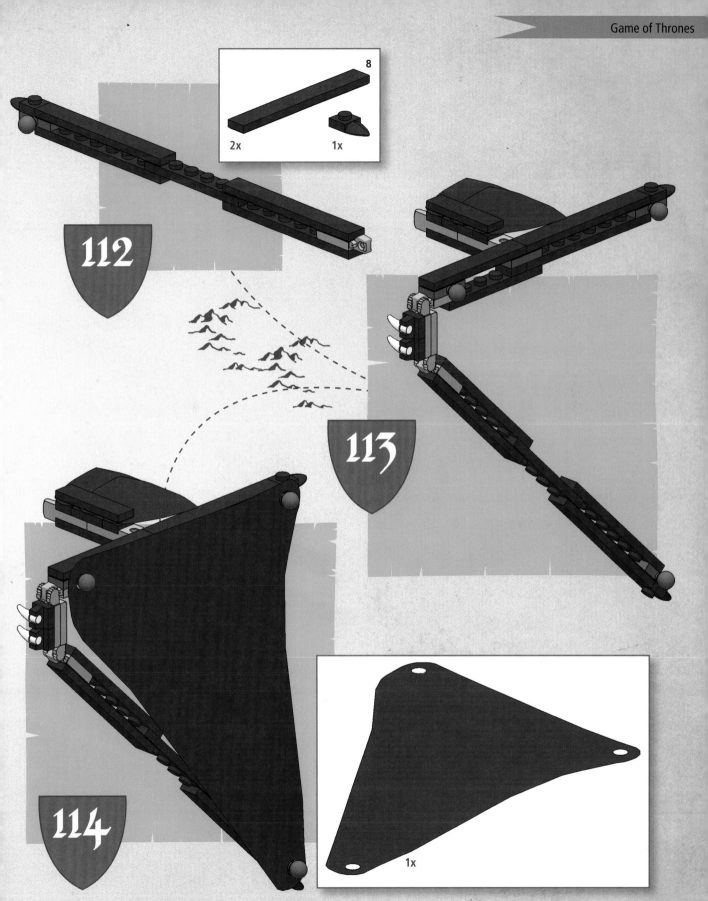

8

2x   1x

112

113

114

1x

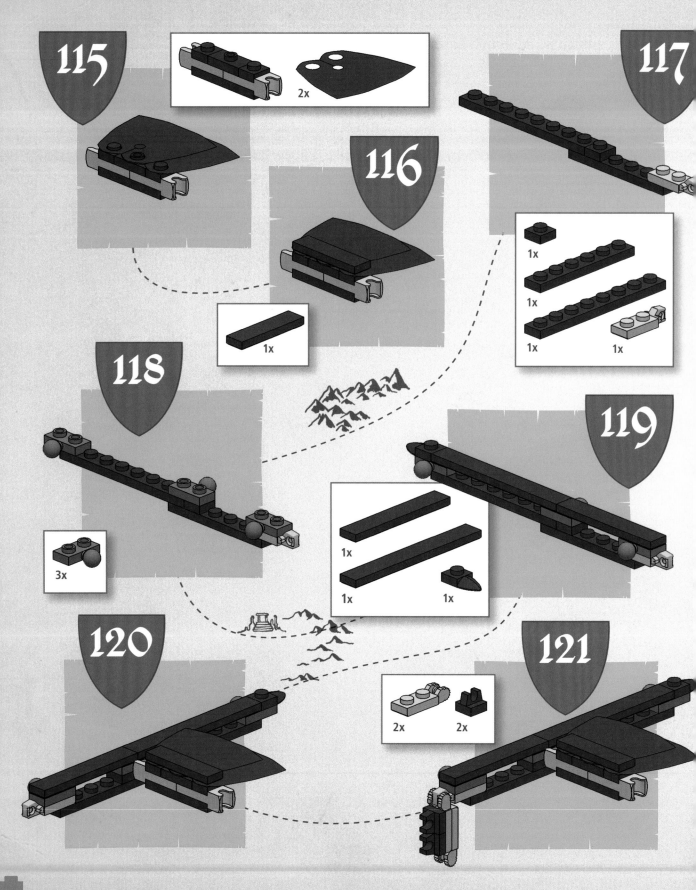

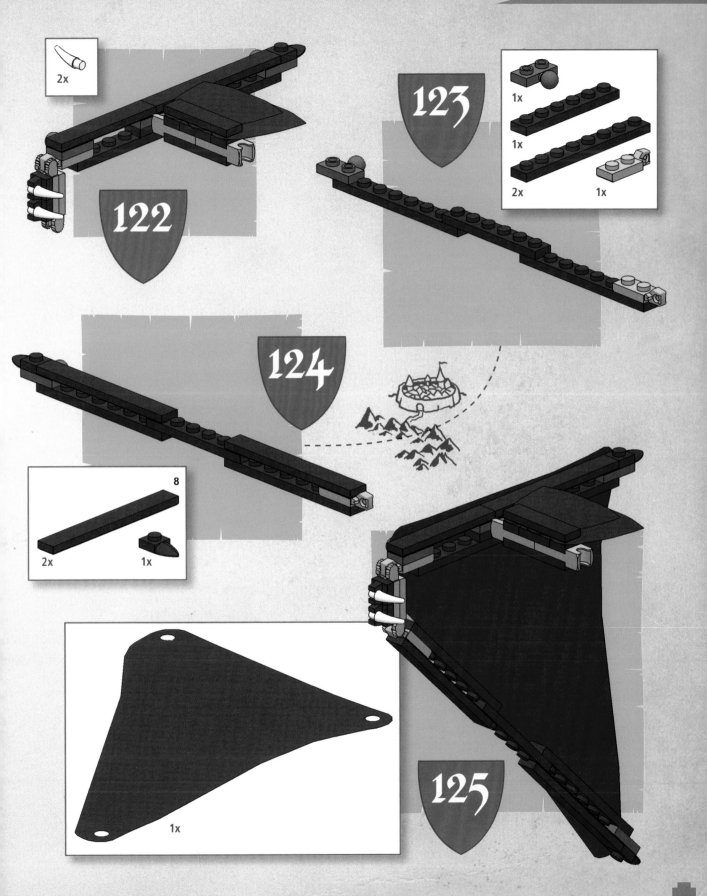

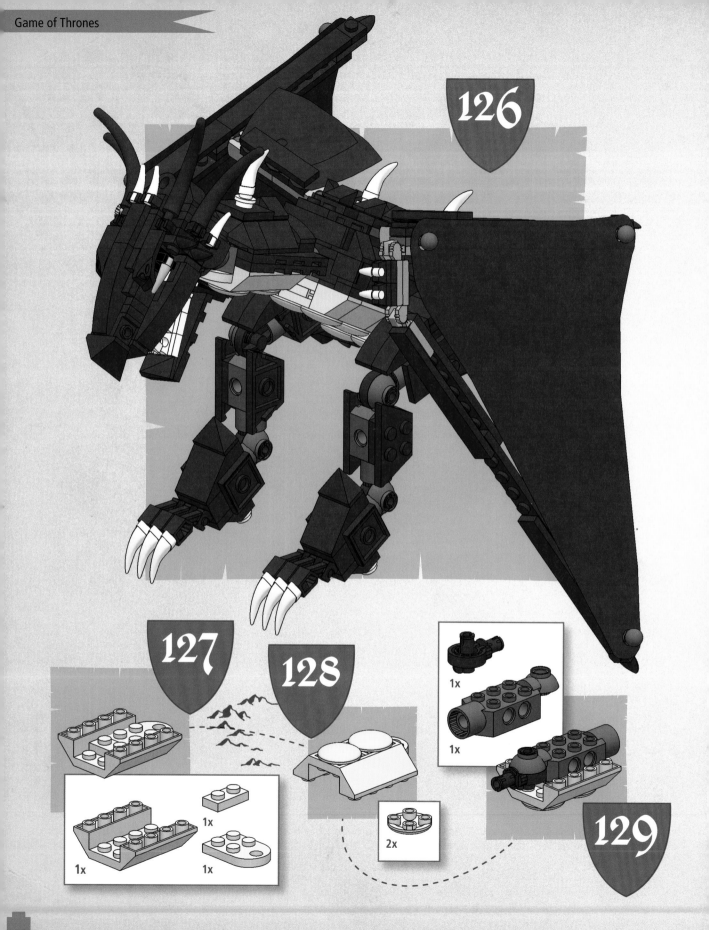

126

127

128

129

1x

1x

1x

1x

1x

2x

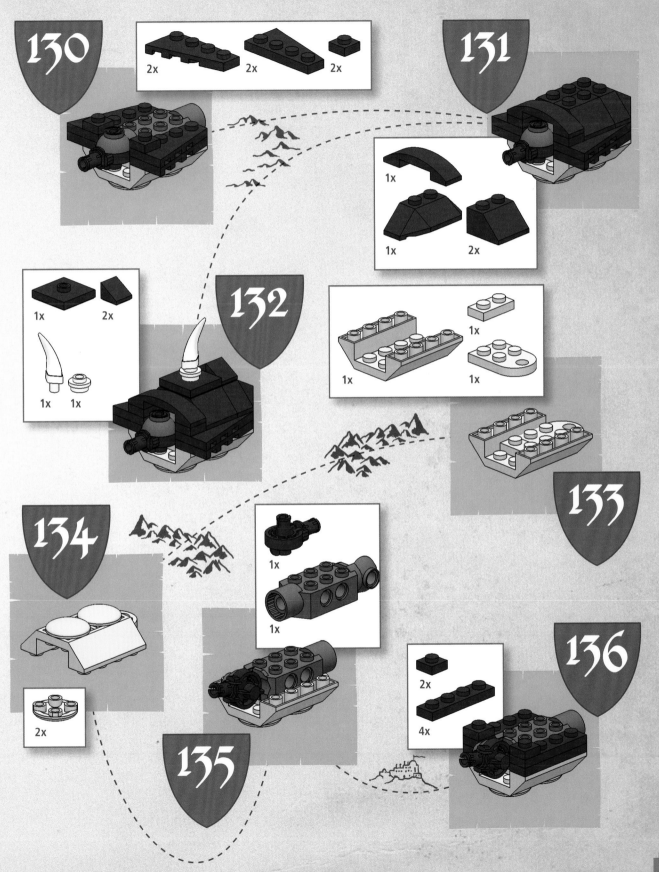

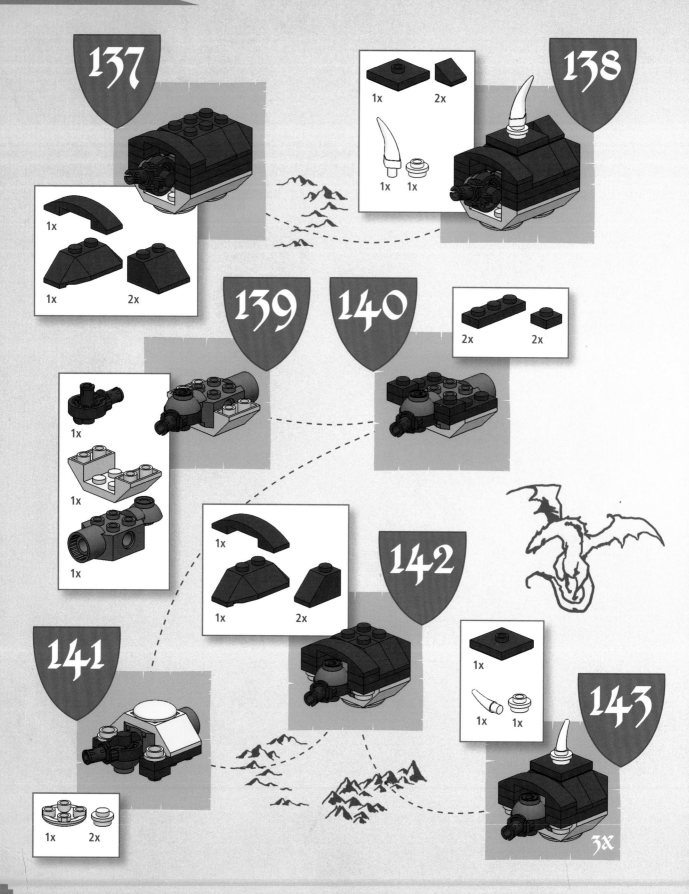

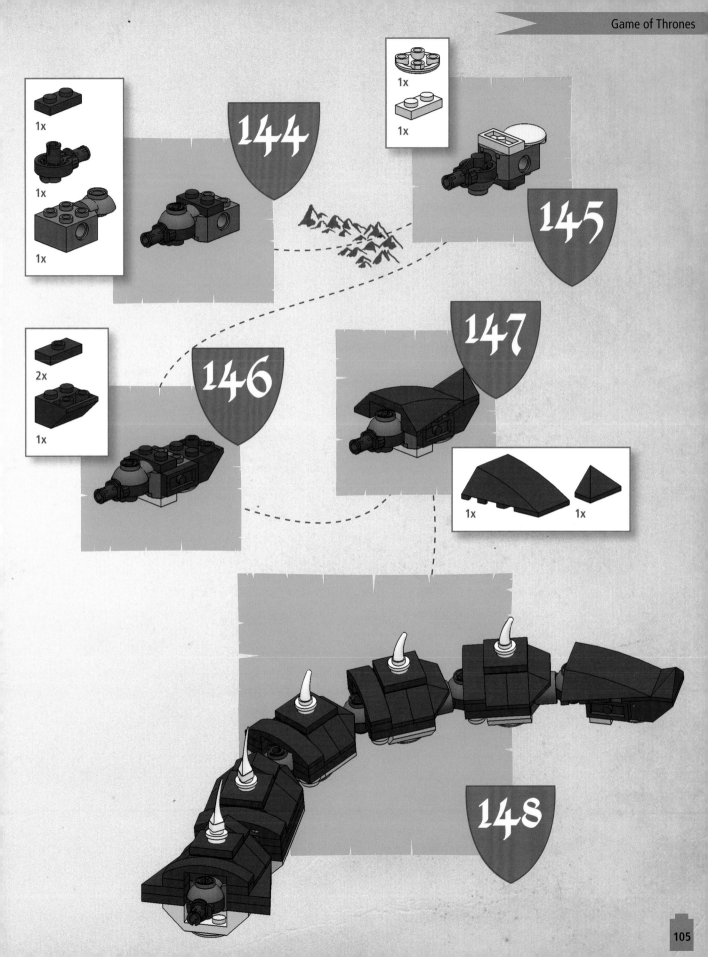

149

1:1,43

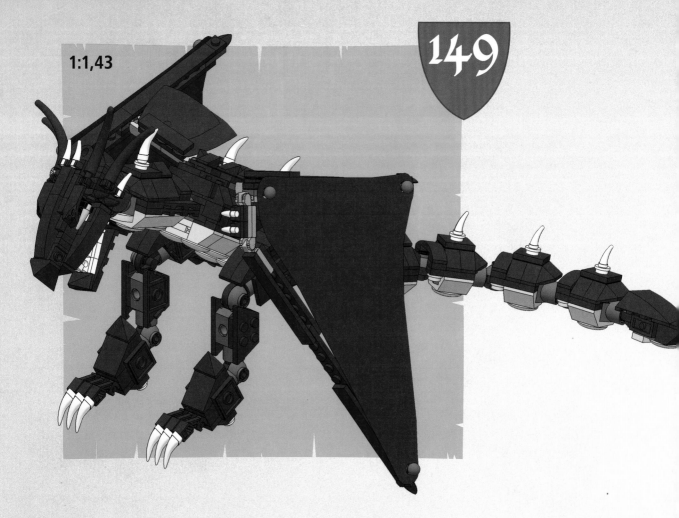

Parts List

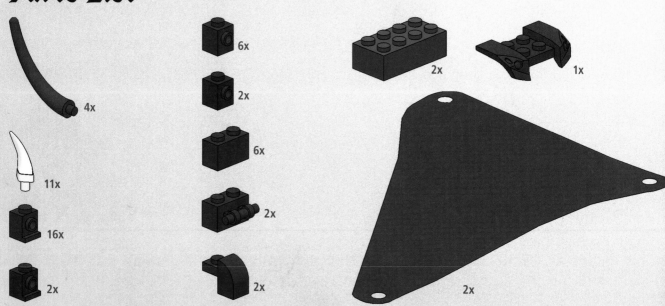

4x

11x

16x

2x

6x

2x

6x

2x

2x

2x

1x

2x

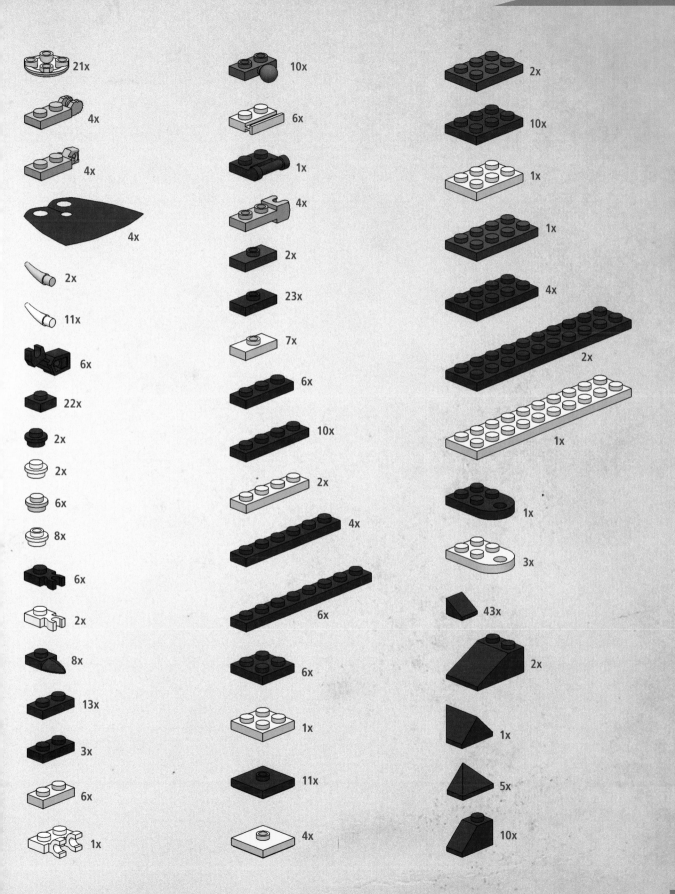

21x
4x
4x
4x
2x
11x
6x
22x
2x
2x
6x
8x
6x
2x
8x
13x
3x
6x
1x

10x
6x
1x
4x
2x
23x
7x
6x
10x
2x
4x
6x
6x
1x
11x
4x

2x
10x
1x
1x
4x
2x
1x
1x
3x
43x
2x
1x
5x
10x

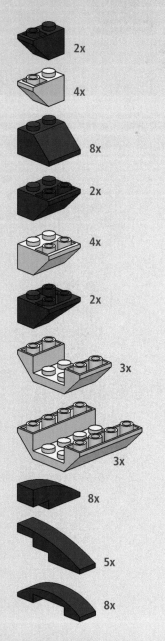

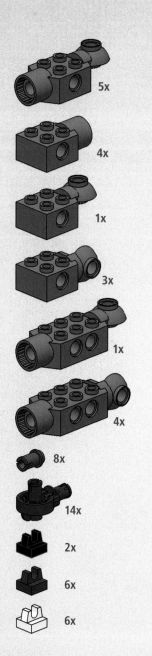

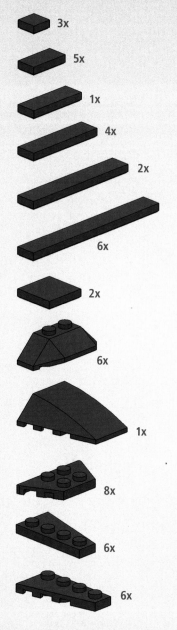

Quantity	Color		Element	Element Name
4		Dark Red	40379	Animal Tail Section End
11		White	87747	Bar 0.5L with Curved Blade 2L
16		Dark Red	4070	Brick 1 x 1 with Headlight
2		Reddish Brown	4070	Brick 1 x 1 with Headlight
6		Dark Red	87087	Brick 1 x 1 with Stud on 1 Side
2		Reddish Brown	87087	Brick 1 x 1 with Stud on 1 Side
6		Dark Red	3004	Brick 1 x 2
2		Dark Red	30236	Brick 1 x 2 with Handle
2		Dark Red	6091	Brick 2 x 1 x 1 & 1/3 with Curved Top

2	Blue	3001	Brick 2 x 4
1	Dark Red	44674	Car Mudguard 3 x 4 Overhanging
2	Dark Red	sailbb38	Cloth Sail Triangular 15 x 22 with 3 Holes
21	Tan	2654	Dish 2 x 2
4	Light Bluish Gray	44302	Hinge Plate 1 x 2 Locking with Dual Finger on End Vertical
4	Light Bluish Gray	44301	Hinge Plate 1 x 2 Locking with Single Finger on End Vertical
4	Dark Red	552	Minifig Cape Cloth, Standard
2	Lime	53451	Minifig Helmet Viking Horn
11	White	53451	Minifig Helmet Viking Horn
6	Dark Red	53989	Minifig Mechanical Arm with Clip and Rod Hole
22	Dark Red	3024	Plate 1 x 1
2	Dark Red	4073	Plate 1 x 1 Round
2	White	4073	Plate 1 x 1 Round
6	Tan	6141	Plate 1 x 1 Round
8	White	85861	Plate 1 x 1 Round with Open Stud
6	Reddish Brown	4085c	Plate 1 x 1 with Clip Vertical Type 3
2	White	4085c	Plate 1 x 1 with Clip Vertical Type 3
8	Dark Red	49673	Plate 1 x 1 with Tooth
13	Dark Red	3023	Plate 1 x 2
3	Reddish Brown	3023	Plate 1 x 2
6	Tan	3023	Plate 1 x 2
1	White	60470	Plate 1 x 2 with 2 Clips Horizontal
10	Dark Bluish Gray	14417	Plate 1 x 2 with Ball Joint-8
6	Tan	32028	Plate 1 x 2 with Door Rail
1	Dark Red	48336	Plate 1 x 2 with Handle Type 2
4	Light Bluish Gray	14418	Plate 1 x 2 with Socket Joint-8 with Friction
2	Blue	3794a	Plate 1 x 2 without Groove with 1 Centre Stud
23	Dark Red	3794a	Plate 1 x 2 without Groove with 1 Centre Stud
7	Tan	3794a	Plate 1 x 2 without Groove with 1 Centre Stud
6	Dark Red	3623	Plate 1 x 3
10	Dark Red	3710	Plate 1 x 4
2	Tan	3710	Plate 1 x 4
4	Dark Red	3666	Plate 1 x 6
6	Dark Red	3460	Plate 1 x 8
6	Dark Red	3022	Plate 2 x 2
1	Tan	3022	Plate 2 x 2
11	Dark Red	87580	Plate 2 x 2 with Groove with 1 Center Stud
4	Tan	87580	Plate 2 x 2 with Groove with 1 Center Stud
2	Blue	3021	Plate 2 x 3
10	Dark Red	3021	Plate 2 x 3
1	Tan	3021	Plate 2 x 3
1	Blue	3020	Plate 2 x 4
4	Dark Red	3020	Plate 2 x 4

2	Dark Red	3832	Plate 2 x 10
1	Tan	3832	Plate 2 x 10
1	Dark Red	3176	Plate 3 x 2 with Hole
3	Tan	3176	Plate 3 x 2 with Hole
43	Dark Red	54200	Slope Brick 31 1 x 1 x 2/3
2	Dark Red	3298	Slope Brick 33 3 x 2
1	Dark Red	3049b	Slope Brick 45 1 x 2 Double / Inverted
5	Dark Red	3048	Slope Brick 45 1 x 2 Triple
10	Dark Red	3040b	Slope Brick 45 2 x 1
2	Dark Red	3665	Slope Brick 45 2 x 1 Inverted
4	Tan	3665	Slope Brick 45 2 x 1 Inverted
8	Dark Red	3039	Slope Brick 45 2 x 2
2	Dark Red	3660	Slope Brick 45 2 x 2 Inverted
4	Tan	3660	Slope Brick 45 2 x 2 Inverted
2	Dark Red	3676	Slope Brick 45 2 x 2 Inverted Double Convex
3	Tan	4871	Slope Brick 45 4 x 2 Double Inverted with Open Center
3	Tan	4854	Slope Brick 45 4 x 4 Double Inverted with Open Center
8	Dark Red	50950	Slope Brick Curved 3 x 1
5	Dark Red	61678	Slope Brick Curved 4 x 1
8	Dark Red	93273	Slope Brick Curved 4 x 1 Double
5	Dark Bluish Gray	47452	Technic Brick 2 x 2 w/ Hole, Click Rot. Hinge (H) and Socket
4	Dark Bluish Gray	48169	Technic Brick 2 x 2 with Hole and Rotation Joint Socket
1	Dark Bluish Gray	48170	Technic Brick 2 x 2 with Hole, Half Rotation Joint Ball Horiz
3	Dark Bluish Gray	48171	Technic Brick 2 x 2 with Hole, Half Rotation Joint Ball Vert
1	Dark Bluish Gray	47454	Technic Brick 2 x 3 w/ Holes, Click Rot. Hinge (H) and Socket
4	Dark Bluish Gray	47432	Technic Brick 2 x 3 w/ Holes, Click Rot. Hinge (V) and Socket
8	Blue	4274	Technic Pin 1/2
14	Dark Red	47455	Technic Pin with Friction with Click Rotation Pin
2	Black	2555	Tile 1 x 1 with Clip
6	Dark Red	2555	Tile 1 x 1 with Clip
6	White	2555	Tile 1 x 1 with Clip
3	Dark Red	3070b	Tile 1 x 1 with Groove
5	Dark Red	3069b	Tile 1 x 2 with Groove
1	Dark Red	63864	Tile 1 x 3 with Groove
4	Dark Red	2431	Tile 1 x 4 with Groove
2	Dark Red	6636	Tile 1 x 6
6	Dark Red	4162	Tile 1 x 8
2	Dark Red	3068b	Tile 2 x 2 with Groove
6	Dark Red	47759	Wedge 2 x 4 Triple
1	Dark Red	47753	Wedge 4 x 4 Triple Curved without Studs
8	Dark Red	51739	Wing 2 x 4
6	Dark Red	41770	Wing 2 x 4 Left
6	Dark Red	41769	Wing 2 x 4 Right

Coach

ere too there is room for experimenting with colors. We don't come across the 3 high inverse sloping pieces very often – We ourselves could never get enough of these, to begin with. But your LEGO® collection may be quite different.

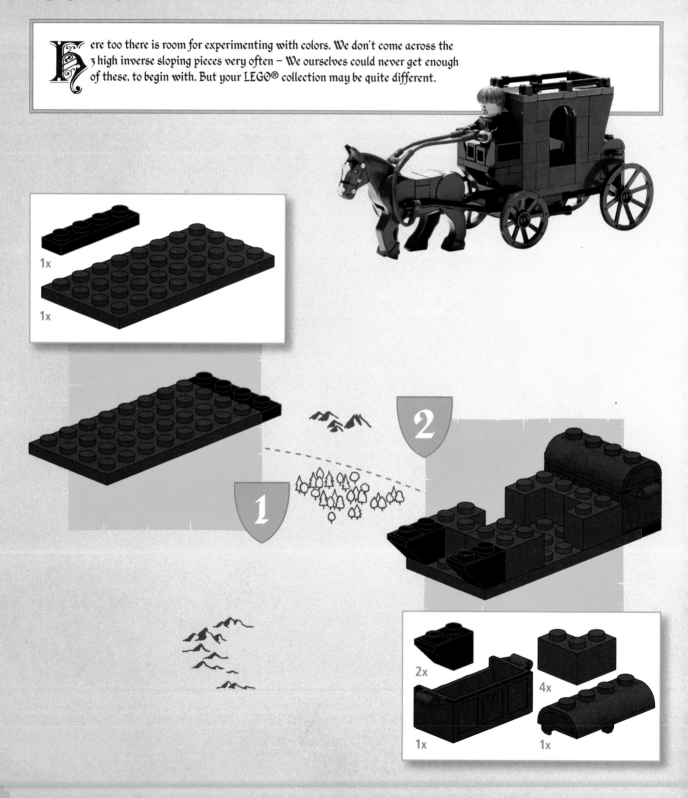

1x

1x

1

2

2x

4x

1x

1x

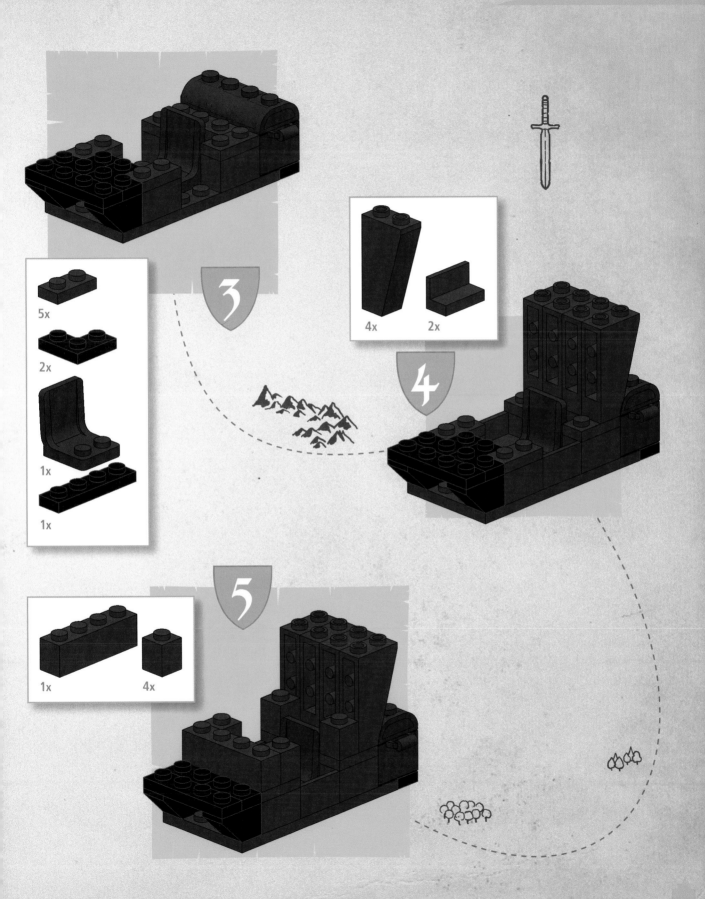

5x

2x

1x

1x

4x   2x

1x   4x

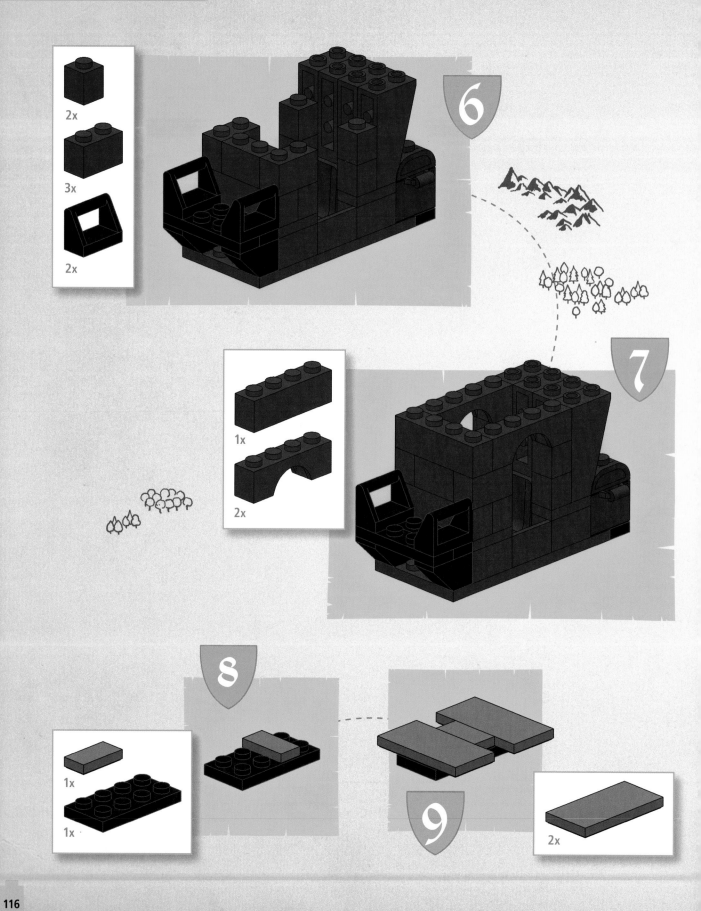

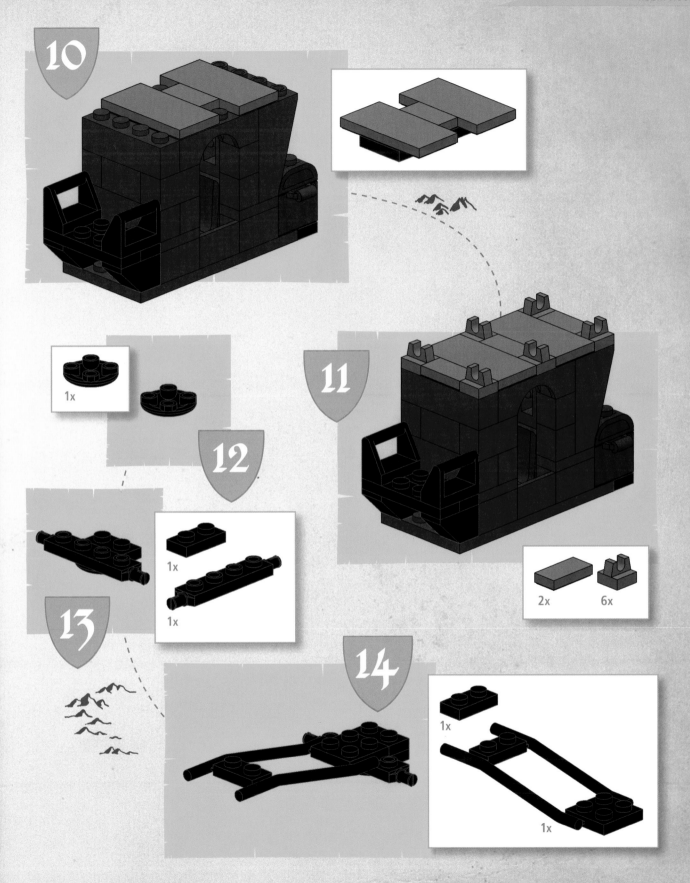

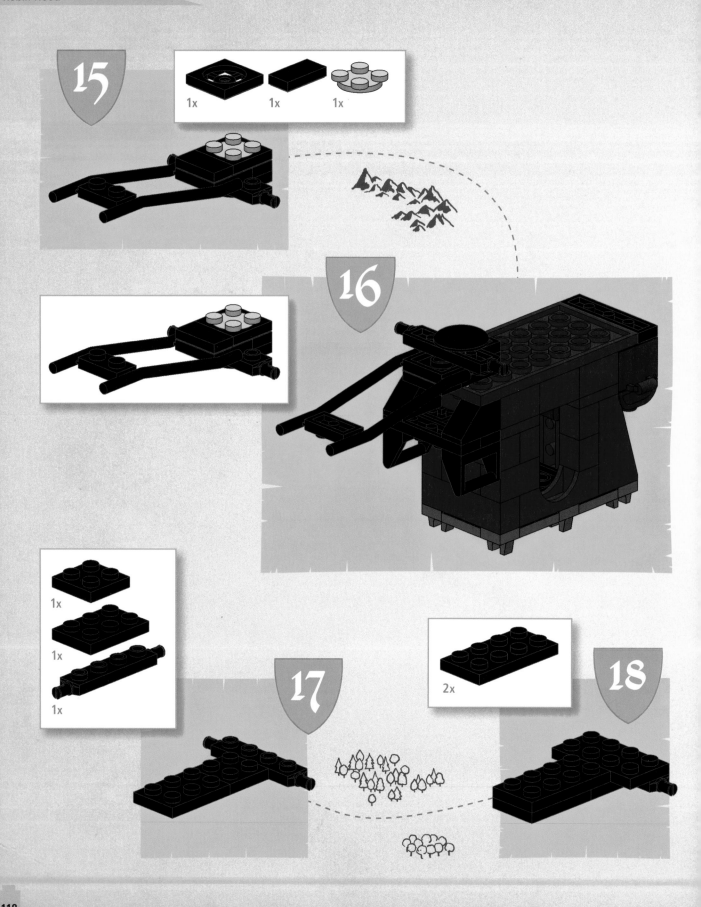

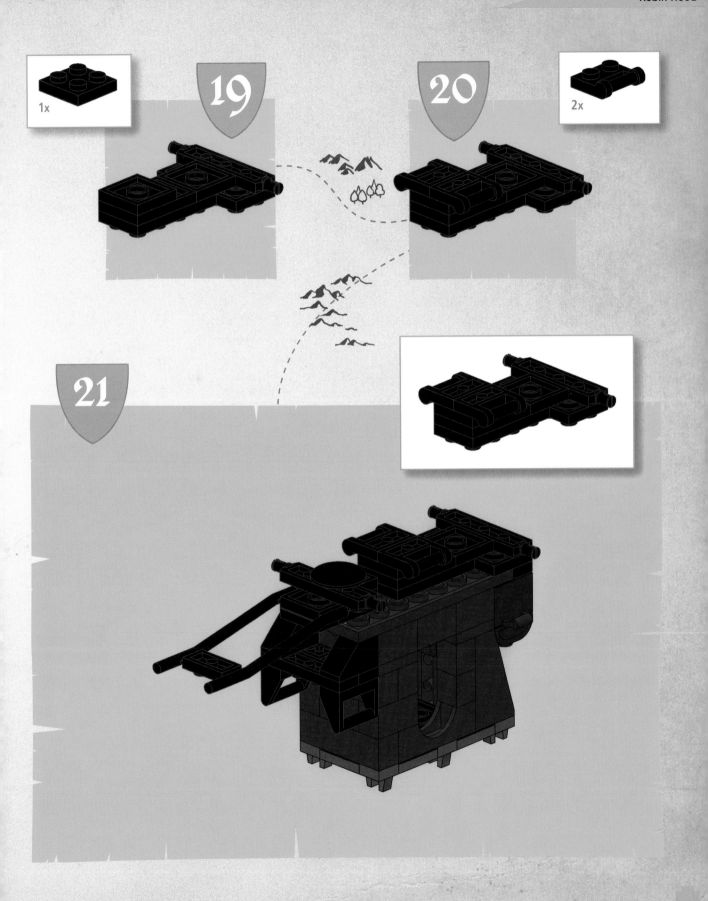

22

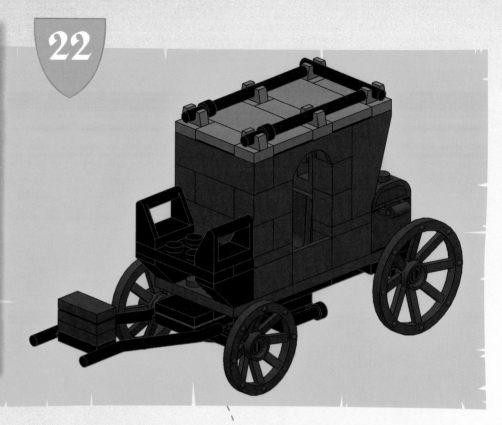

23

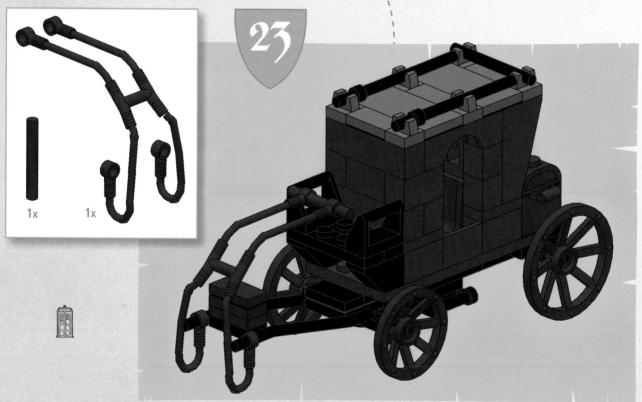

The new "Mos Eisley Cantina" for the Star Wars set includes a new rein that you can here put to alternative use.

24

1x

Parts List

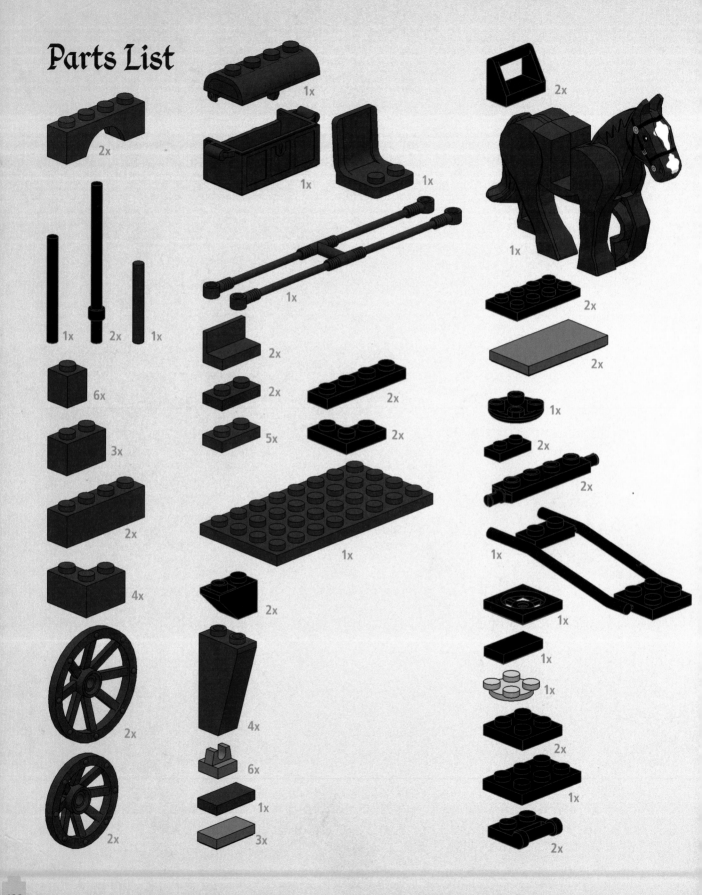

2x

1x

2x

1x

1x

1x

1x

1x

2x

1x

1x

1x

2x

2x

2x

2x

1x

5x

2x

2x

2x

1x

2x

2x

1x

2x

6x

3x

2x

4x

2x

2x

1x

1x

1x

2x

1x

2x

2x

4x

6x

1x

3x

Quantity	Color		Element	Element Name
2		Dark Red	3659	Arch 1 x 4
1		Black	30374	Bar 4L Light Sabre Blade
2		Black	63965	Bar 6L with Thick Stop
1		Reddish Brown	87994	Bar 3L
6		Dark Red	3005	Brick 1 x 1
3		Dark Red	3004	Brick 1 x 2
2		Dark Red	3010	Brick 1 x 4
4		Dark Red	2357	Brick 2 x 2 Corner
2		Reddish Brown	4489	Castle Wagon Wheel Large
2		Reddish Brown	2470	Castle Wagon Wheel Small
1		Reddish Brown	4739	Container Treasure Chest Lid
1		Reddish Brown	4738b	Container Treasure Chest without Slots
1		Reddish Brown	4079	Minifig Seat 2 x 2
1		Reddish Brown	30191	Minifig Stretcher Holder
2		Dark Red	4865a	Panel 1 x 2 x 1 with Square Corners
2		Reddish Brown	3023	Plate 1 x 2
5		Dark Red	3023	Plate 1 x 2
2		Black	3710	Plate 1 x 4
2		Black	2420	Plate 2 x 2 Corner
1		Dark Red	3035	Plate 4 x 8
2		Black	3665	Slope Brick 45 2 x 1 Inverted
4		Dark Red	2449	Slope Brick 75 2 x 1 x 3 Inverted
6		Dark Bluish Gray	2555	Tile 1 x 1 with Clip
1		Reddish Brown	3069b	Tile 1 x 2 with Groove
3		Dark Bluish Gray	3069b	Tile 1 x 2 with Groove
2		Black	2432	Tile 1 x 2 with Handle
1		Reddish Brown	10509p01	Animal Horse Poseable with Black Bridle and White Blaze Pattern
2		Black	3020	Plate 2 x 4
2		Dark Bluish Gray	87079	Tile 2 x 4
1		Black	2654	Plate, Round 2 x 2 with Rounded Bottom
2		Black	3023	Plate 1 x 2
2		Black	2926	Plate, Modified 1 x 4 with Wheels Holder
1		Black	2397	Horse Hitching
1		Black	3680	Turntable 2 x 2 Plate, Base
1		Black	3069b	Tile 1 x 2 with Groove
1		Light Bluish Gray	3679	Turntable 2 x 2 Plate, Top
2		Black	3022	Plate 2 x 2
1		Black	3021	Plate 2 x 3
2		Black	48336	Plate, Modified 1 x 2 with Handle on Side - Closed Ends

Tree

This very sturdy leafy tree was designed by Christian Treczoks. It's already made quite an impact on the scene. We've already used it in another book (Build your own car – Joe's Garage) as decoration.

Now, finally, we show you how it's built.

2x

A

Here, we first show you how the leaves are put in place and then begin with the building instructions.

1x   1x

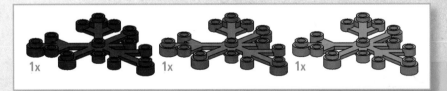

1x   1x   1x

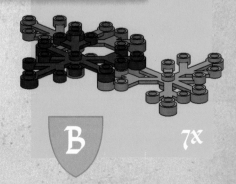

B   7x

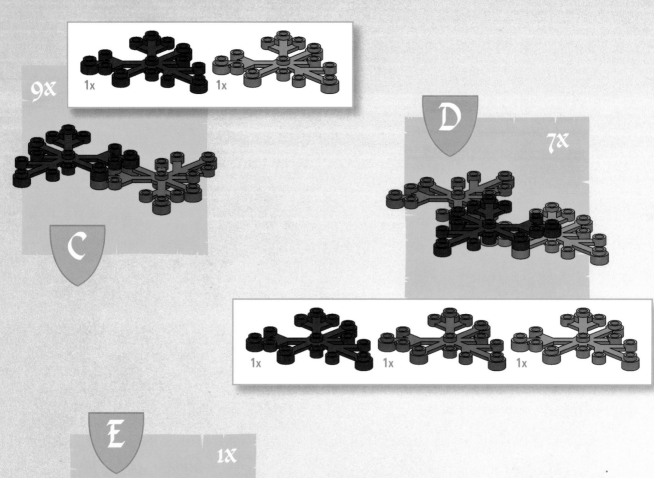

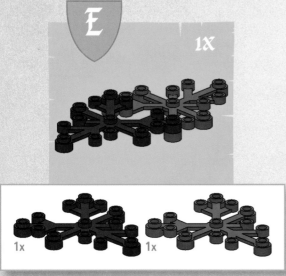

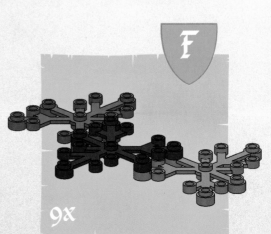

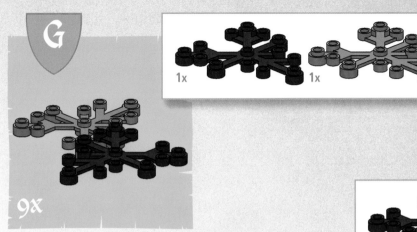

G

9x

1x 1x

H

8x

1x 1x

I

6x

1x 1x

J

3x

1x 1x

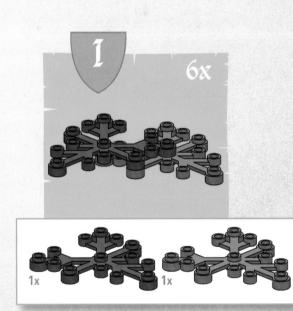

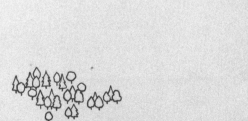

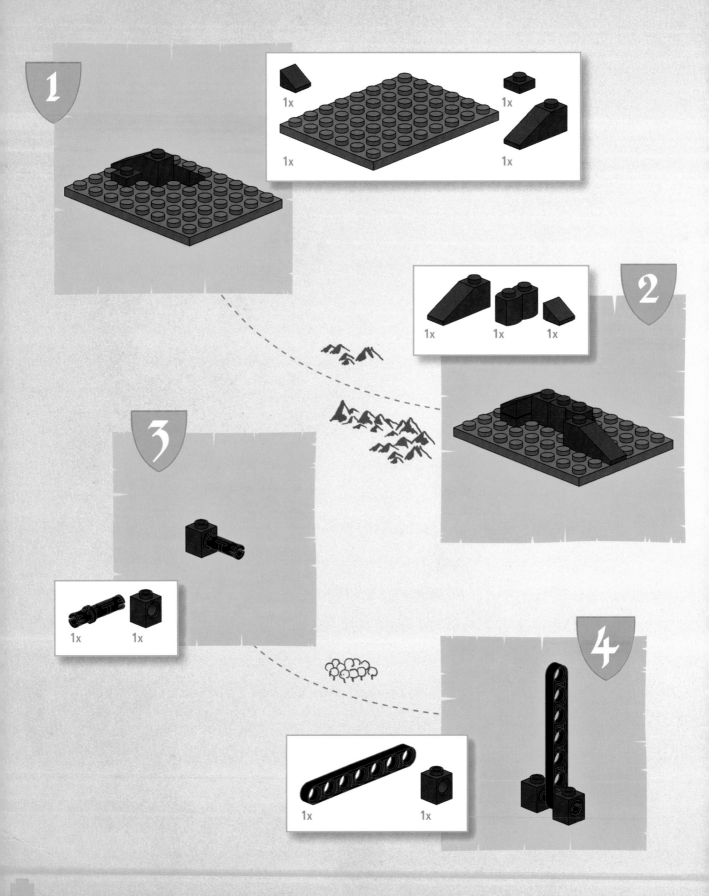

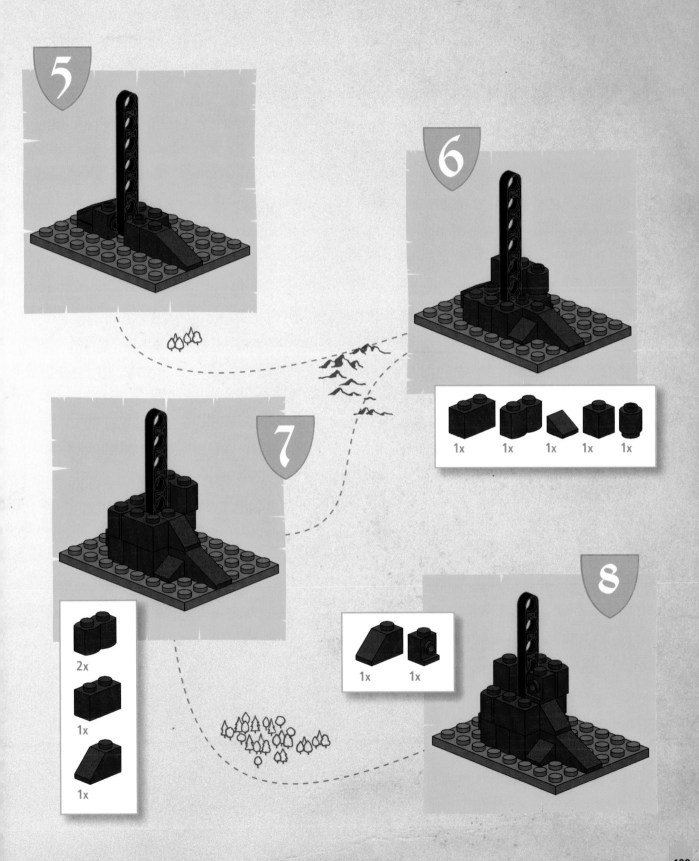

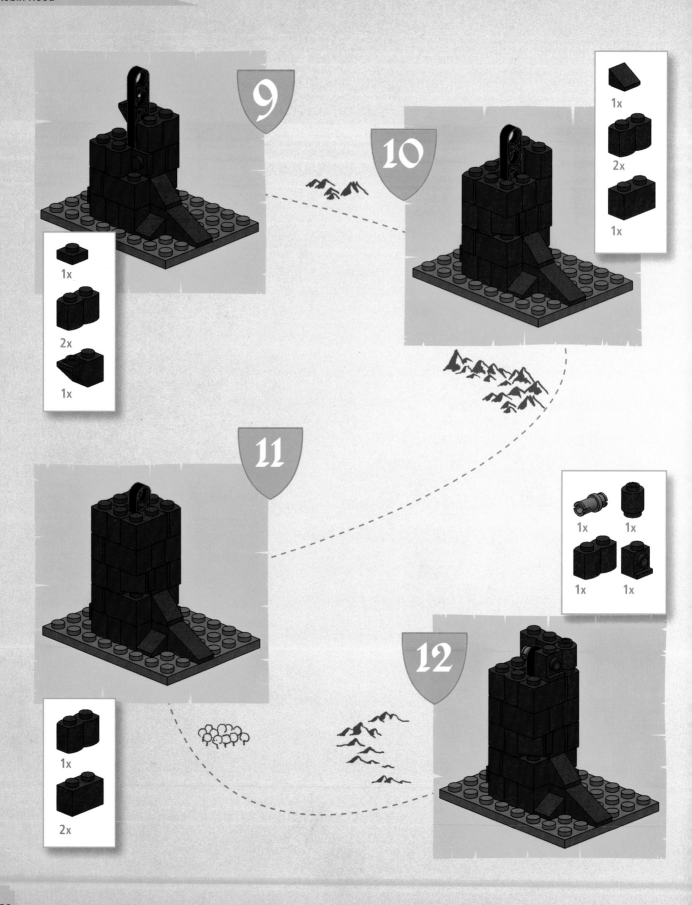

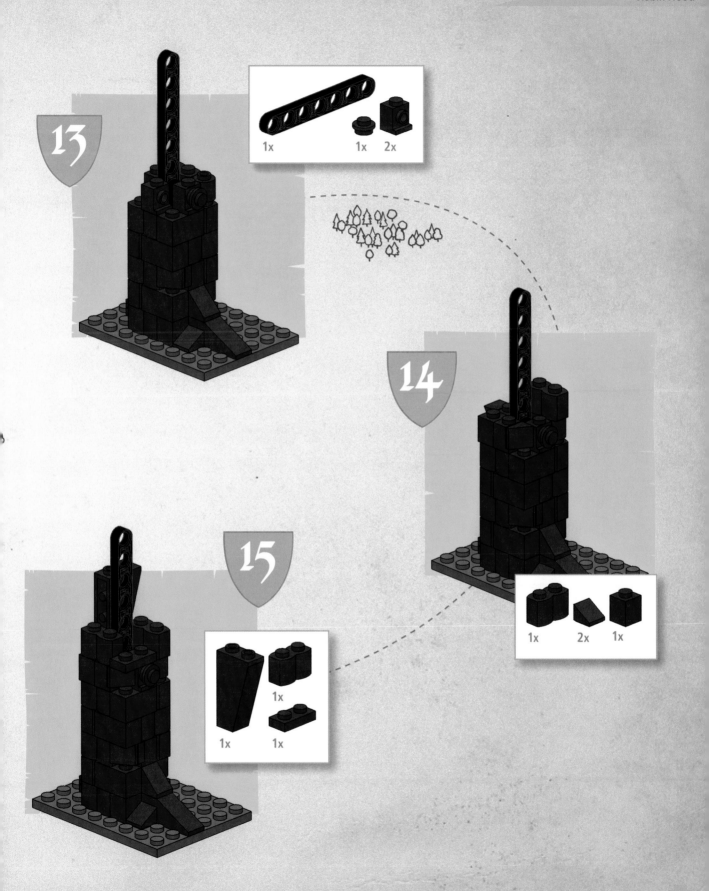

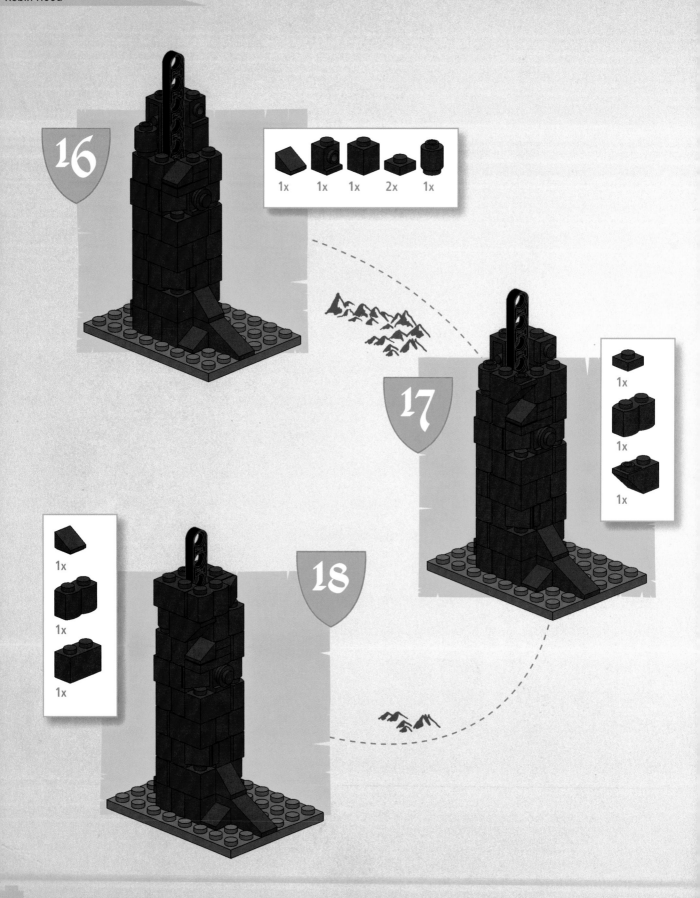

16

1x 1x 1x 2x 1x

17

1x

1x

1x

18

1x

1x

1x

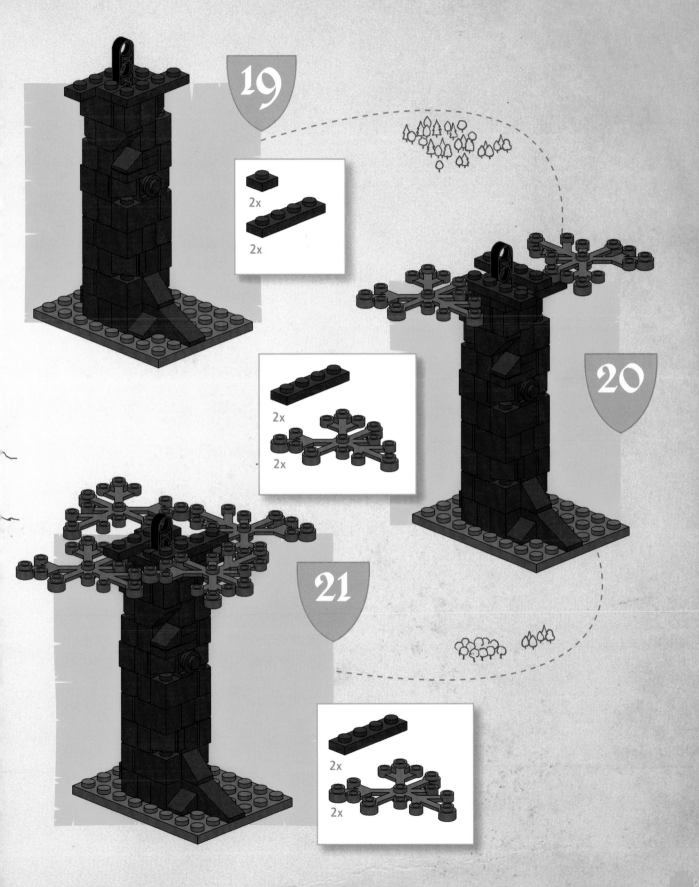

27

2x

28

2x
2x

2x
1x
1x

29

So far, we've used only individual leaves, but here we also need the pre-made, multi-leaved elements.

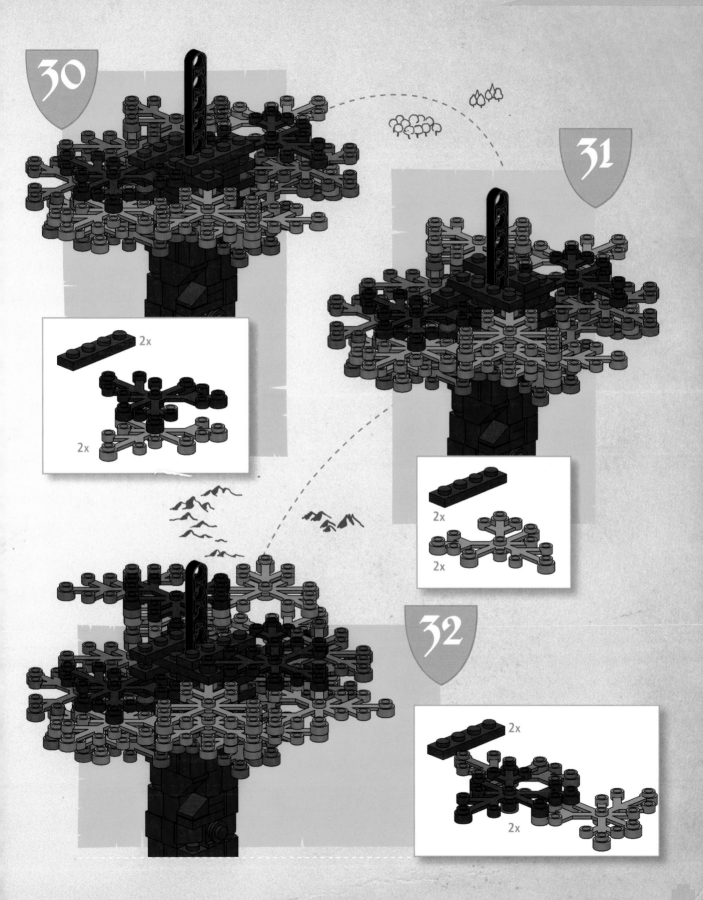

30

31

2x

2x

2x

2x

32

2x

2x

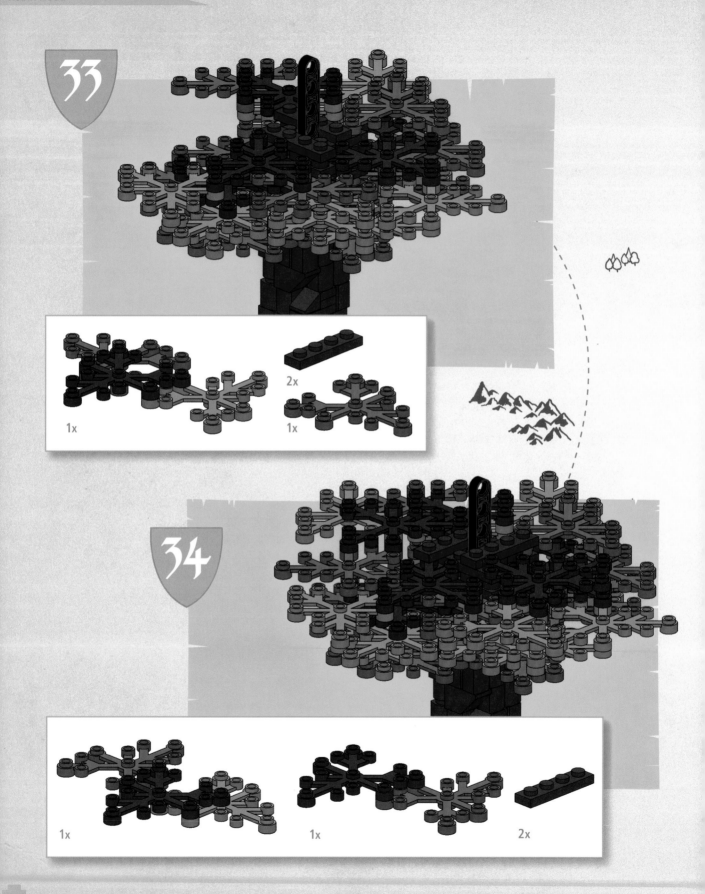

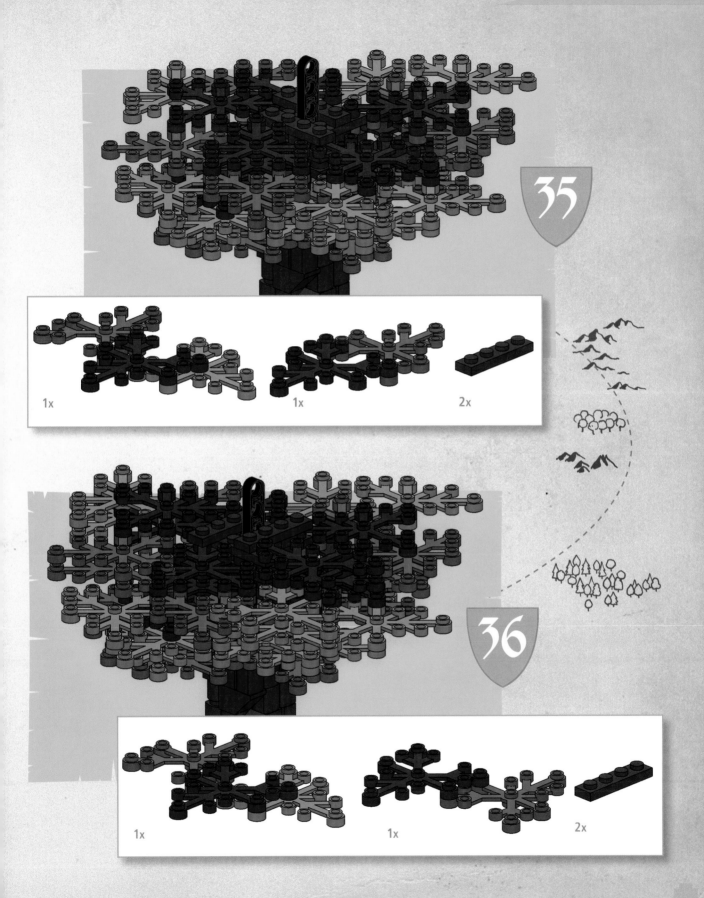

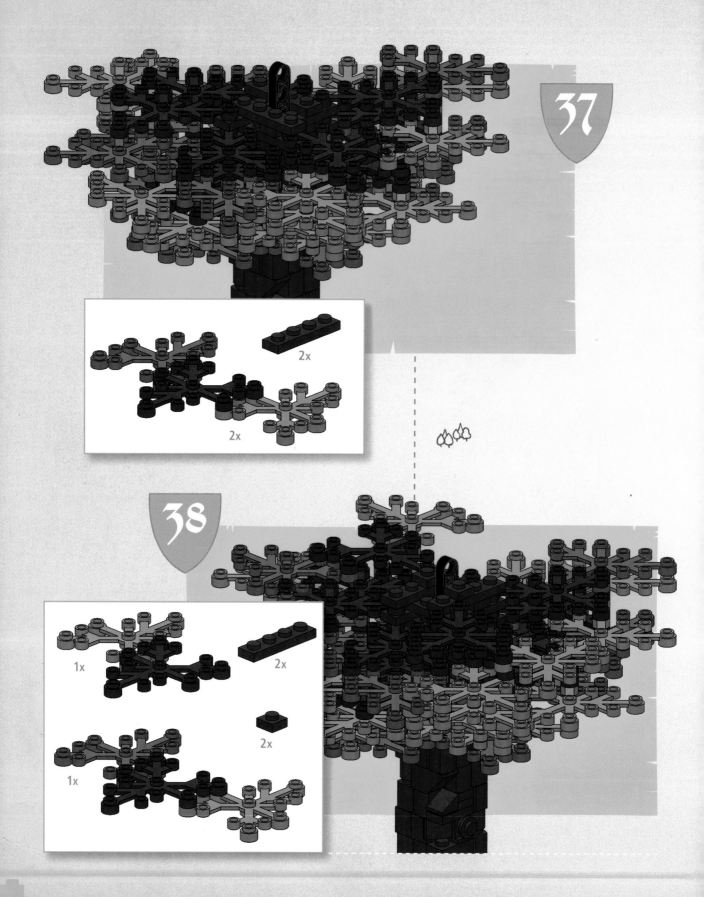

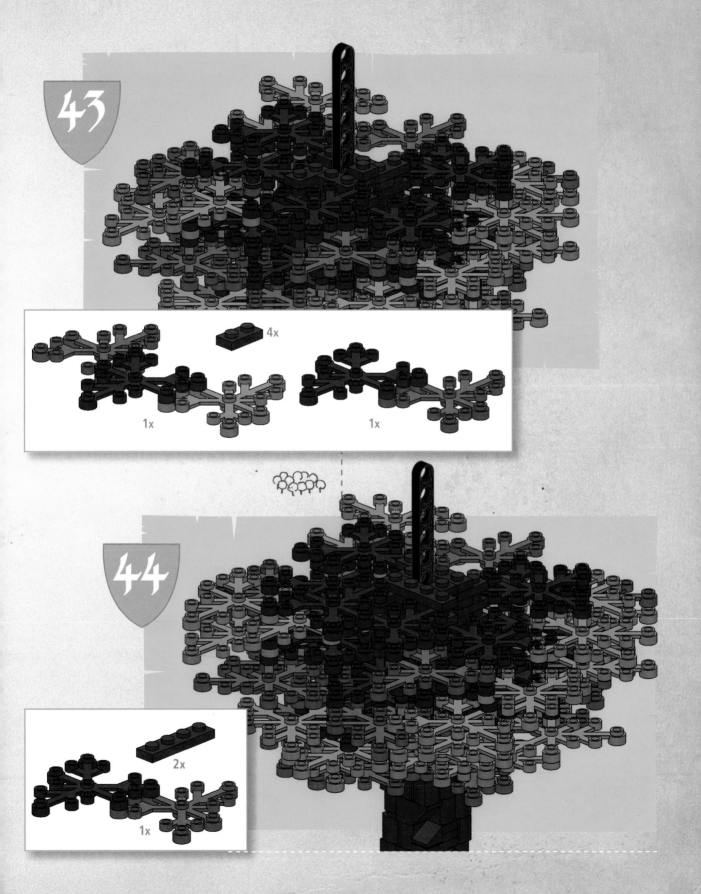

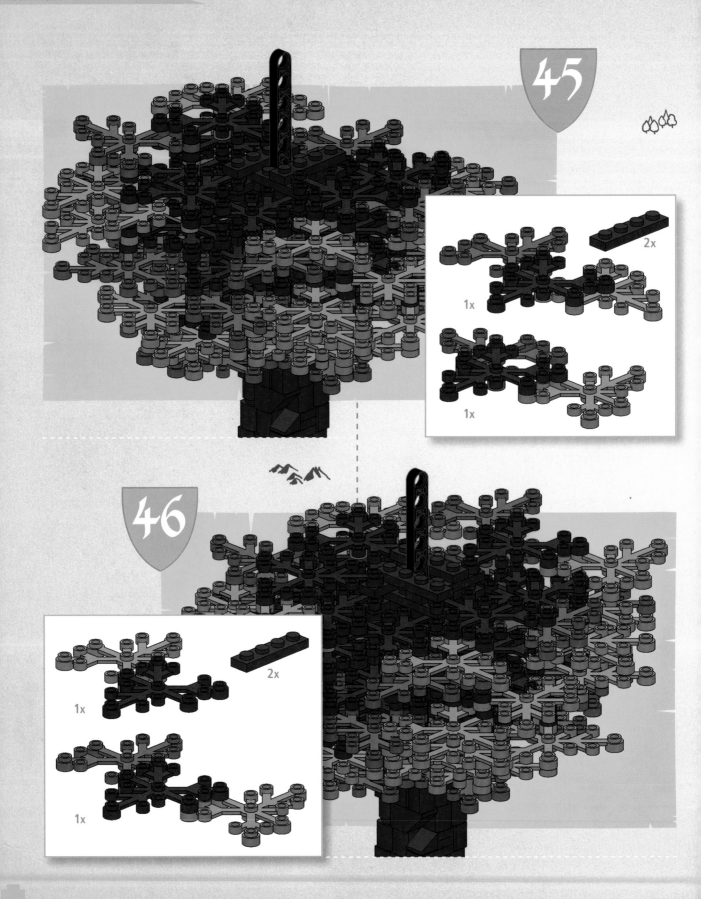

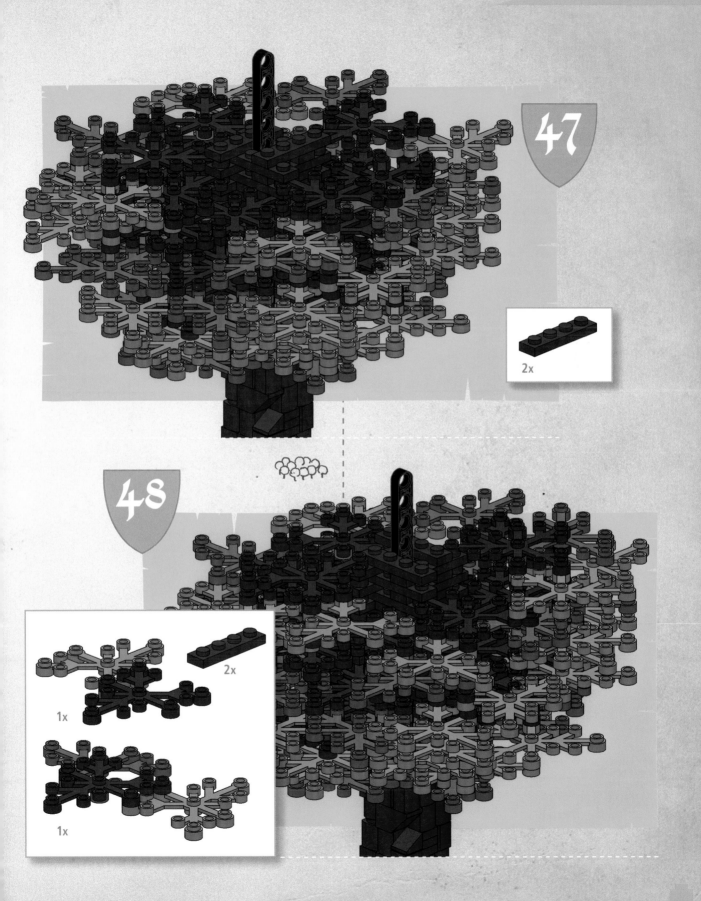

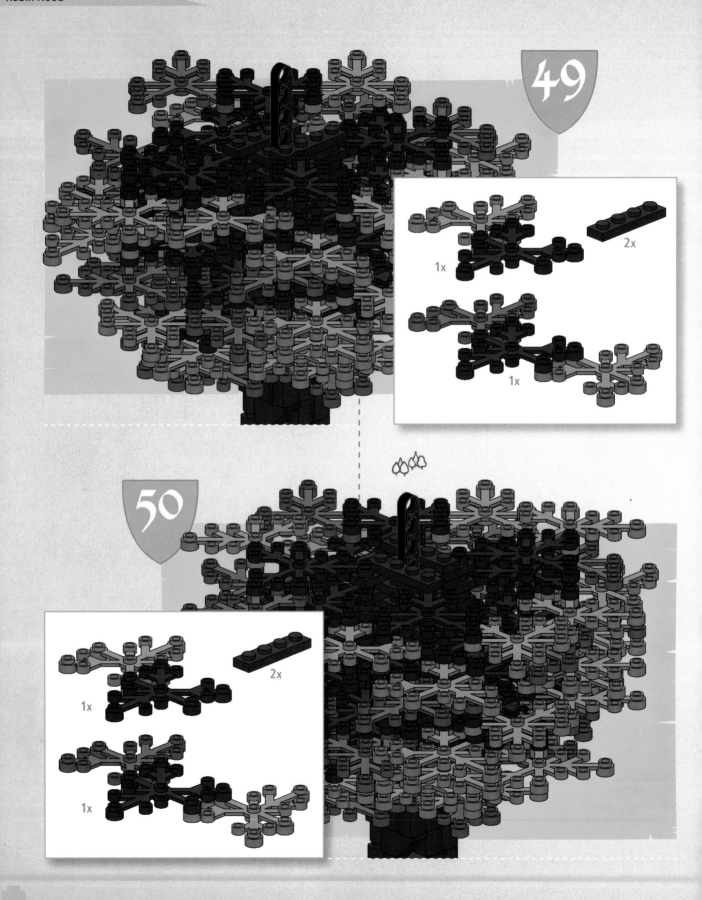

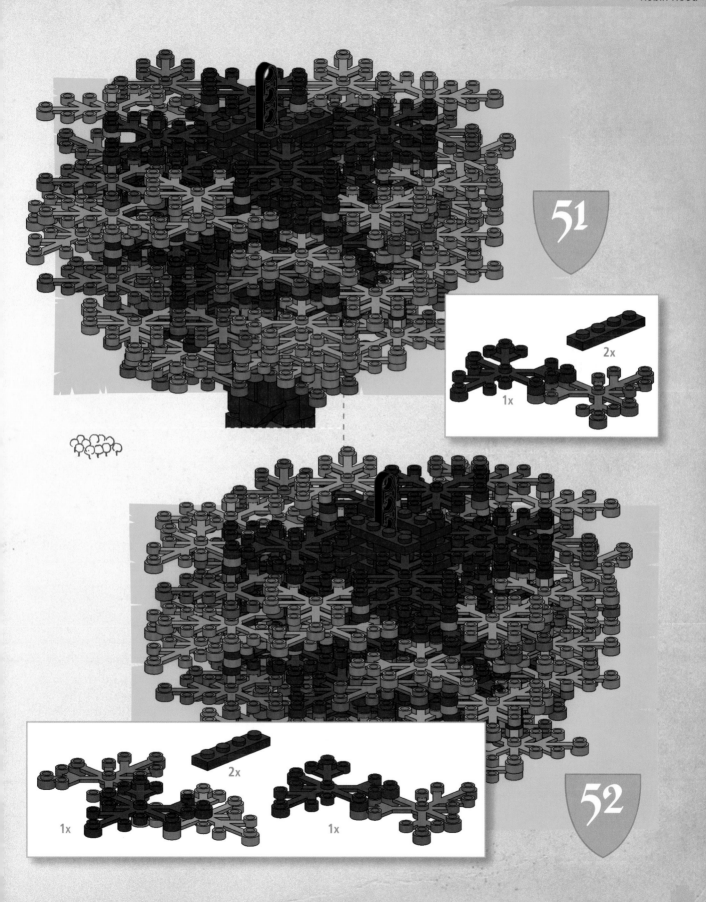

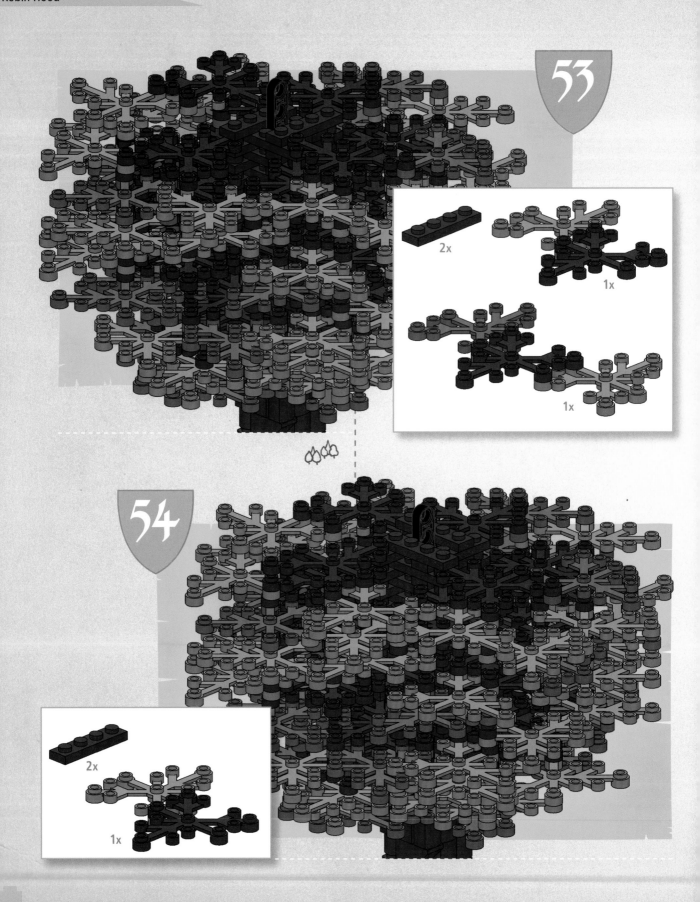

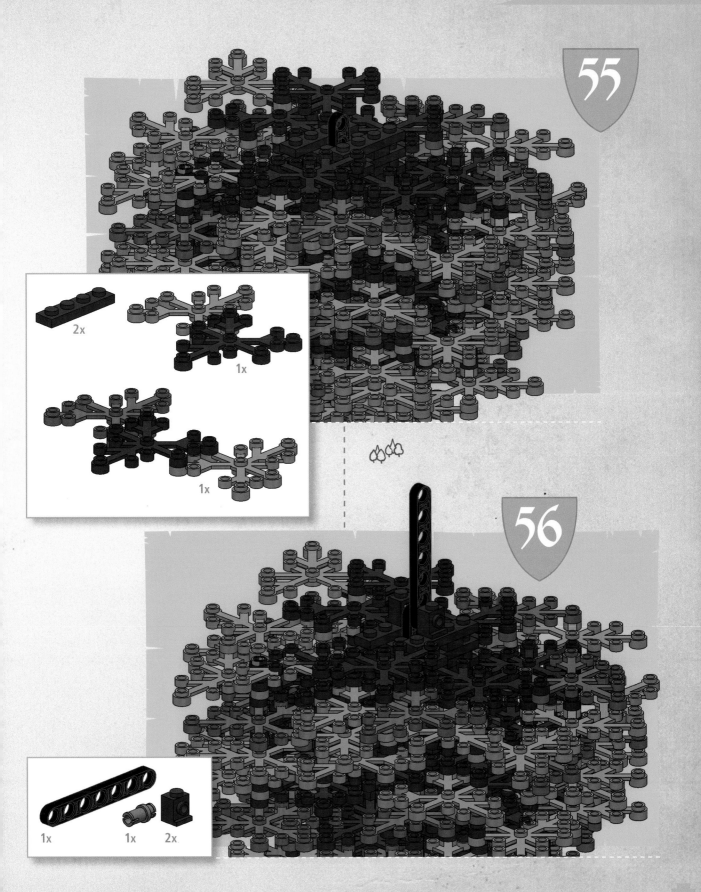

55

56

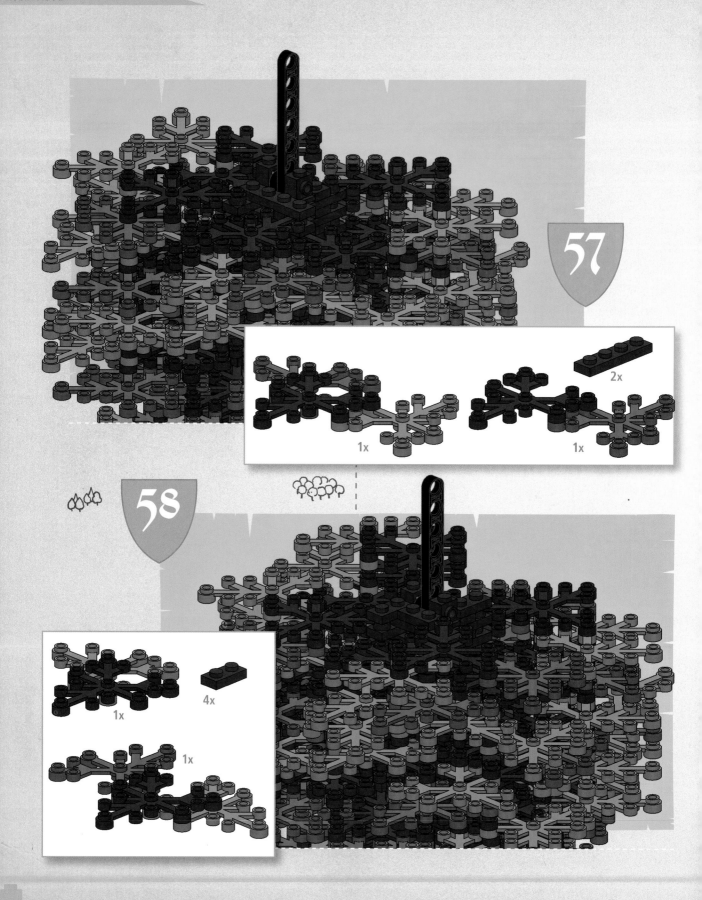

59

2x

1x

60

1x

1x

2x

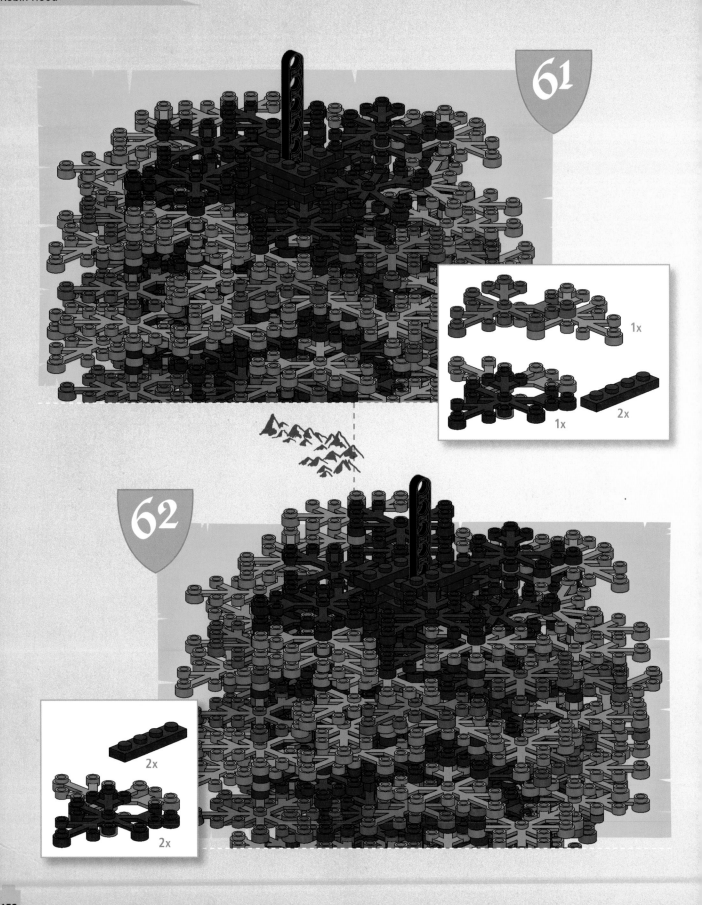

61

1x

1x

2x

62

2x

2x

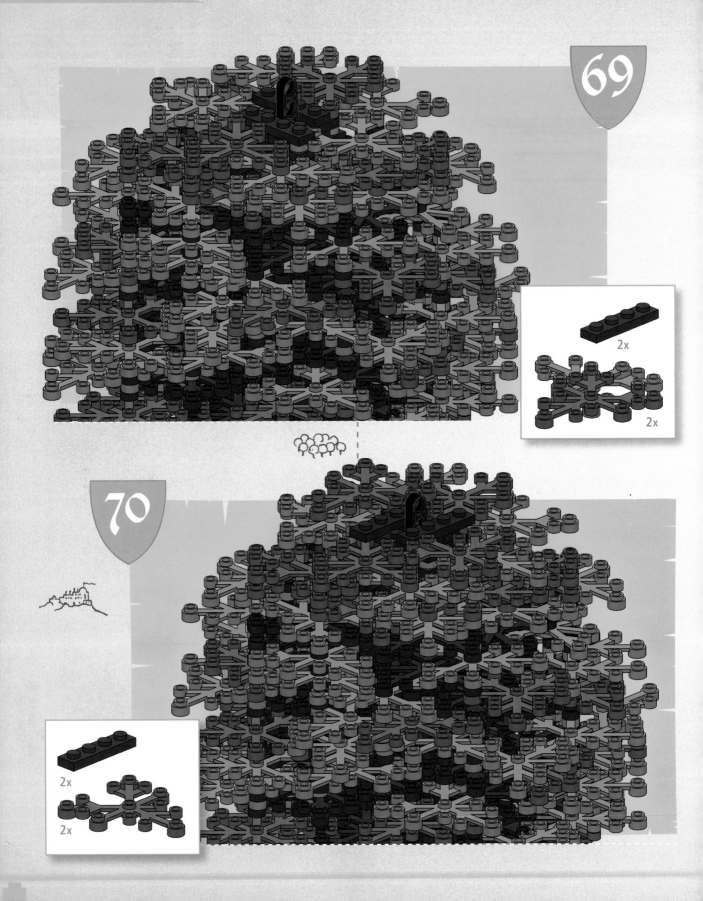

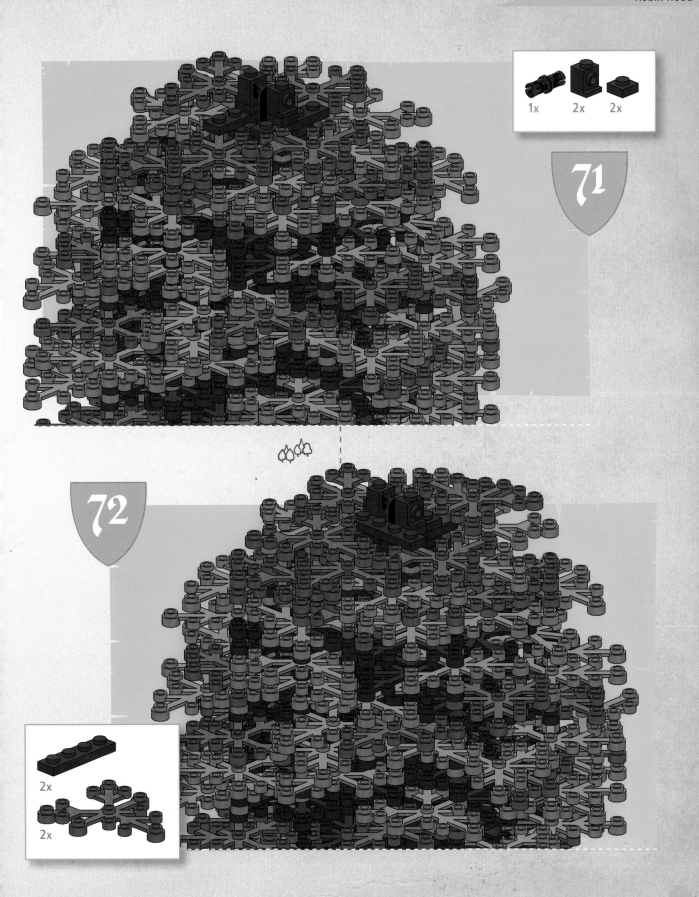

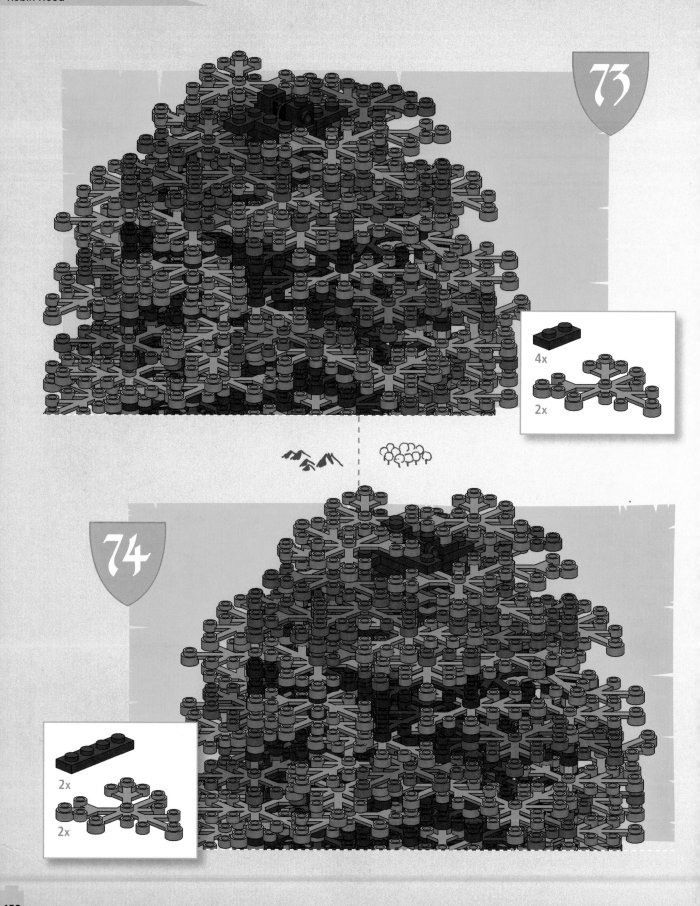

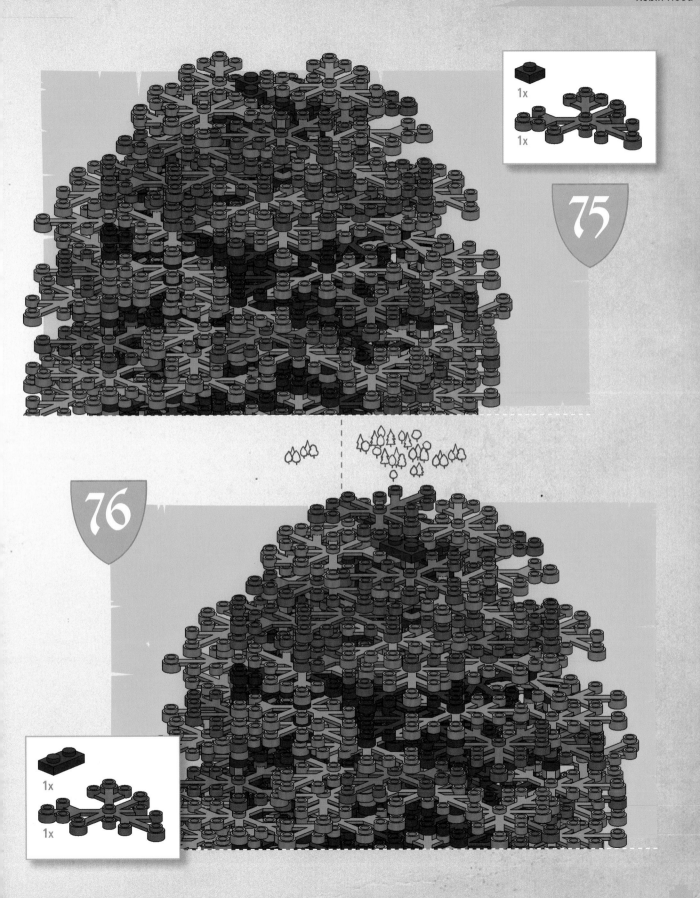

77

1x

Parts List

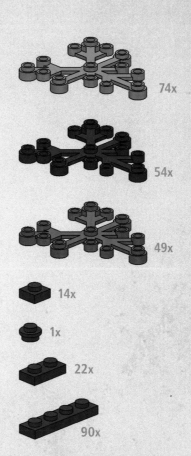

Quantity	Color		Element	Element Name
3		Reddish Brown	3005	Brick 1 x 1
3		Reddish Brown	3062b	Brick 1 x 1 Round with Hollow Stud
13		Reddish Brown	4070	Brick 1 x 1 with Headlight
6		Reddish Brown	3004	Brick 1 x 2
14		Reddish Brown	30136	Brick 1 x 2 Log
74		Bright Green	2417	Plant Leaves 6 x 5
54		Dark Green	2417	Plant Leaves 6 x 5
49		Green	2417	Plant Leaves 6 x 5
14		Reddish Brown	3024	Plate 1 x 1
1		Reddish Brown	4073	Plate 1 x 1 Round
22		Reddish Brown	3023	Plate 1 x 2
90		Reddish Brown	3710	Plate 1 x 4

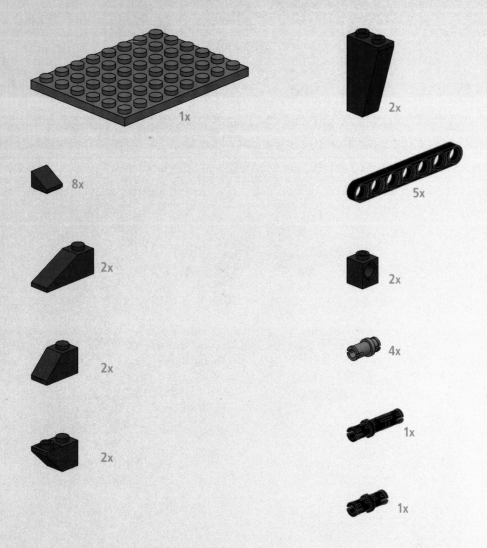

Quantity	Color	Element	Element Name
1	Green	3036	Plate 6 x 8
8	Reddish Brown	54200	Slope Brick 31 1 x 1 x 2/3
2	Reddish Brown	4286	Slope Brick 33 3 x 1
2	Reddish Brown	3040b	Slope Brick 45 2 x 1
2	Reddish Brown	3665	Slope Brick 45 2 x 1 Inverted
2	Reddish Brown	2449	Slope Brick 75 2 x 1 x 3 Inverted
5	Black	32065	Technic Beam 7 x 1/2
2	Reddish Brown	6541	Technic Brick 1 x 1 with Hole
4	Dark Bluish Gray	32002	Technic Pin 3/4
1	Black	6558	Technic Pin Long with Friction and Slot
1	Black	2780	Technic Pin with Friction and Slots

Oxcart

The size of this cart was a challenge. We came across various carts on the Internet, but we wanted to find a particular design that in our view would be consistent with the miniature size of the figures. Of course, you can choose whatever shade of brown you prefer, as they all reflect nature.

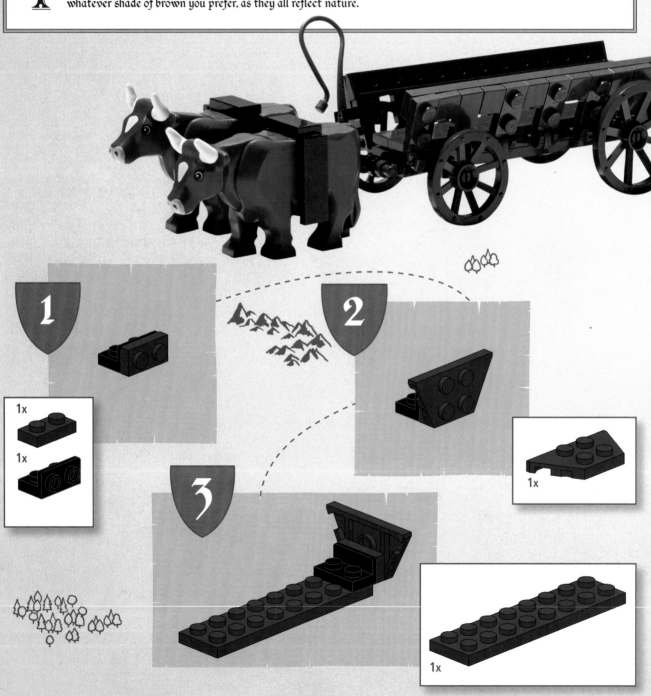

1

1x

1x

2

1x

3

1x

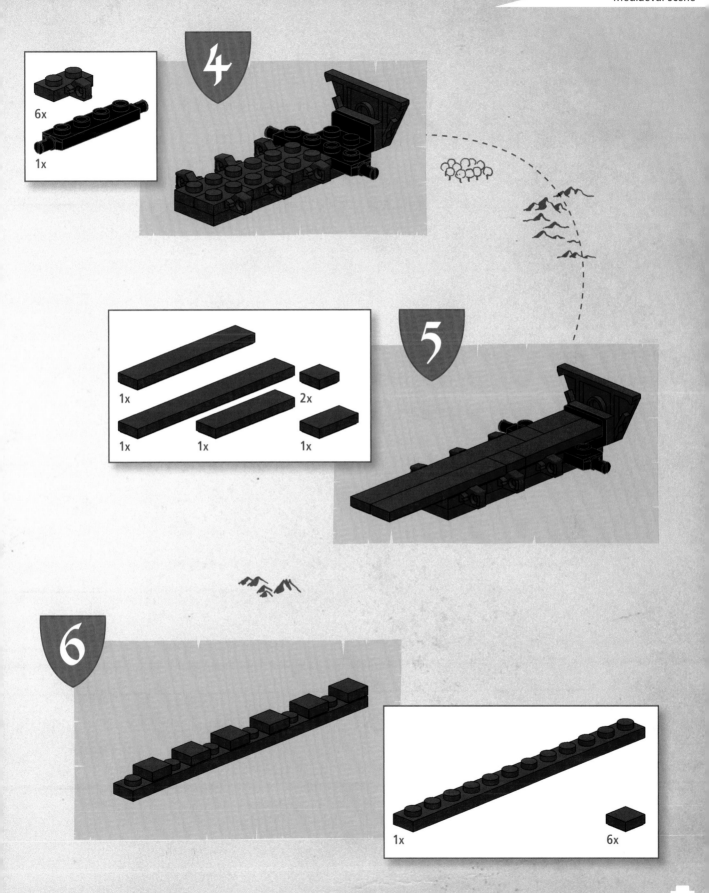

6x

1x

1x
1x
1x
2x
1x

1x
6x

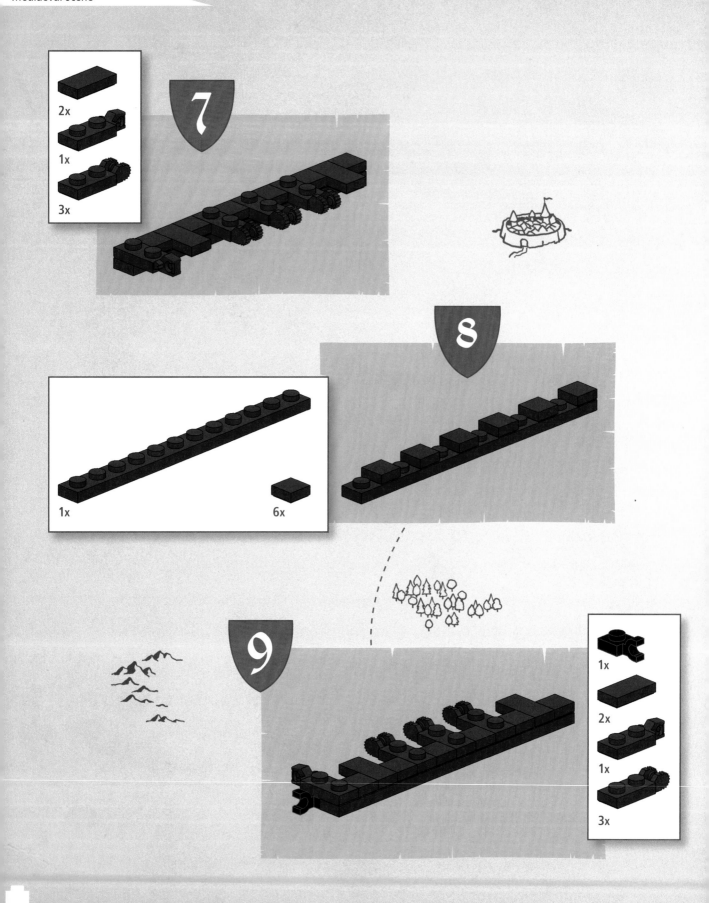

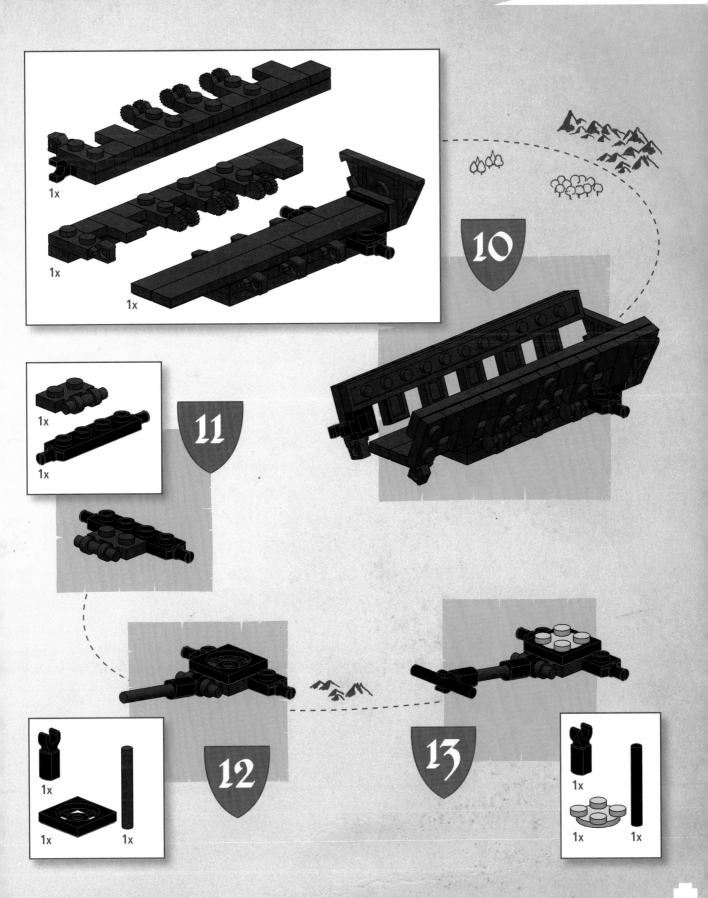

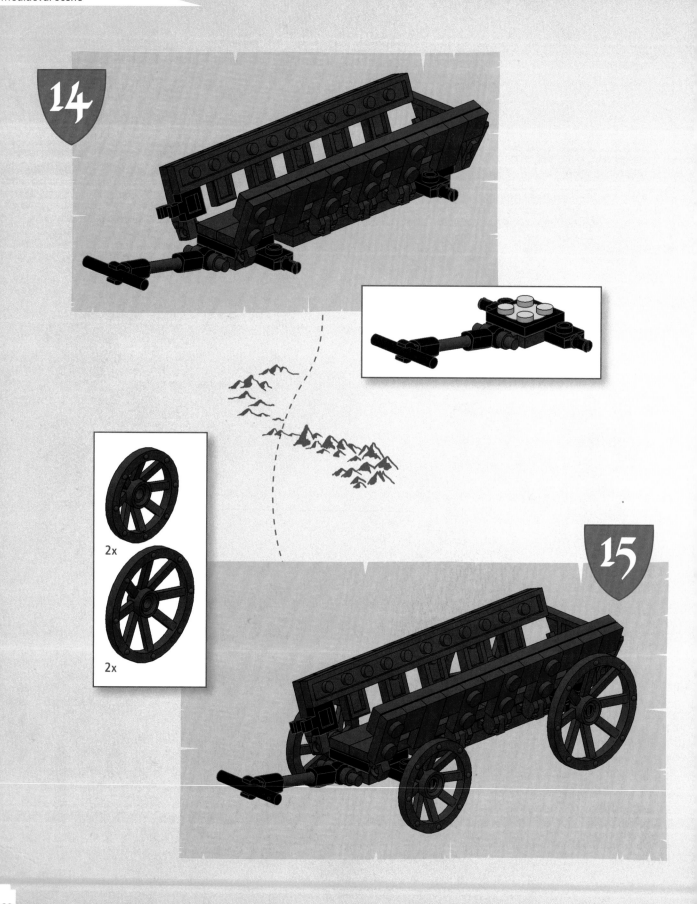

14

15

2x

2x

16

2x

1x

1x

1x

17

2x

18

2x

4x

Put a whip in the black clip, so as to give your model the finishing touch.

Parts List

2x

 4x

 1x

1x

 2x

 1x

 4x

 2x

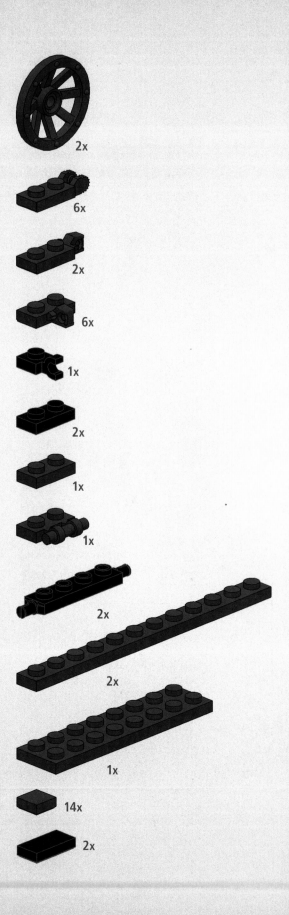

2x

6x

2x

6x

1x

2x

1x

1x

2x

2x

1x

14x

2x

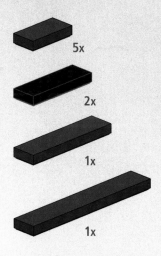

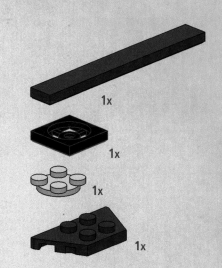

Quantity	Color		Element	Element Name
2		Reddish Brown	64452	Animal Cow
4		White	64847	Animal Cow Horn
1		Black	87994	Bar 3L
1		Reddish Brown	87994	Bar 3L
2		Black	11090	Bar Tube with Clip
1		Black	99780	Bracket 1 x 2 - 1 x 2 Up
4		Black	87087	Brick 1 x 1 with Stud on 1 Side
2		Reddish Brown	4489	Castle Wagon Wheel Large
2		Reddish Brown	2470	Castle Wagon Wheel Small
6		Reddish Brown	44302	Hinge Plate 1 x 2 Locking with Dual Finger on End Vertical
2		Reddish Brown	44301	Hinge Plate 1 x 2 Locking with Single Finger on End Vertical
6		Reddish Brown	44567	Hinge Plate 1 x 2 Locking with Single Finger On Side Vertical
1		Black	6019	Plate 1 x 1 with Clip Horizontal
2		Black	3023	Plate 1 x 2
1		Reddish Brown	3023	Plate 1 x 2
1		Reddish Brown	2540	Plate 1 x 2 with Handle
2		Black	2926	Plate 1 x 4 with Wheels Holder
2		Reddish Brown	60479	Plate 1 x 12
1		Reddish Brown	3034	Plate 2 x 8
14		Reddish Brown	3070b	Tile 1 x 1 with Groove
2		Black	3069b	Tile 1 x 2 with Groove
5		Reddish Brown	3069b	Tile 1 x 2 with Groove
2		Black	63864	Tile 1 x 3 with Groove
1		Reddish Brown	2431	Tile 1 x 4 with Groove
1		Reddish Brown	6636	Tile 1 x 6
1		Reddish Brown	4162	Tile 1 x 8
1		Black	3680	Turntable 2 x 2 Plate Base
1		Light Bluish Gray	3679	Turntable 2 x 2 Plate Top
1		Reddish Brown	51739	Wing 2 x 4

Catapult

esieging a castle was a common activity in the time of knights. In the Middle Ages, they devoted a considerable amount of time to creating ingenious mechanisms: even now, we view their catapults as masterpieces. Our version is fully functional, too.

1x

2x

2x

1x

1

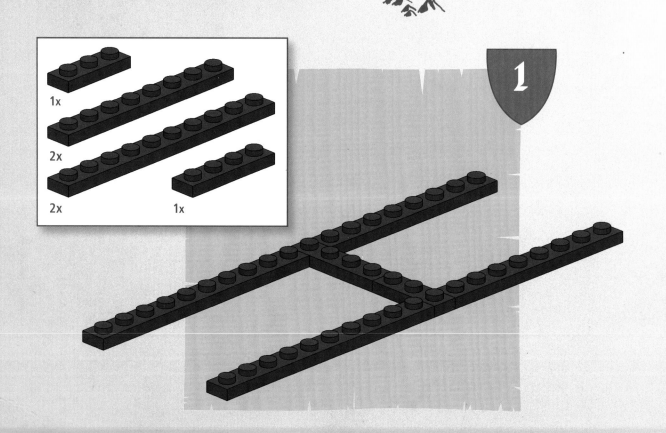

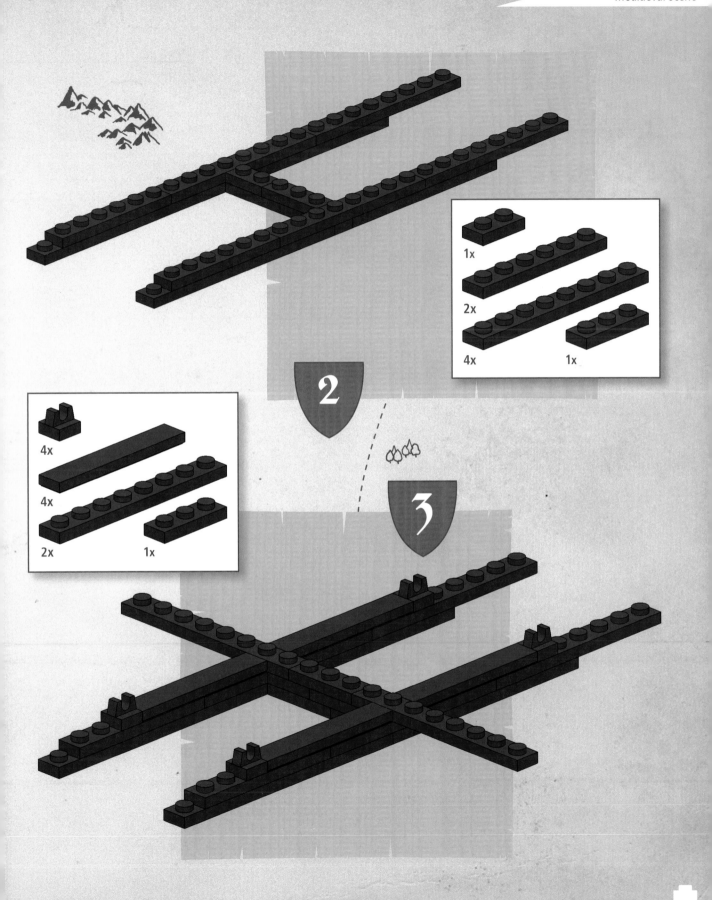

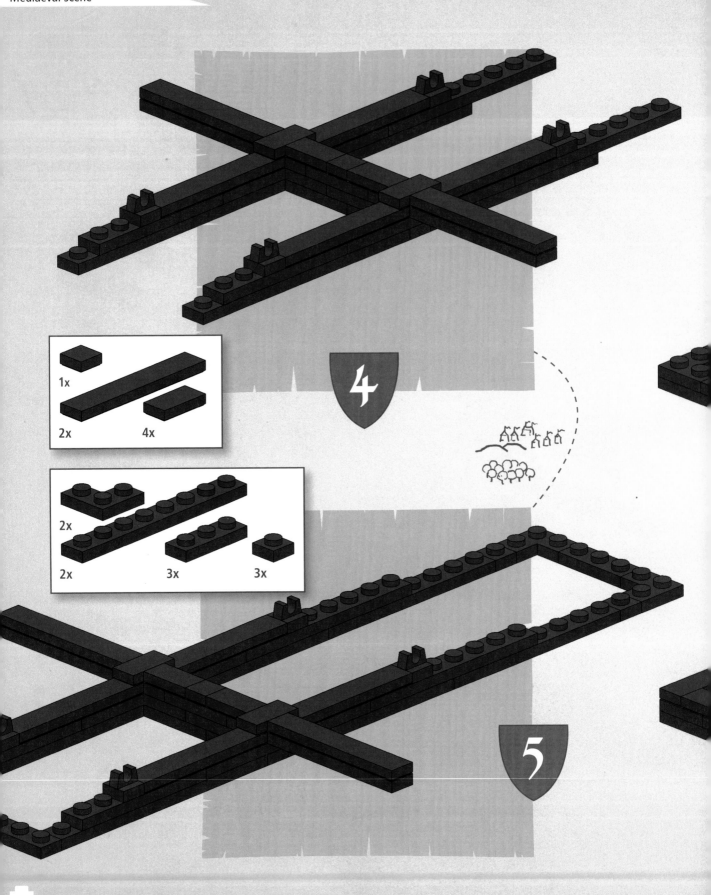

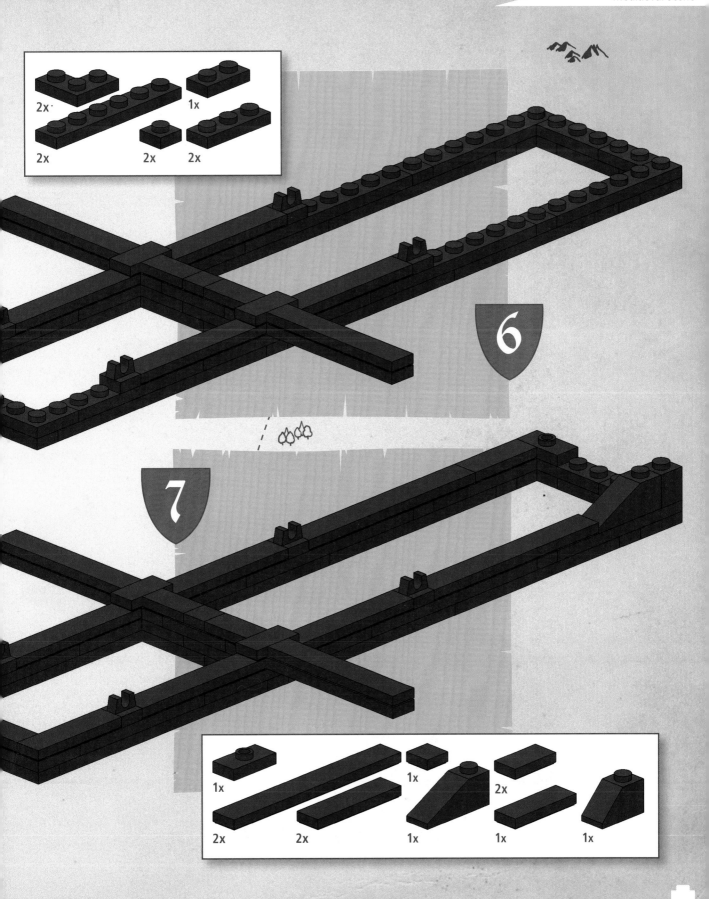

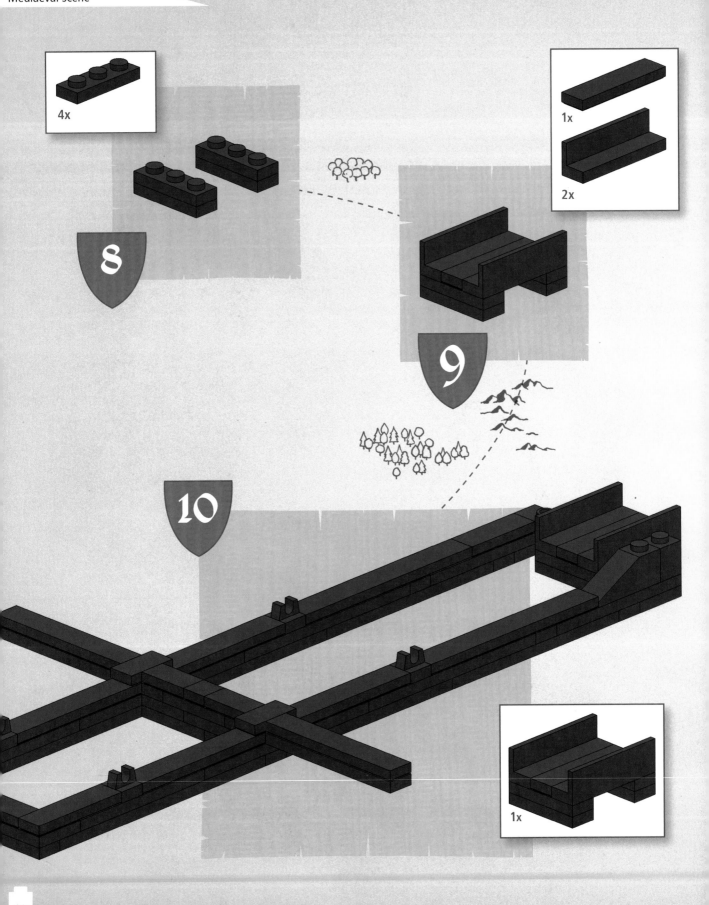

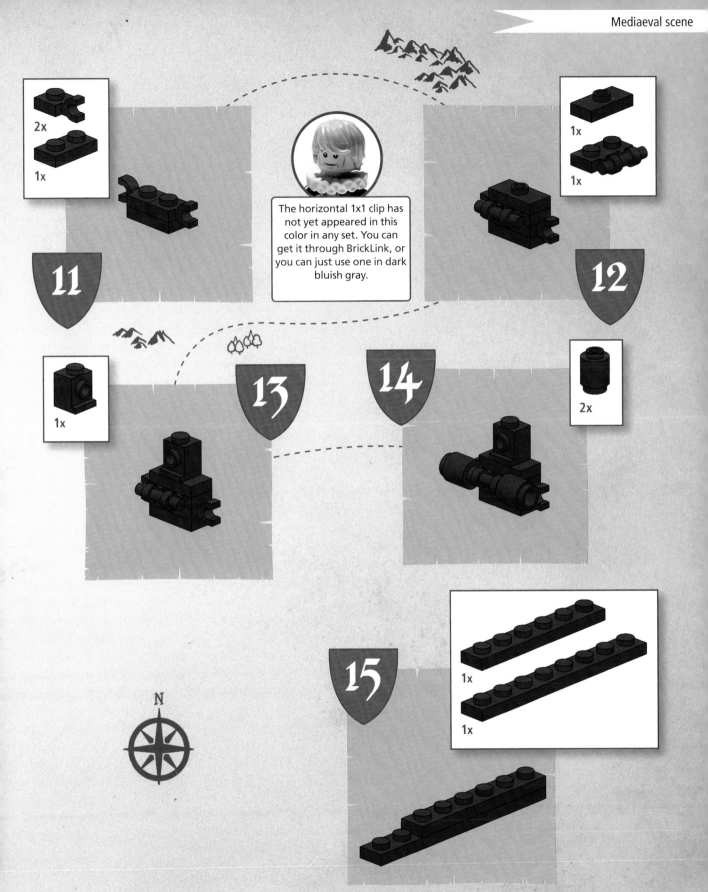

2x

1x

1x

1x

The horizontal 1x1 clip has not yet appeared in this color in any set. You can get it through BrickLink, or you can just use one in dark bluish gray.

11

12

1x

2x

13

14

15

1x

1x

N

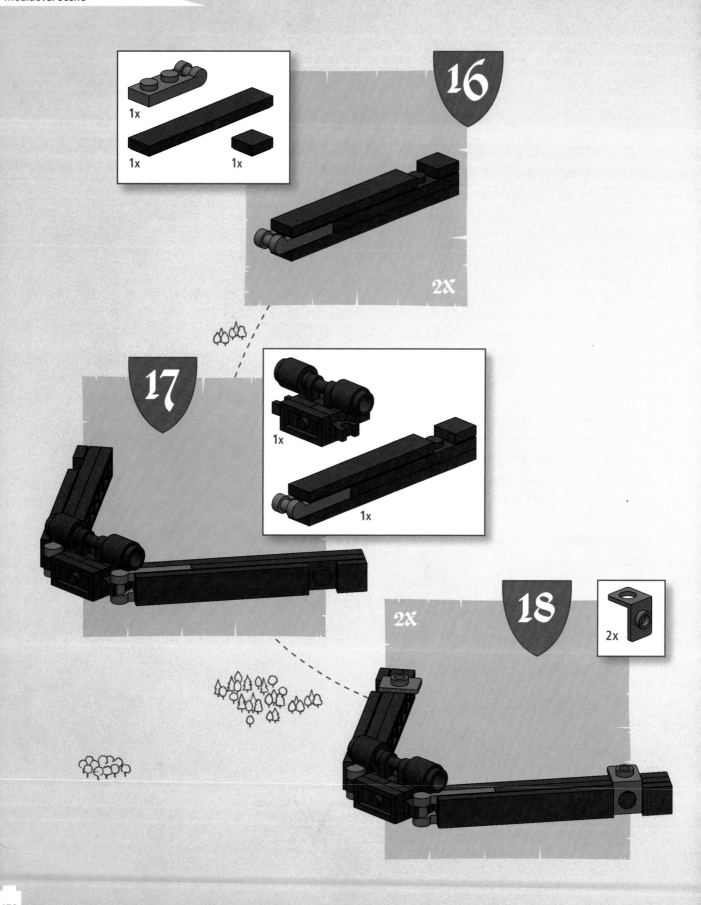

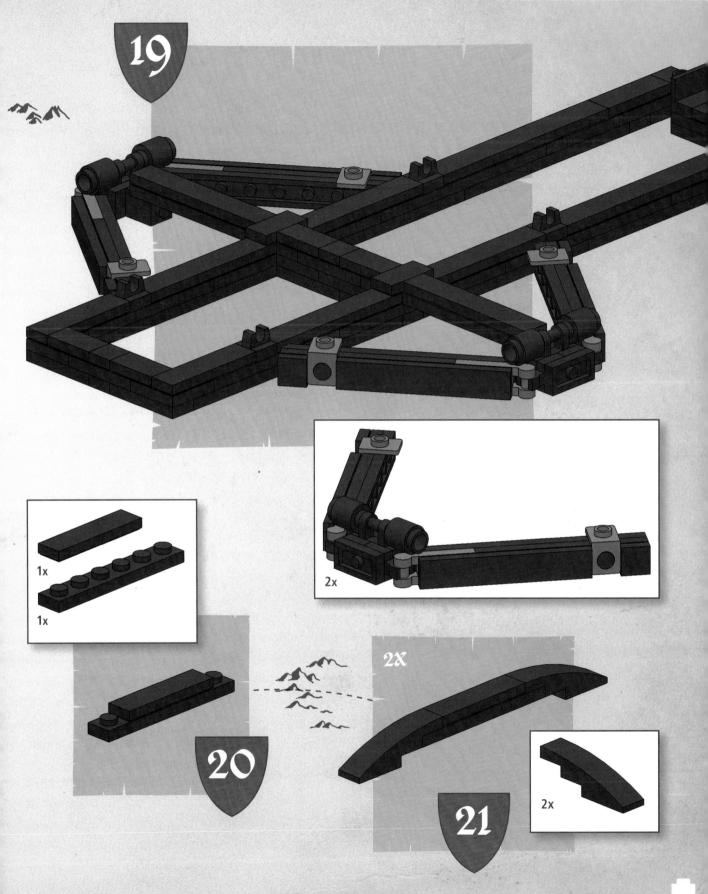

19

1x

1x

2x

20

2x

21

2x

22

23

2x

5

1x

1x

1x

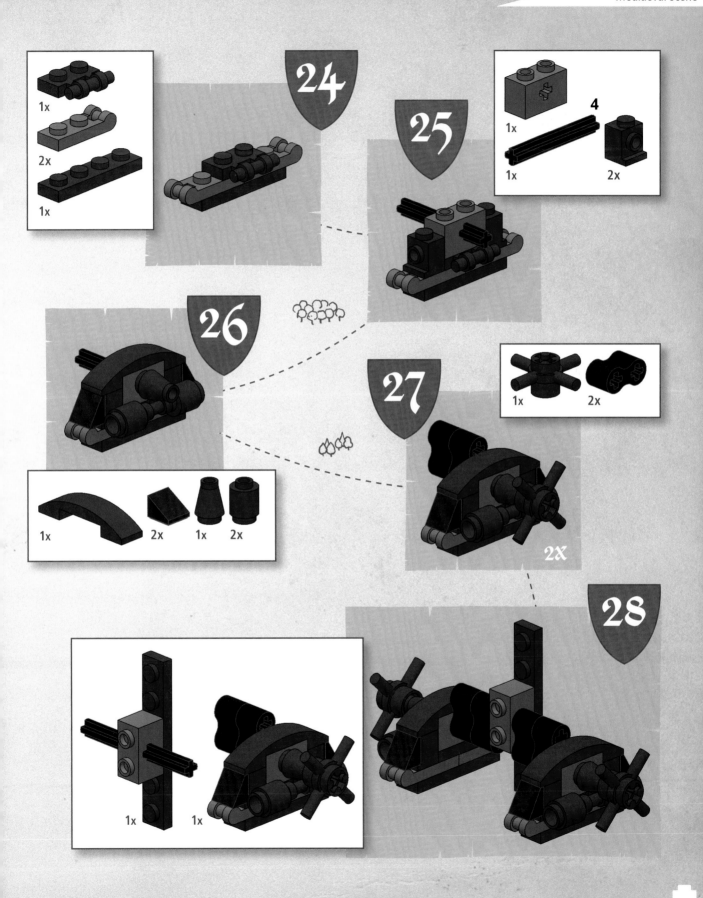

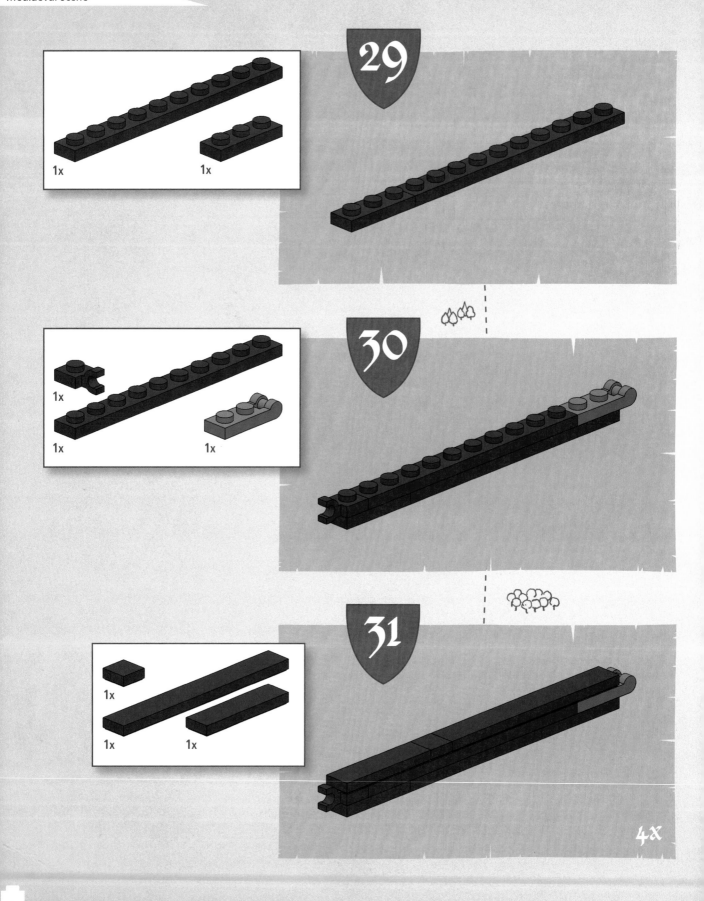

4x

32

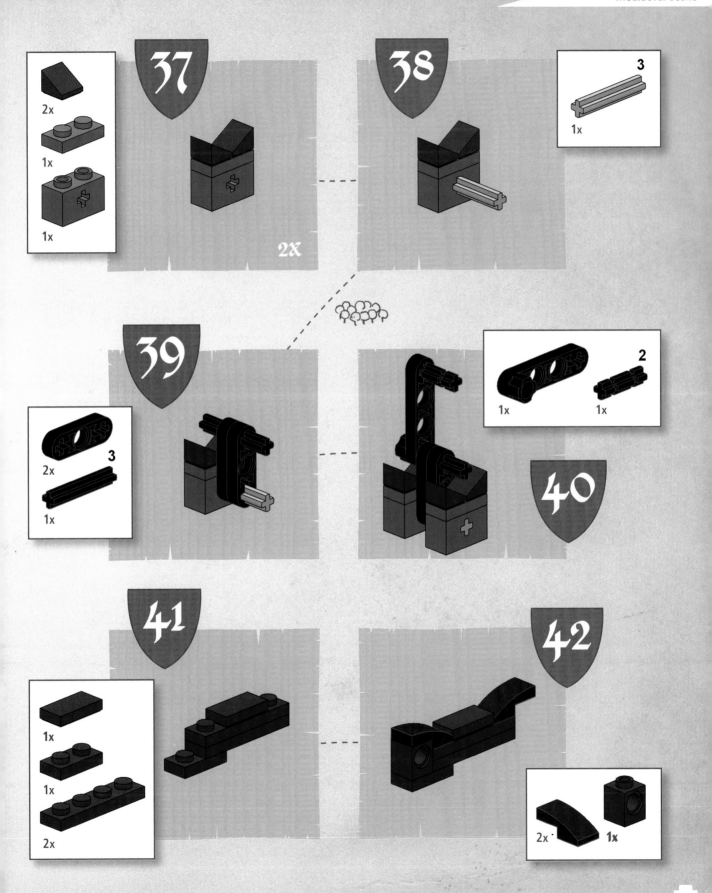

2x

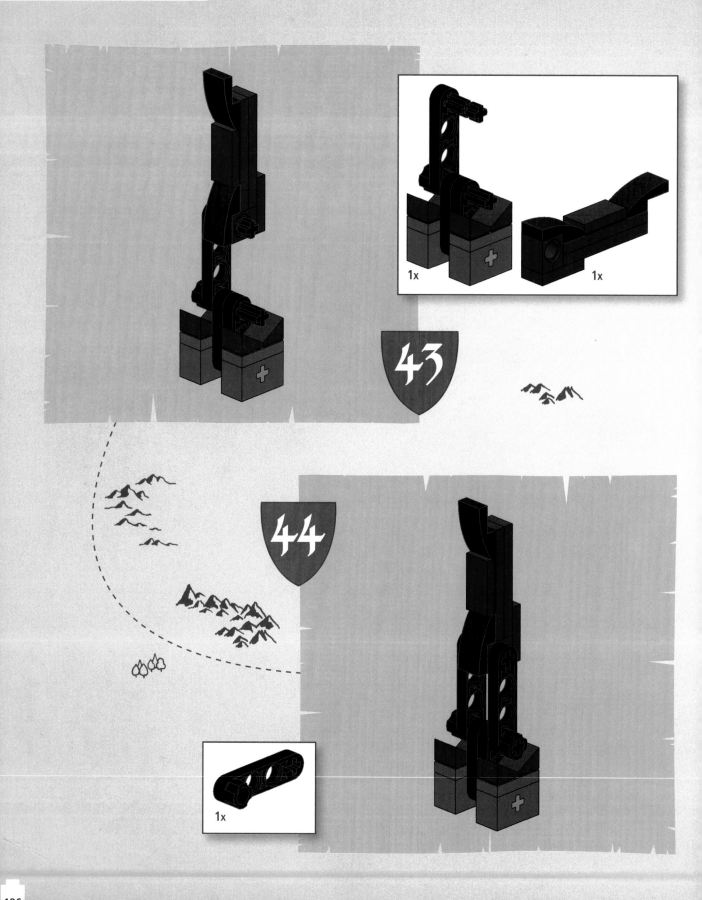

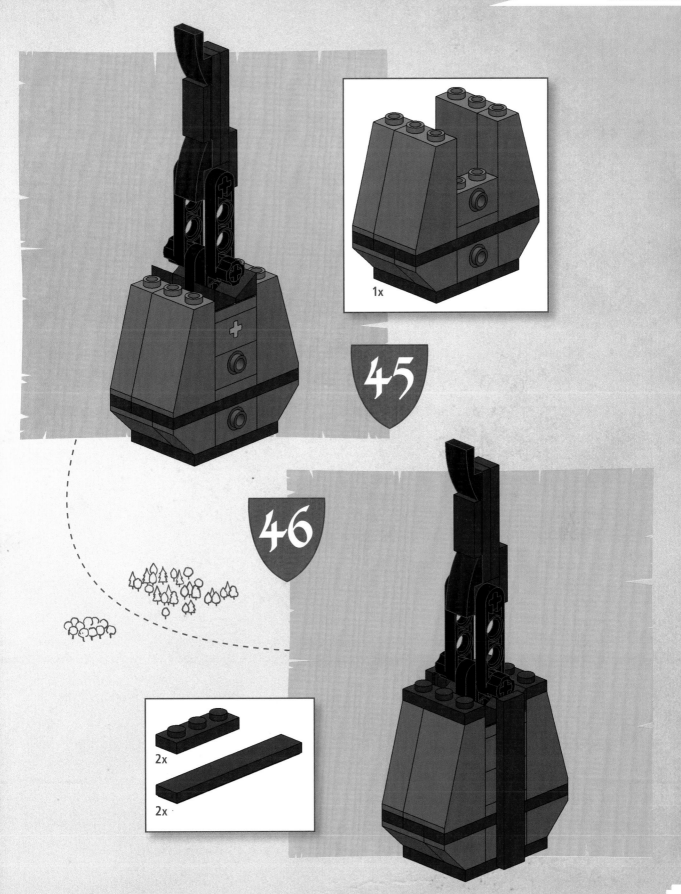

45

46

1x

2x

2x

1x

47

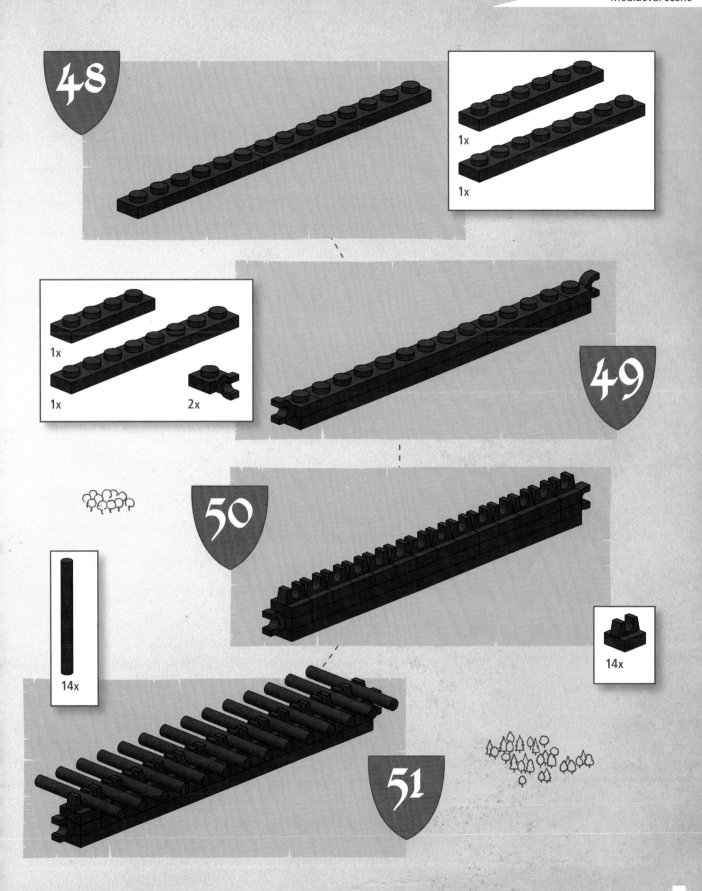

55

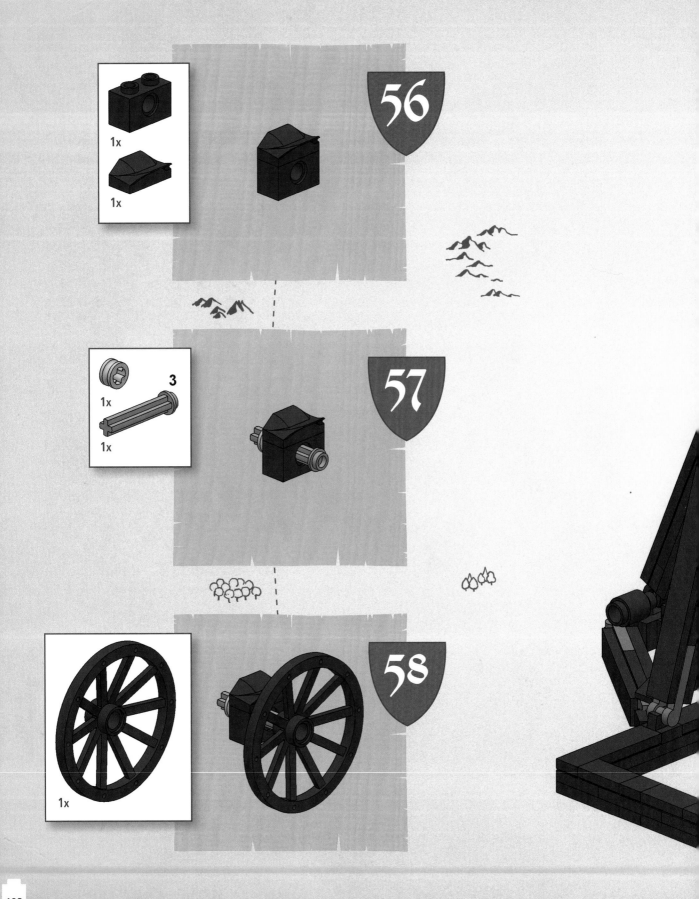

59

1x

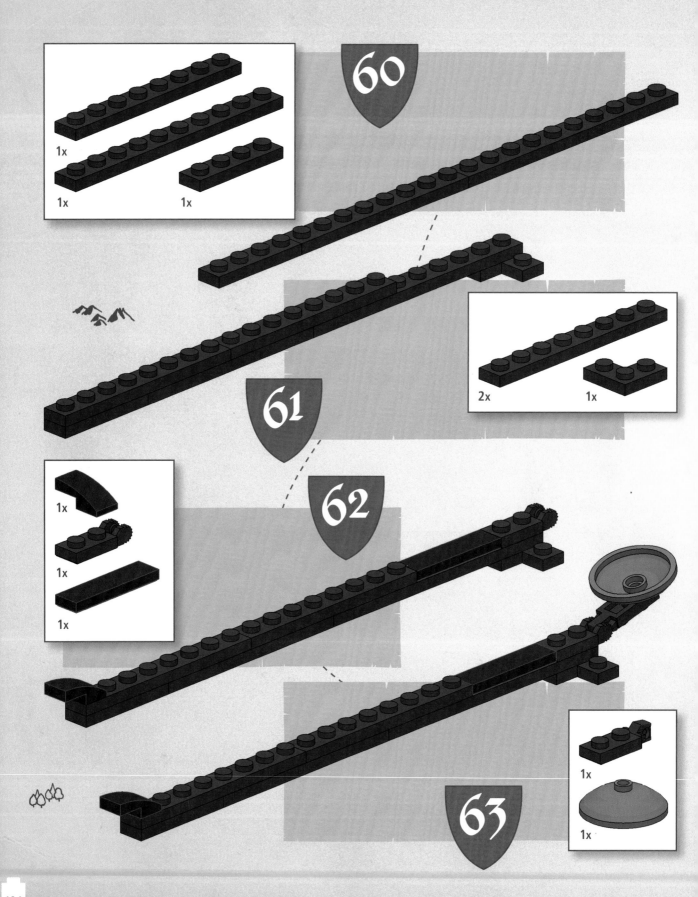

1x

1:1,66

64

Parts List

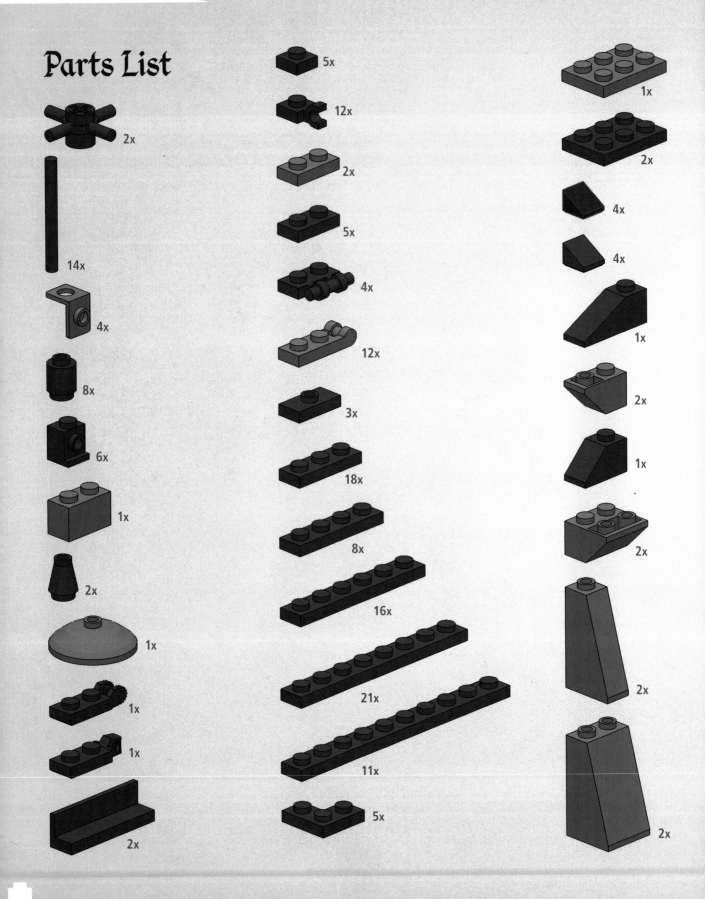

2x

14x

4x

8x

6x

1x

2x

1x

1x

1x

2x

5x

12x

2x

5x

4x

12x

3x

18x

8x

16x

21x

11x

5x

1x

2x

4x

4x

1x

2x

1x

2x

2x

2x

Quantity	Color		Element	Element Name
2		Reddish Brown	48723	Bar 1L Quadruple with Axlehole Hub
14		Reddish Brown	30374	Bar 4L Light Sabre Blade
4		Dark Bluish Gray	42446	Bracket 1 x 1 - 1 x 1
8		Reddish Brown	3062b	Brick 1 x 1 Round with Hollow Stud
6		Reddish Brown	4070	Brick 1 x 1 with Headlight
1		Dark Bluish Gray	3004	Brick 1 x 2
2		Reddish Brown	6188	Cone 1 x 1
1		Dark Bluish Gray	43898	Dish 3 x 3 Inverted
1		Reddish Brown	44302	Hinge Plate 1 x 2 Locking with Dual Finger on End Vertical
1		Reddish Brown	44301	Hinge Plate 1 x 2 Locking with Single Finger on End Vertical
2		Reddish Brown	30413	Panel 1 x 4 x 1
5		Reddish Brown	3024	Plate 1 x 1
12		Reddish Brown	6019	Plate 1 x 1 with Clip Horizontal
2		Dark Bluish Gray	3023	Plate 1 x 2
5		Reddish Brown	3023	Plate 1 x 2
4		Reddish Brown	2540	Plate 1 x 2 with Handle
12		Dark Bluish Gray	60478	Plate 1 x 2 with Handle on End
3		Reddish Brown	3794a	Plate 1 x 2 without Groove with 1 Centre Stud
18		Reddish Brown	3623	Plate 1 x 3
8		Reddish Brown	3710	Plate 1 x 4

Quantity	Color	Element	Element Name
16	Reddish Brown	3666	Plate 1 x 6
21	Reddish Brown	3460	Plate 1 x 8
11	Reddish Brown	4477	Plate 1 x 10
5	Reddish Brown	2420	Plate 2 x 2 Corner
1	Dark Bluish Gray	3021	Plate 2 x 3
2	Reddish Brown	3021	Plate 2 x 3
4	Dark Brown	54200	Slope Brick 31 1 x 1 x 2/3
4	Reddish Brown	54200	Slope Brick 31 1 x 1 x 2/3
1	Reddish Brown	4286	Slope Brick 33 3 x 1
2	Dark Bluish Gray	3665	Slope Brick 45 2 x 1 Inverted
1	Reddish Brown	3040	Slope Brick 45 2 x 1 without Centre Stud
2	Dark Bluish Gray	3660	Slope Brick 45 2 x 2 Inverted
2	Dark Bluish Gray	4460	Slope Brick 75 2 x 1 x 3
2	Dark Bluish Gray	3684	Slope Brick 75 2 x 2 x 3
1	Reddish Brown	47458	Slope Brick Curved 1 x 2 x 2/3 with Fin without Studs
3	Dark Brown	11477	Slope Brick Curved 2 x 1
4	Reddish Brown	61678	Slope Brick Curved 4 x 1
2	Reddish Brown	93273	Slope Brick Curved 4 x 1 Double
1	Black	32062	Technic Axle 2 Notched
1	Black	4519	Technic Axle 3
1	Light Bluish Gray	4519	Technic Axle 3
1	Dark Tan	6587	Technic Axle 3 with Stud
2	Black	3705	Technic Axle 4
1	Black	32073	Technic Axle 5
4	Rubber Black	45590	Technic Axle Joiner Double Flexible
2	Black	6632	Technic Beam 3 x 1/2 Liftarm
2	Black	2825	Technic Beam 4 x 1/2 Liftarm with Boss
1	Reddish Brown	6541	Technic Brick 1 x 1 with Hole
5	Dark Bluish Gray	32064a	Technic Brick 1 x 2 with Axlehole Type 1
4	Dark Bluish Gray	3700	Technic Brick 1 x 2 with Hole
1	Reddish Brown	3700	Technic Brick 1 x 2 with Hole
1	Light Bluish Gray	32123a	Technic Bush 1/2 Smooth with Axle Hole Reduced
4	Blue	4274	Technic Pin 1/2
18	Reddish Brown	2555	Tile 1 x 1 with Clip
10	Reddish Brown	3070b	Tile 1 x 1 with Groove
7	Reddish Brown	3069b	Tile 1 x 2 with Groove
1	Reddish Brown	63864	Tile 1 x 3 with Groove
1	Dark Brown	2431	Tile 1 x 4 with Groove
9	Reddish Brown	2431	Tile 1 x 4 with Groove
13	Reddish Brown	6636	Tile 1 x 6
7	Reddish Brown	4162	Tile 1 x 8
1	Reddish Brown	33211	Wheel Spoked 5 & 1/2 x 5 & 1/2

Modular Castle

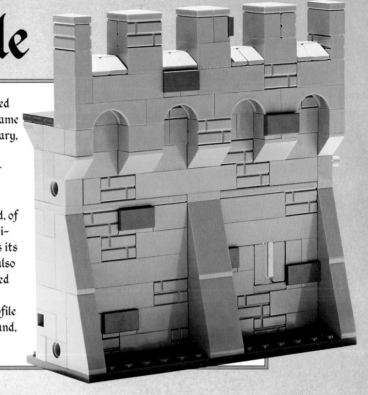

This castle is the heart of our theme. We discussed the matter at great length and we eventually came up with a very clear idea: it had to be easy to vary, not too hard to build and at the same time of a substantial size. The modular design unites all the requirements.

We show you the basic elements, such as walls, towers and, of course, a drawbridge. But you are all lords of your own individual castles, and the construction of every castle follows its own aesthetic and tactical considerations. Thus, you can also discover on the photos a few buildings that we've integrated into our castle site. Be creative, and decide for yourselves how big you want your castle to be! If you don't have a profile brick, just use an ordinary one. If there's no light gray to hand, dark gray will do as well.

Wide wall section

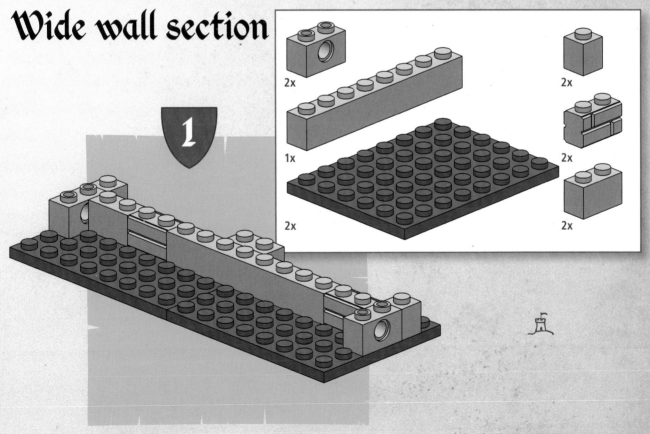

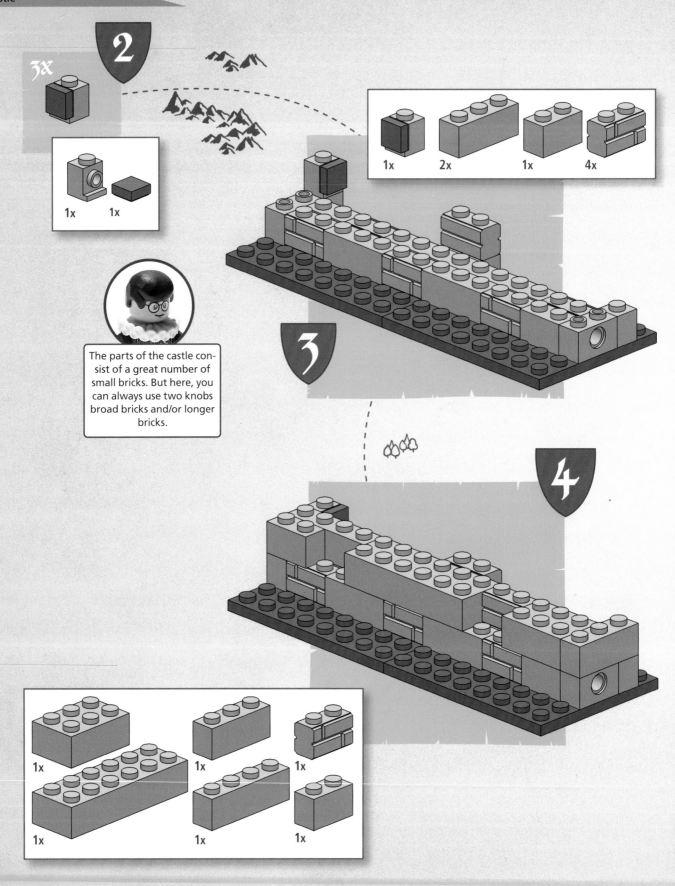

3x

1x   1x

1x   2x   1x   4x

The parts of the castle consist of a great number of small bricks. But here, you can always use two knobs broad bricks and/or longer bricks.

1x   1x   1x

1x   1x   1x

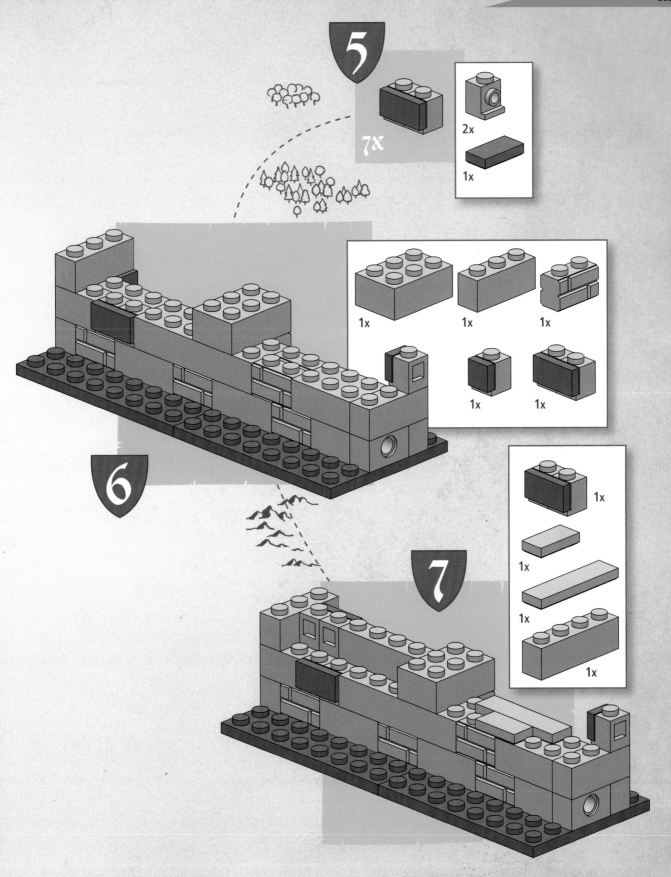

5

7x

2x

1x

6

1x   1x   1x

1x   1x

7

1x

1x

1x

1x

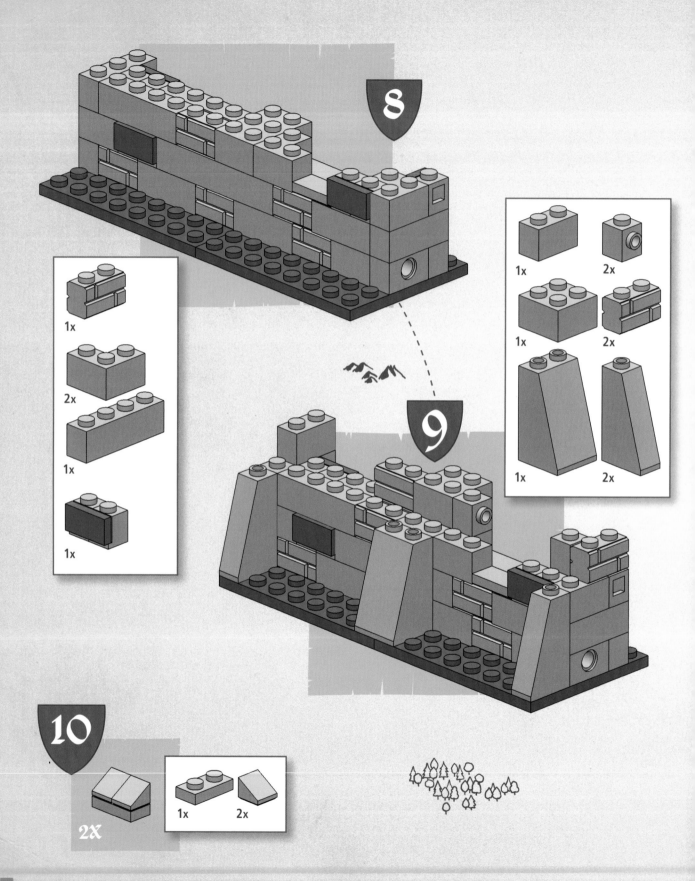

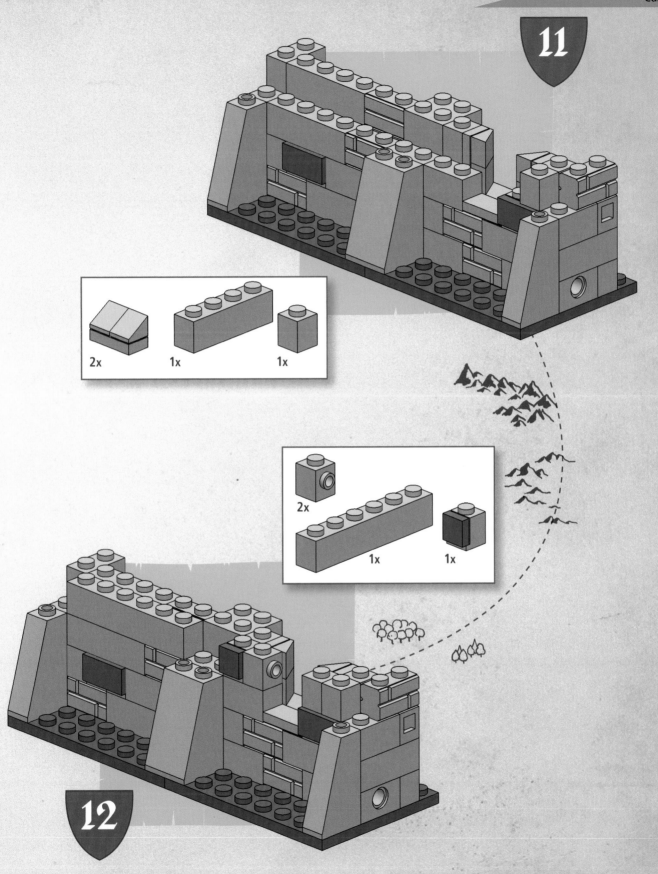

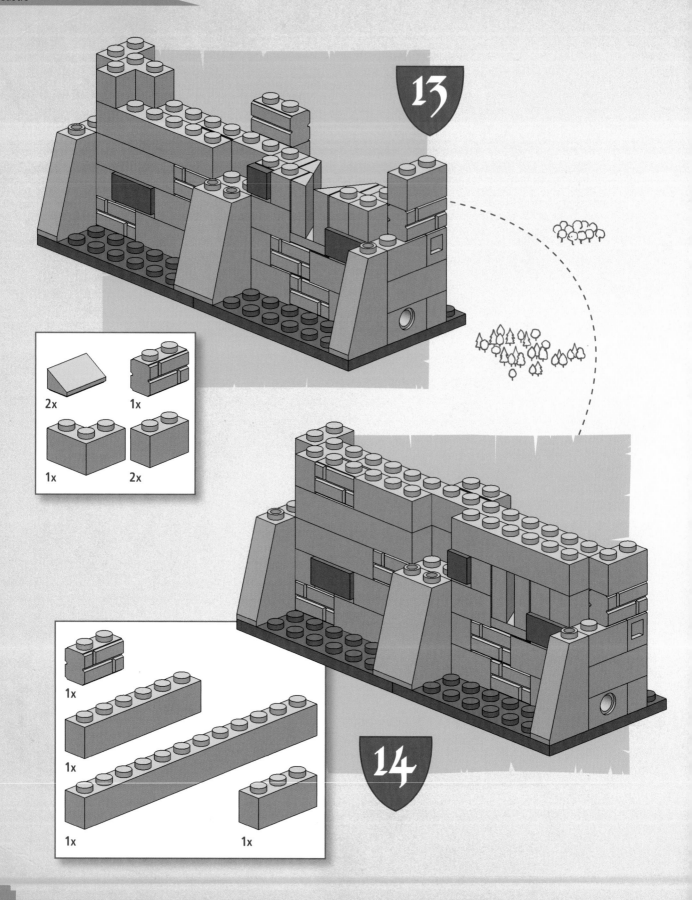

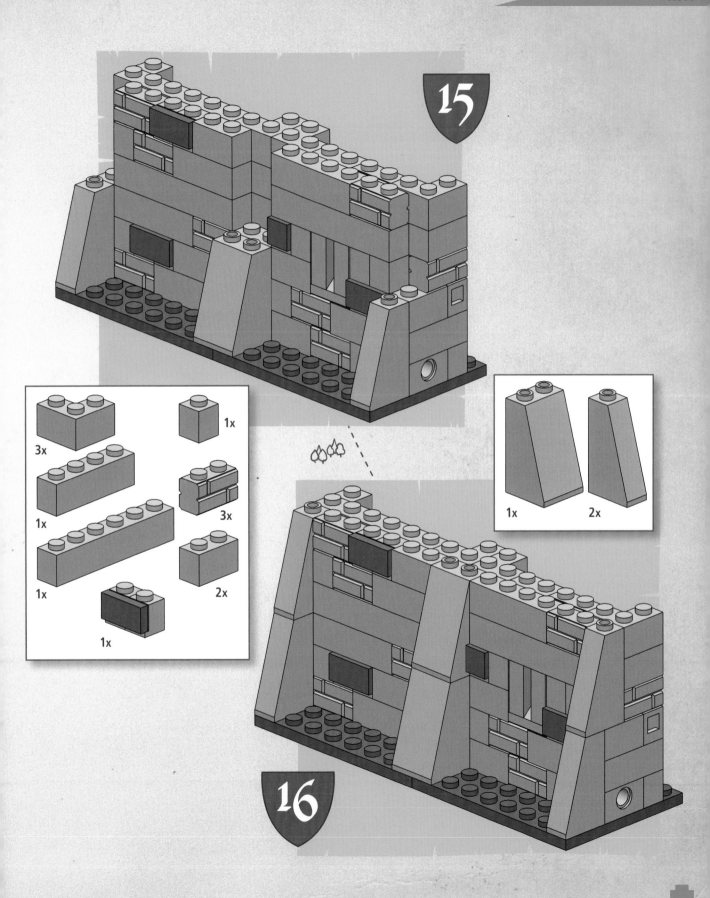

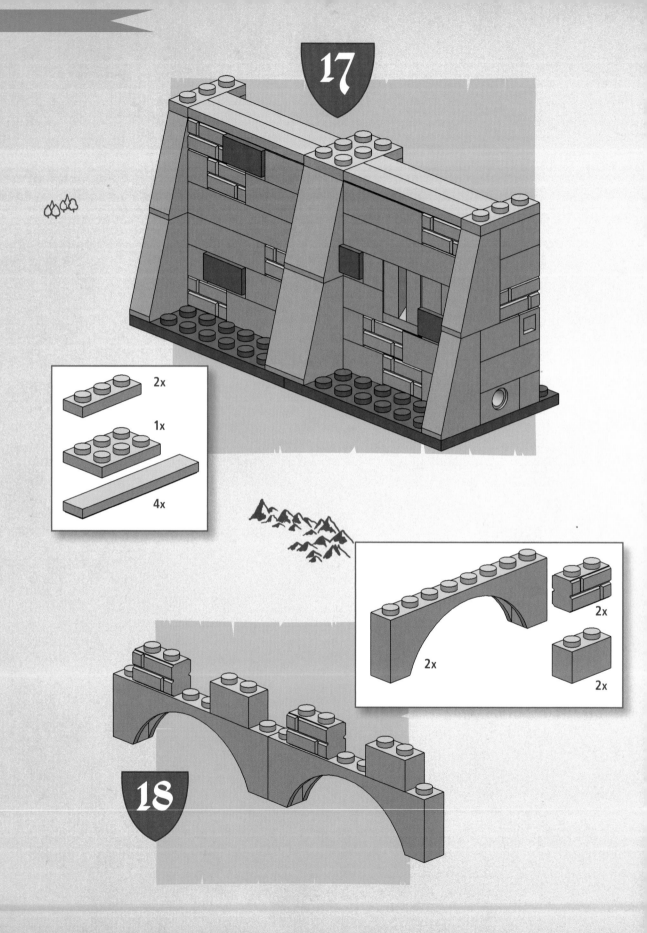

17

2x

1x

4x

18

2x

2x

2x

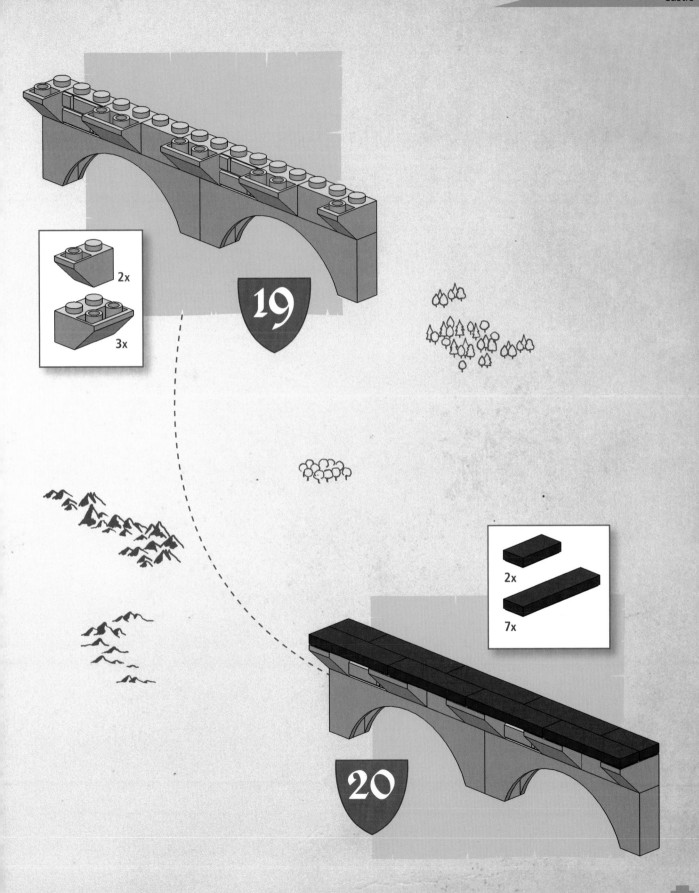

19

2x

3x

20

2x

7x

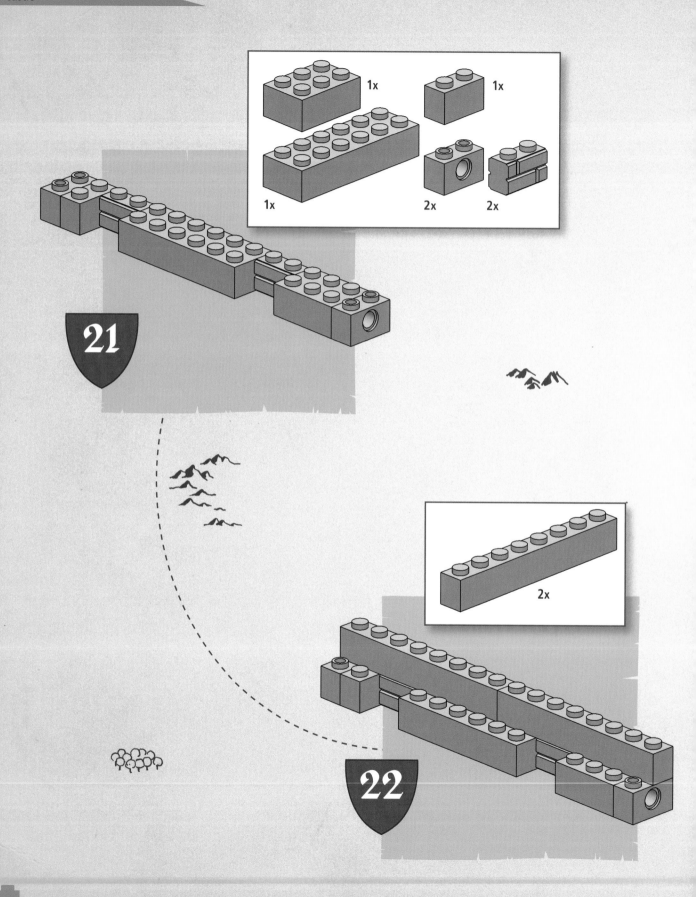

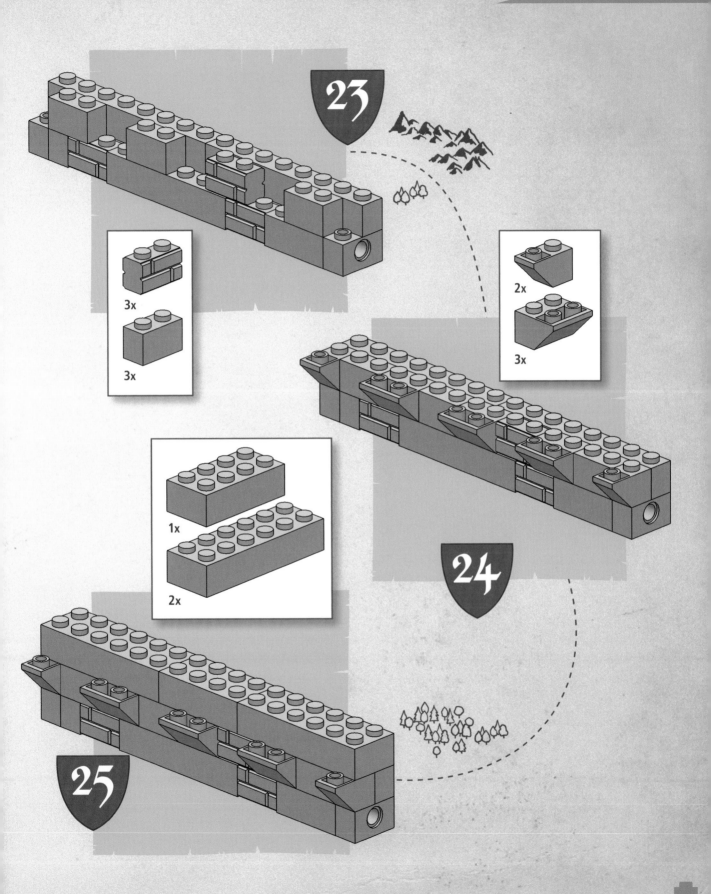

23

3x

3x

2x

3x

1x

2x

24

25

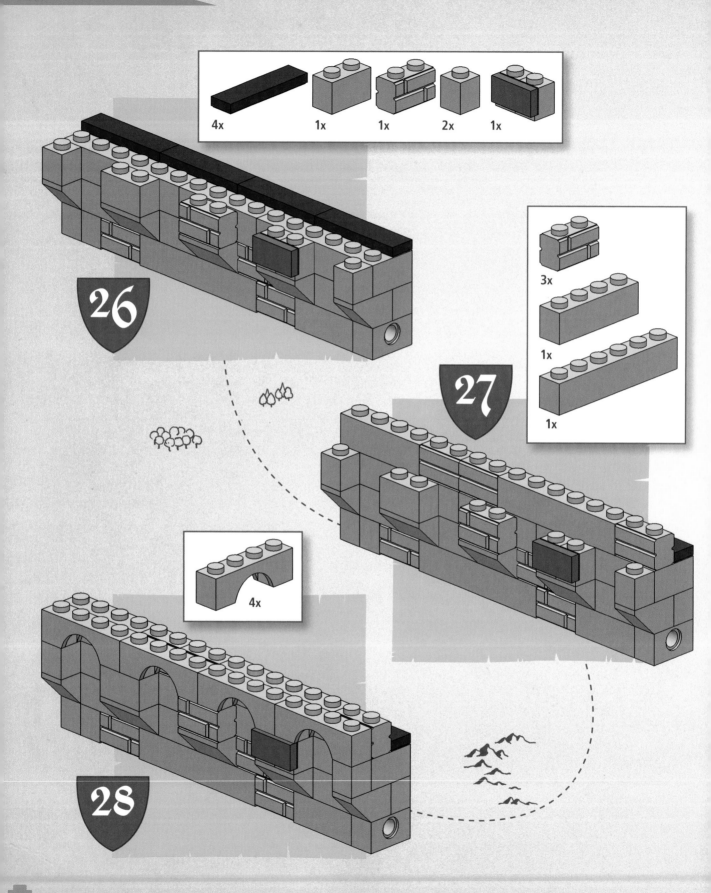

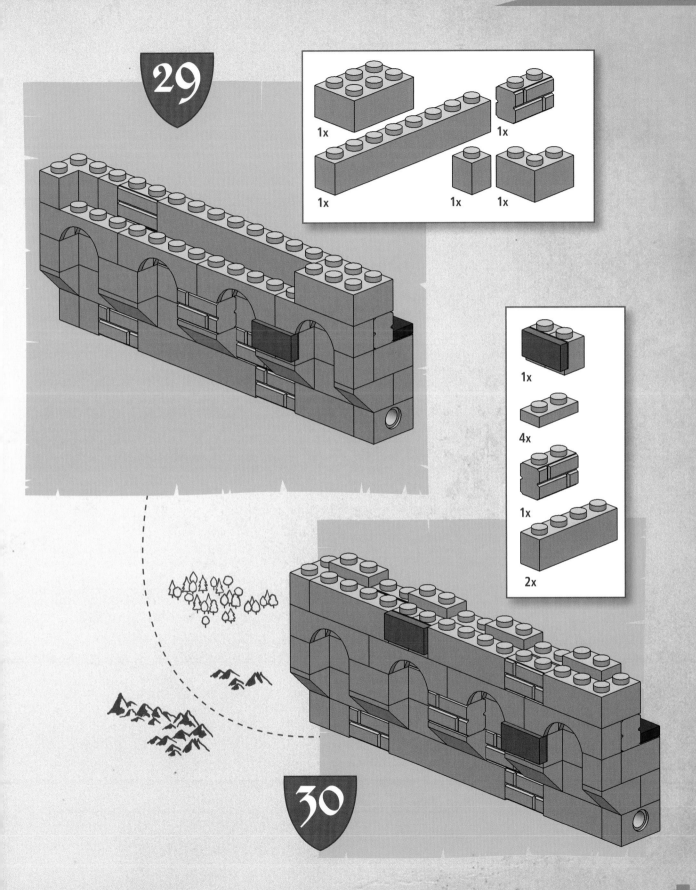

29

1x
1x
1x
1x
1x

1x
4x
1x
2x

30

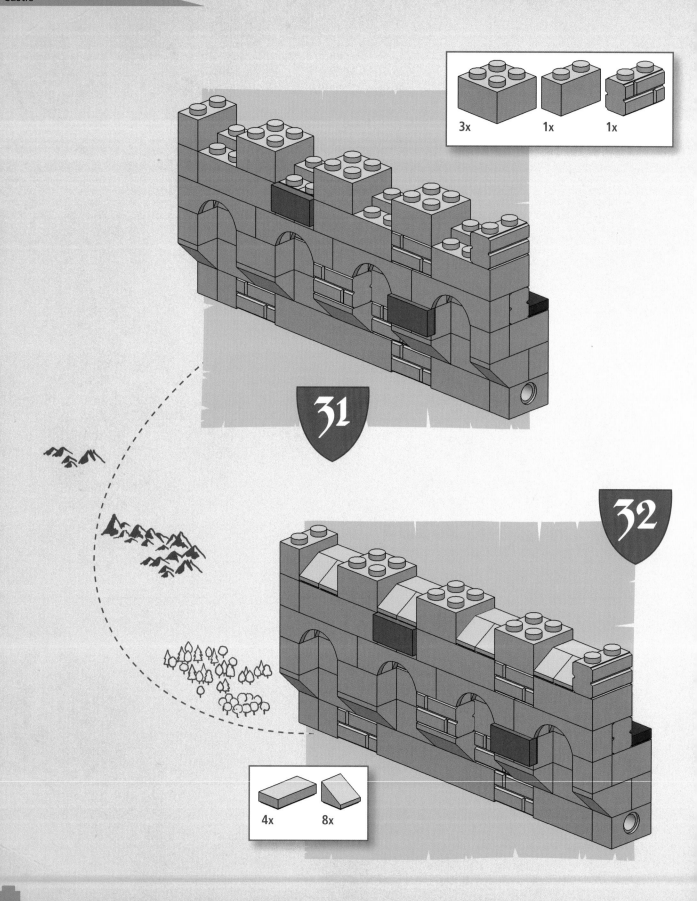

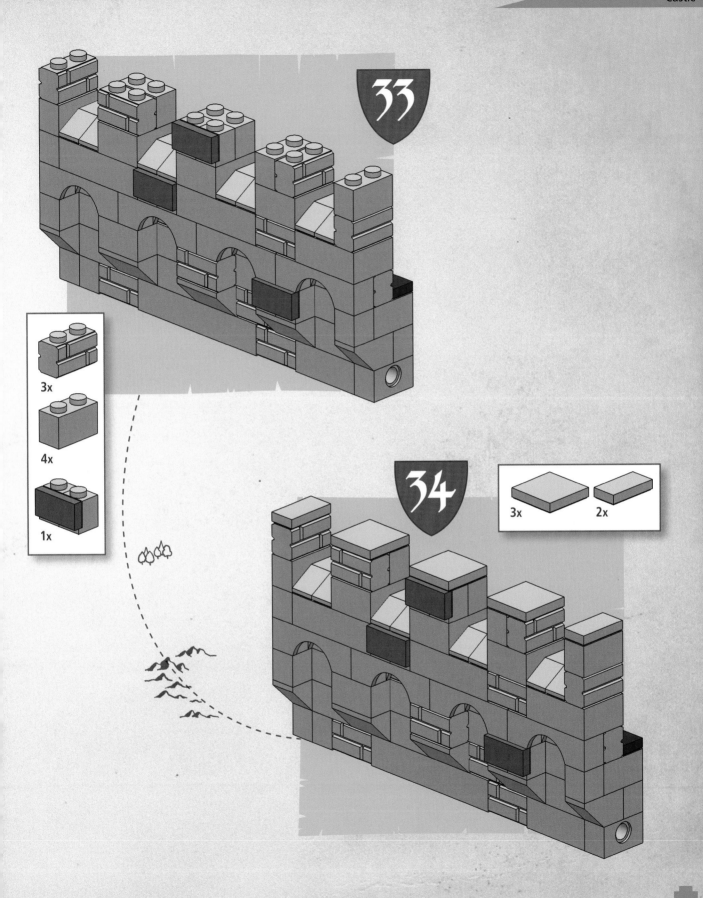

33

3x
4x
1x

34

3x
2x

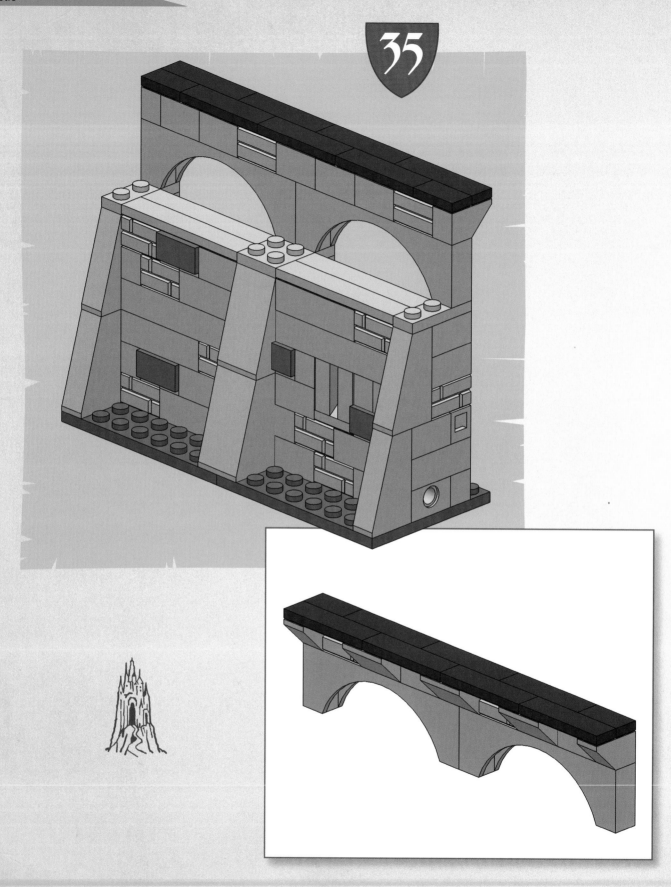

2x

36

Parts List

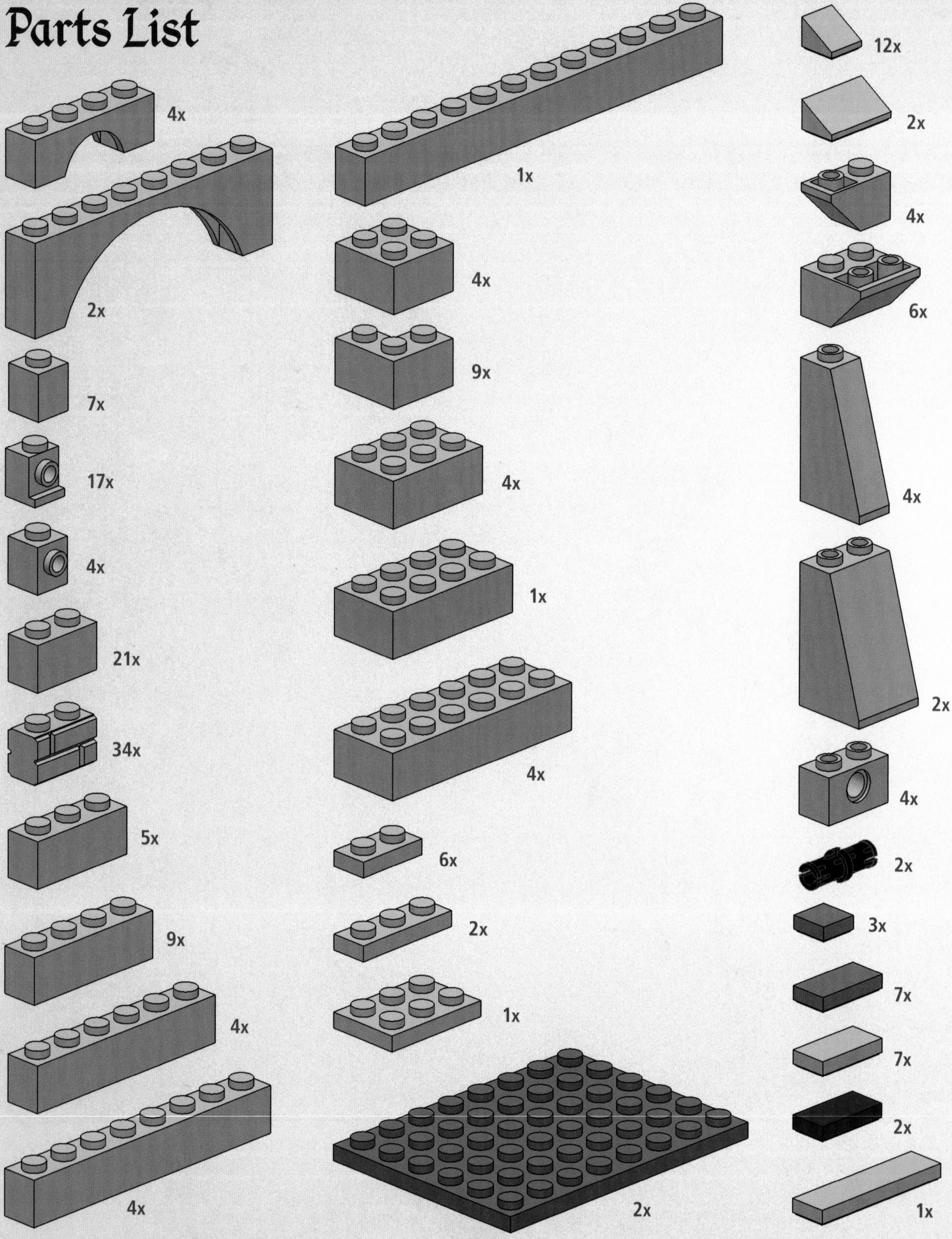

4x

2x

7x

17x

4x

21x

34x

5x

9x

4x

4x

1x

4x

9x

4x

1x

4x

4x

6x

2x

1x

2x

12x

2x

4x

6x

4x

2x

4x

2x

3x

7x

7x

2x

1x

11x

4x

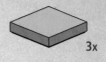

3x

Quantity		Color	Element	Element Name
4		Light Bluish Gray	3659	Arch 1 x 4
2		Light Bluish Gray	3308	Arch 1 x 8 x 2
7		Light Bluish Gray	3005	Brick 1 x 1
17		Light Bluish Gray	4070	Brick 1 x 1 with Headlight
4		Light Bluish Gray	87087	Brick 1 x 1 with Stud on 1 Side
21		Light Bluish Gray	3004	Brick 1 x 2
34		Light Bluish Gray	98283	Brick 1 x 2 with Embossed Bricks
5		Light Bluish Gray	3622	Brick 1 x 3
9		Light Bluish Gray	3010	Brick 1 x 4
4		Light Bluish Gray	3009	Brick 1 x 6
4		Light Bluish Gray	3008	Brick 1 x 8
1		Light Bluish Gray	6112	Brick 1 x 12
4		Light Bluish Gray	3003	Brick 2 x 2
9		Light Bluish Gray	2357	Brick 2 x 2 Corner
4		Light Bluish Gray	3002	Brick 2 x 3
1		Light Bluish Gray	3001	Brick 2 x 4
4		Light Bluish Gray	2456	Brick 2 x 6
6		Light Bluish Gray	3023	Brick 1 x 2
2		Light Bluish Gray	3623	Brick 1 x 3
1		Light Bluish Gray	3021	Plate 2 x 3
2		Green	3036	Plate 6 x 8
12		Light Bluish Gray	54200	Slope Brick 31 1 x 1 x 2/3
2		Light Bluish Gray	85984	Slope Brick 31 1 x 2 x 2/3
4		Light Bluish Gray	3665	Slope Brick 45 2 x 1 Inverted
6		Light Bluish Gray	3660	Slope Brick 45 2 x 2 Inverted
4		Light Bluish Gray	4460	Slope Brick 75 2 x 1 x 3
2		Light Bluish Gray	3684	Slope Brick 75 2 x 2 x 3
4		Light Bluish Gray	3700	Technic Brick 1 x 2 with Hole
2		Black	2780	Technic Pin with Friction and Slots
3		Dark Bluish Gray	3070b	Tile 1 x 1 with Groove
7		Dark Bluish Gray	3069b	Tile 1 x 2 with Groove
7		Light Bluish Gray	3069b	Tile 1 x 2 with Groove
2		Reddish Brown	3069b	Tile 1 x 2 with Groove
1		Light Bluish Gray	2431	Tile 1 x 4 with Groove
11		Reddish Brown	2431	Tile 1 x 4 with Groove
4		Light Bluish Gray	6636	Tile 1 x 6
3		Light Bluish Gray	3068b	Tile 2 x 2 with Groove

Narrow wall section

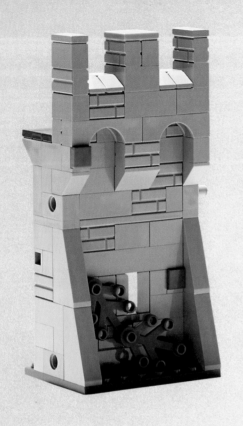

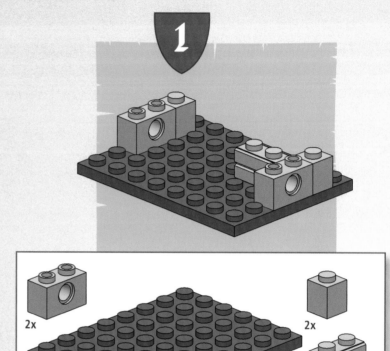

1

2x

1x

2x

1x

2

1x 1x

4x

1x 1x 1x 2x

3

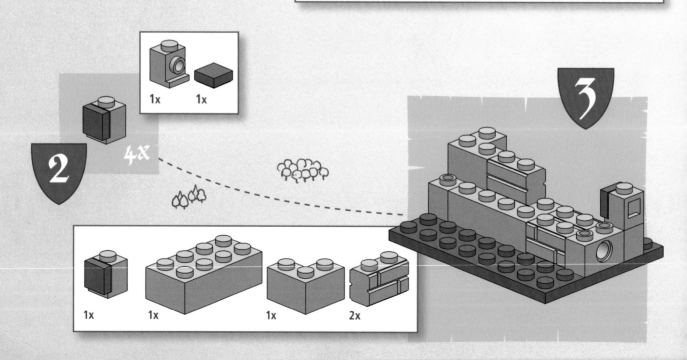

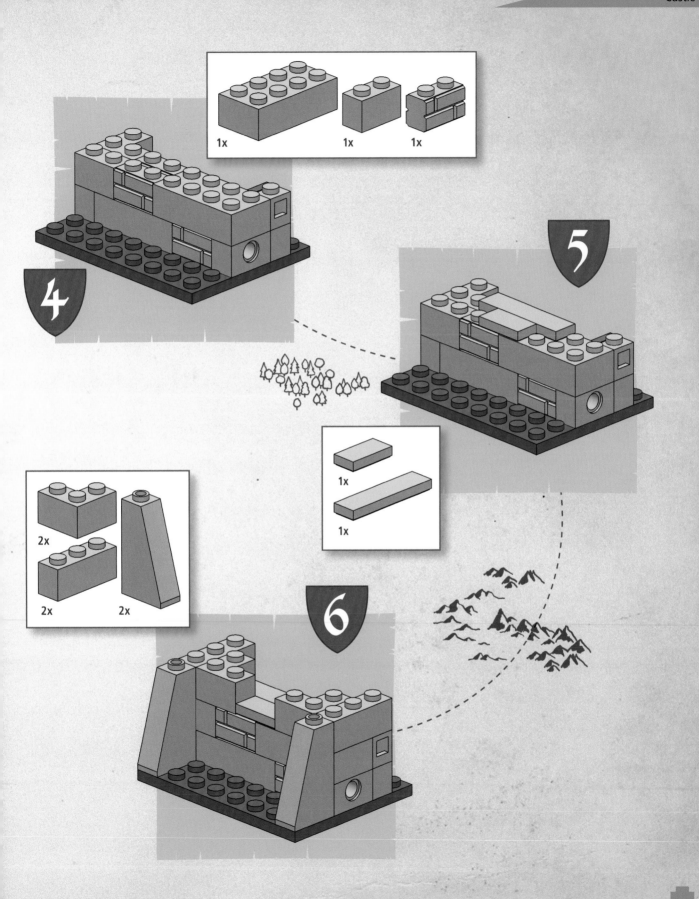

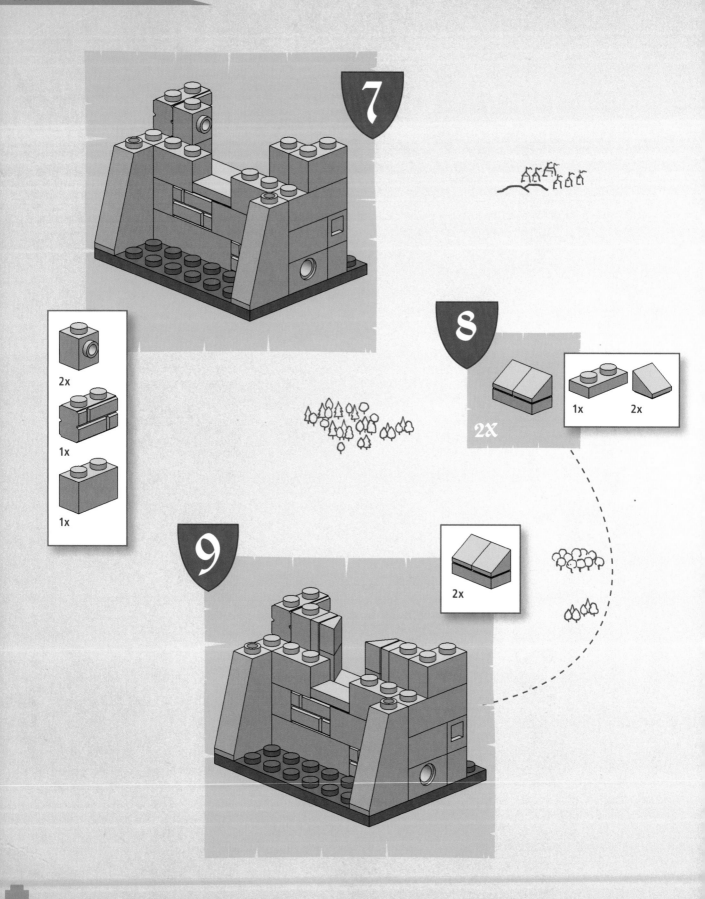

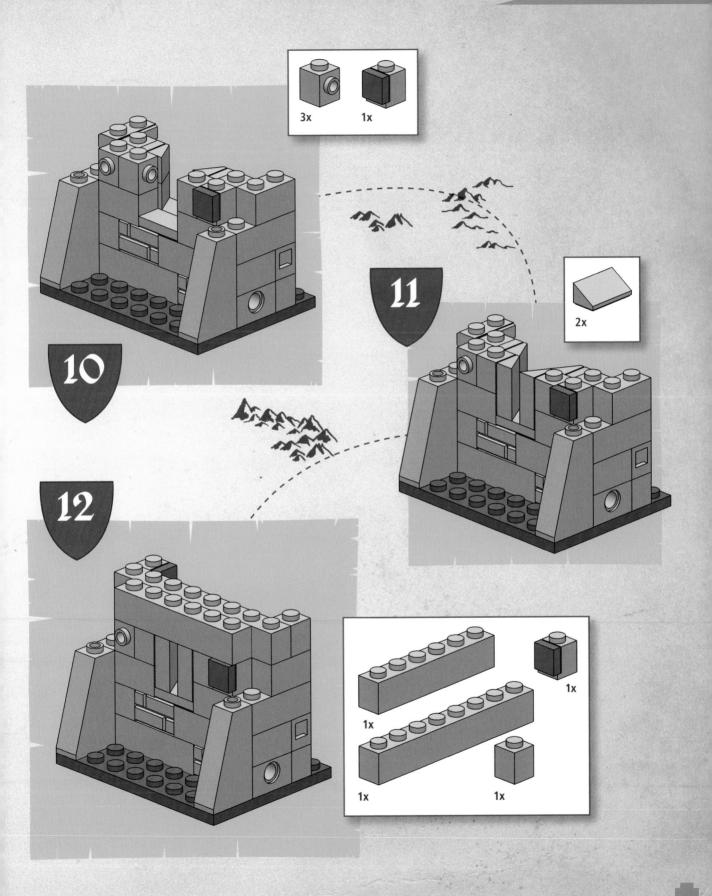

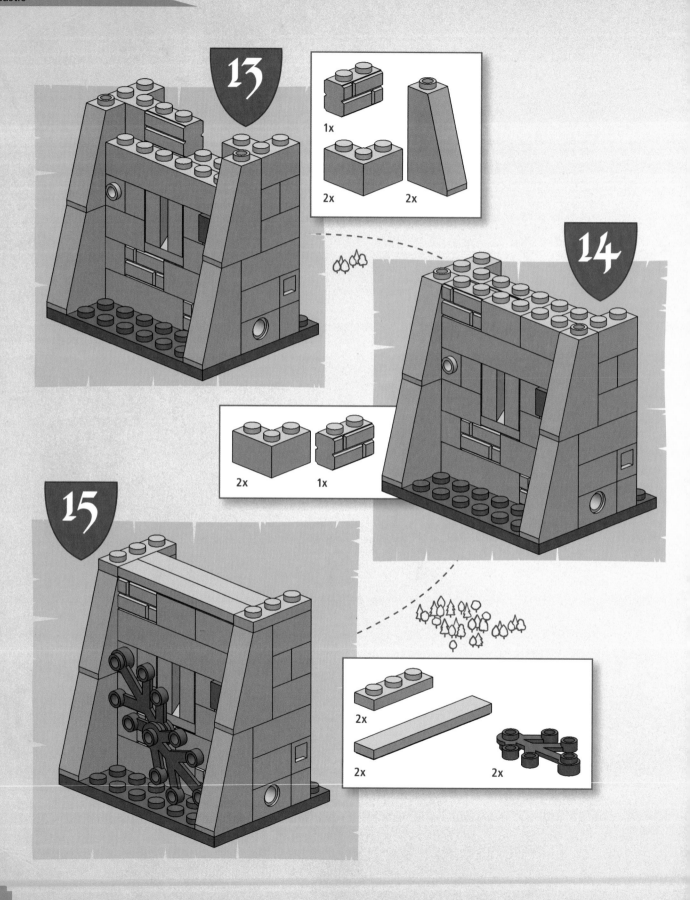

13

1x

2x　　2x

14

2x　　1x

15

2x

2x　　2x

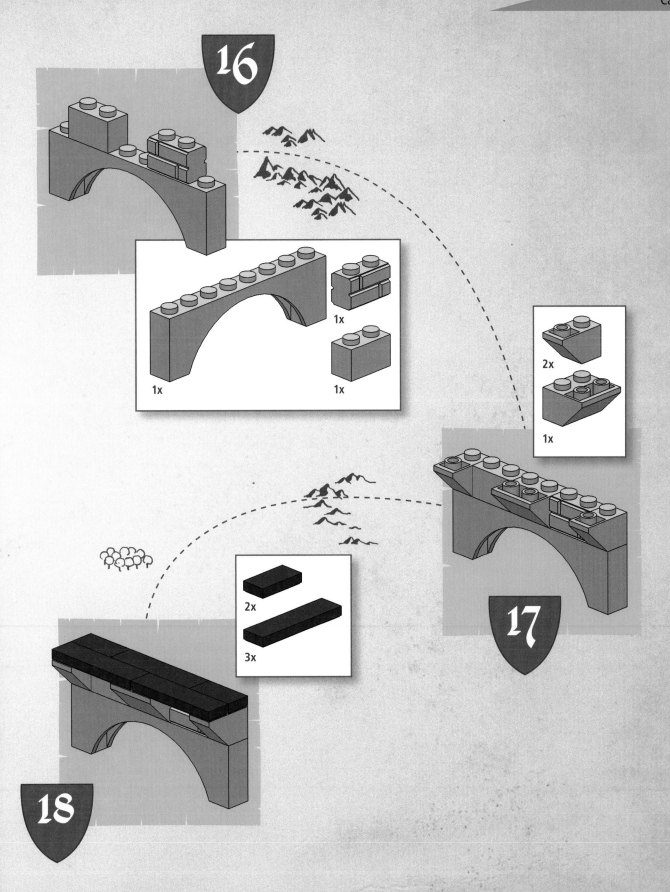

16

1x

1x 1x

2x

1x

17

2x

3x

18

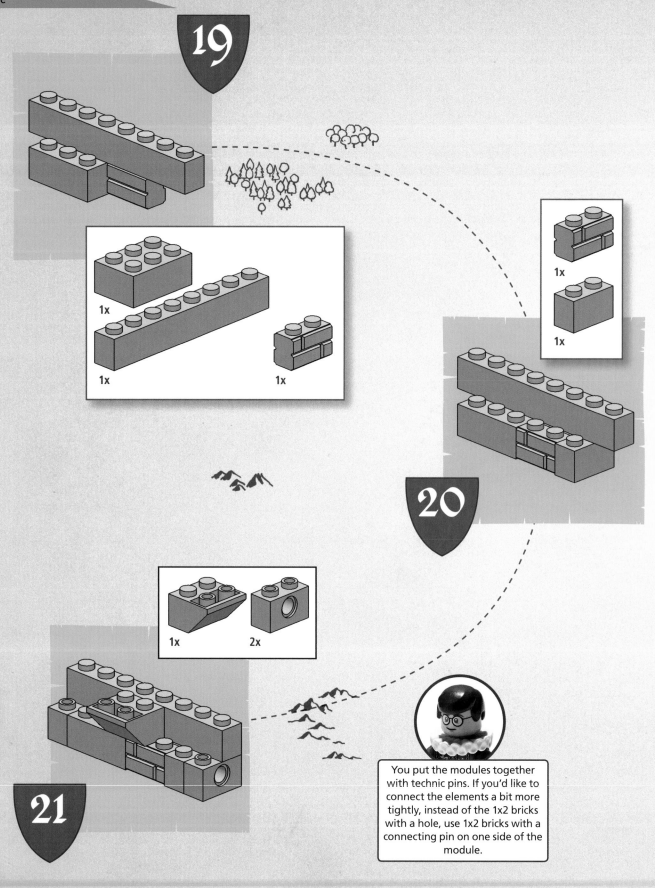

19

1x
1x
1x

20

1x
1x

21

1x
2x

You put the modules together with technic pins. If you'd like to connect the elements a bit more tightly, instead of the 1x2 bricks with a hole, use 1x2 bricks with a connecting pin on one side of the module.

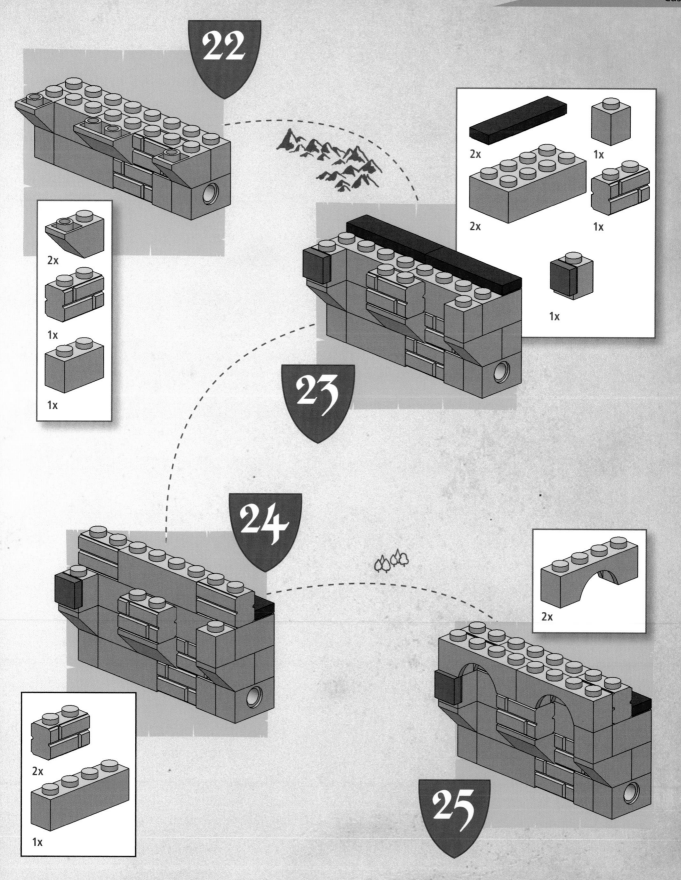

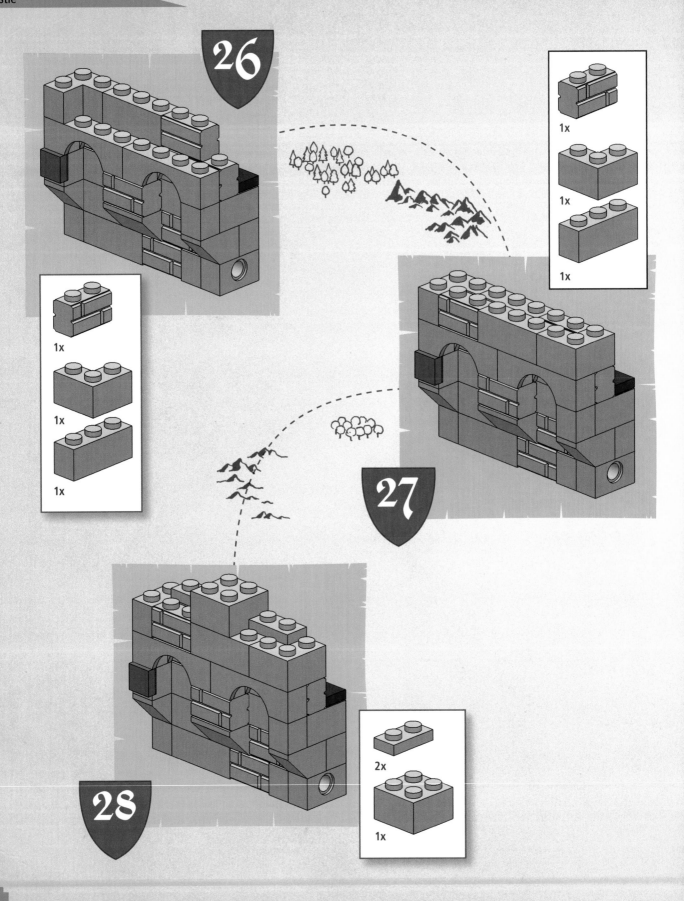

26

1x

1x

1x

1x

1x

1x

27

28

2x

1x

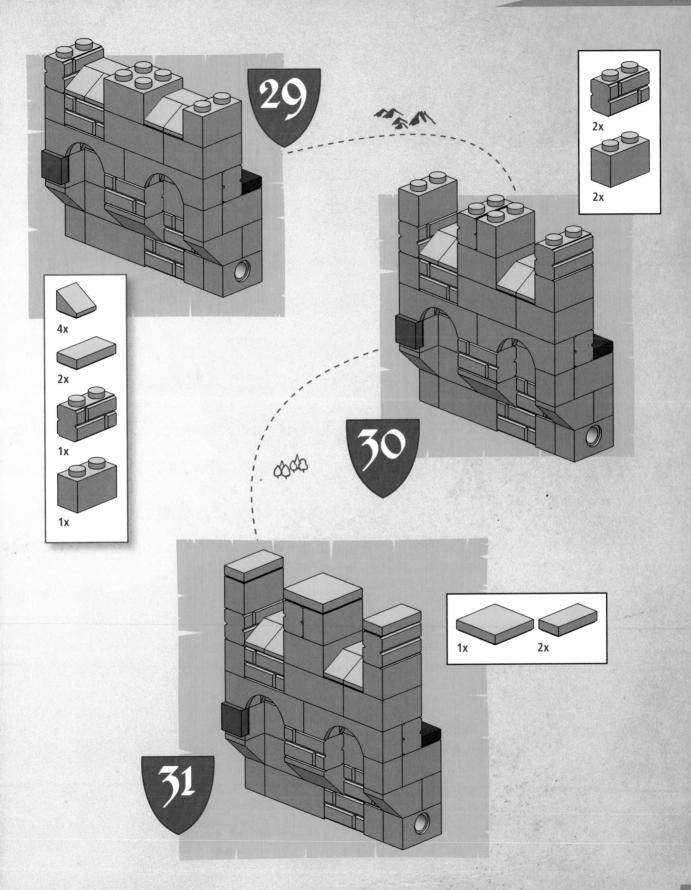

29

30

31

2x

2x

4x

2x

1x

1x

1x

2x

32

2x

33

Parts List

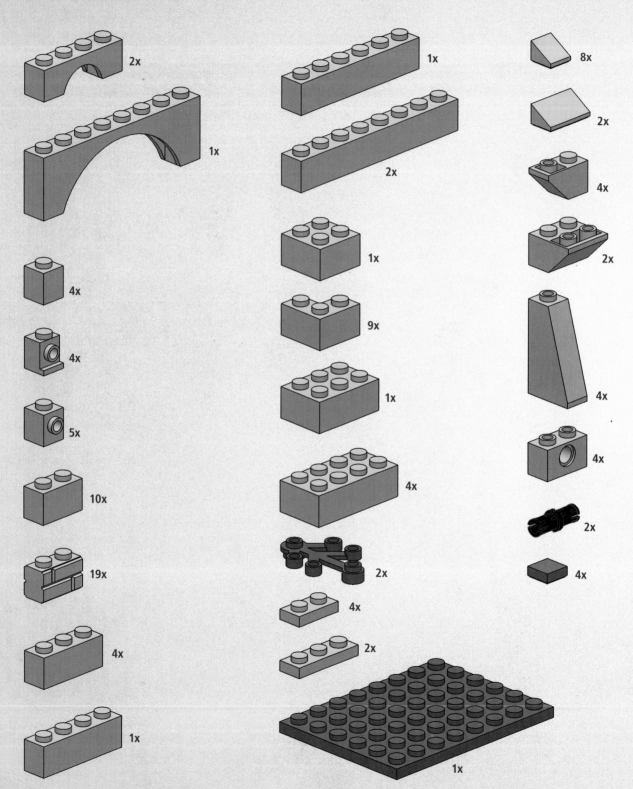

2x

1x

1x

2x

8x

2x

4x

2x

4x

4x

4x

5x

1x

9x

1x

10x

1x

4x

19x

2x

2x

4x

4x

4x

2x

1x

1x

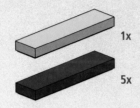 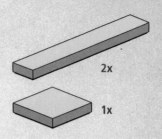

Quantity	Color		Element	Element Name
2		Light Bluish Gray	3659	Arch 1 x 4
1		Light Bluish Gray	3308	Arch 1 x 8 x 2
4		Light Bluish Gray	3005	Brick 1 x 1
4		Light Bluish Gray	4070	Brick 1 x 1 with Headlight
5		Light Bluish Gray	87087	Brick 1 x 1 with Stud on 1 Side
10		Light Bluish Gray	3004	Brick 1 x 2
19		Light Bluish Gray	98283	Brick 1 x 2 with Embossed Bricks
4		Light Bluish Gray	3622	Brick 1 x 3
1		Light Bluish Gray	3010	Brick 1 x 4
1		Light Bluish Gray	3009	Brick 1 x 6
2		Light Bluish Gray	3008	Brick 1 x 8
1		Light Bluish Gray	3003	Brick 2 x 2
9		Light Bluish Gray	2357	Brick 2 x 2 Corner
1		Light_Bluish_Gray	3002	Brick 2 x 3
4		Light Bluish Gray	3001	Brick 2 x 4
2		Green	2423	Plant Leaves 4 x 3
4		Light Bluish Gray	3023	Plate 1 x 2
2		Light Bluish Gray	3623	Plate 1 x 3
1		Green	3036	Plate 6 x 8
8		Light Bluish Gray	54200	Slope Brick 31 1 x 1 x 2/3
2		Light Bluish Gray	85984	Slope Brick 31 1 x 2 x 2/3
4		Light Bluish Gray	3665	Slope Brick 45 2 x 1 Inverted
2		Light Bluish Gray	3660	Slope Brick 45 2 x 2 Inverted
4		Light Bluish Gray	4460	Slope Brick 75 2 x 1 x 3
4		Light Bluish Gray	3700	Technic Brick 1 x 2 with Hole
2		Black	2780	Technic Pin with Friction and Slots
4		Dark Bluish Gray	3070b	Tile 1 x 1 with Groove
5		Light Bluish Gray	3069b	Tile 1 x 2 with Groove
2		Reddish Brown	3069b	Tile 1 x 2 with Groove
1		Light Bluish Gray	2431	Tile 1 x 4 with Groove
5		Reddish Brown	2431	Tile 1 x 4 with Groove
2		Light Bluish Gray	6636	Tile 1 x 6
1		Light Bluish Gray	3068b	Tile 2 x 2 with Groove

Corner piece

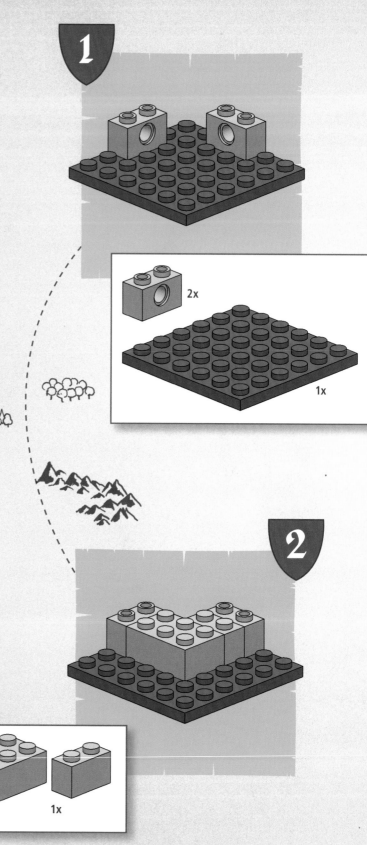

1

2x

1x

2

1x   1x

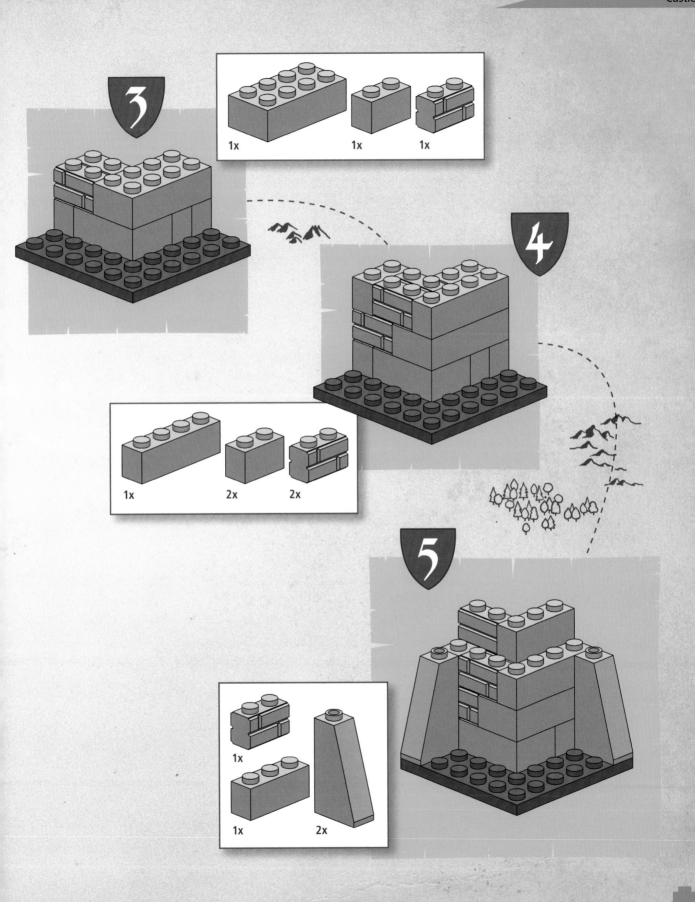

3

1x   1x   1x

4

1x   2x   2x

5

1x

1x   2x

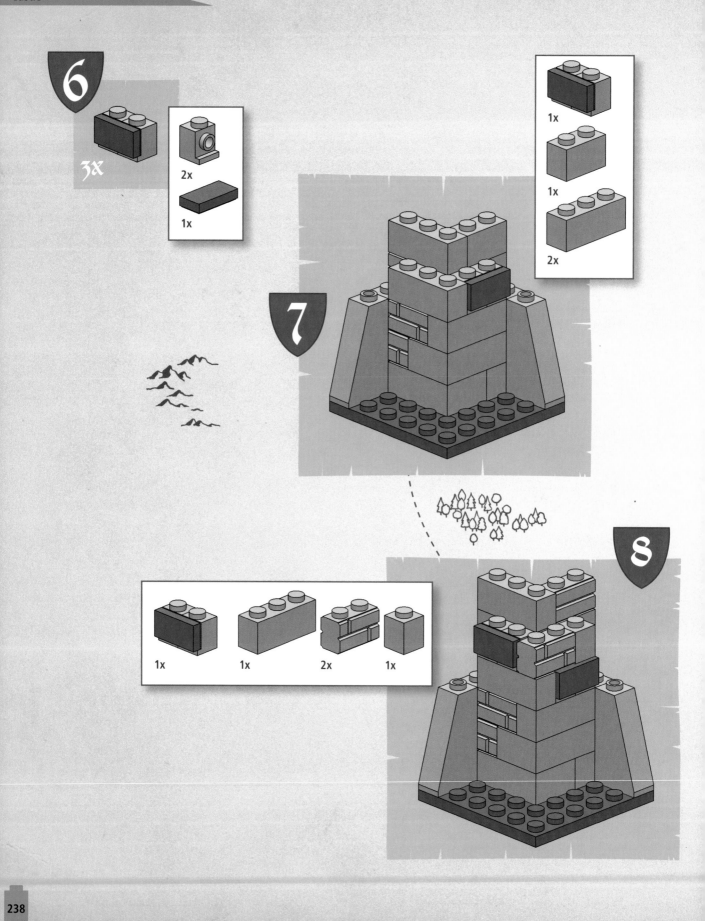

6

3x

2x

1x

1x

1x

2x

7

1x

1x

2x

1x

8

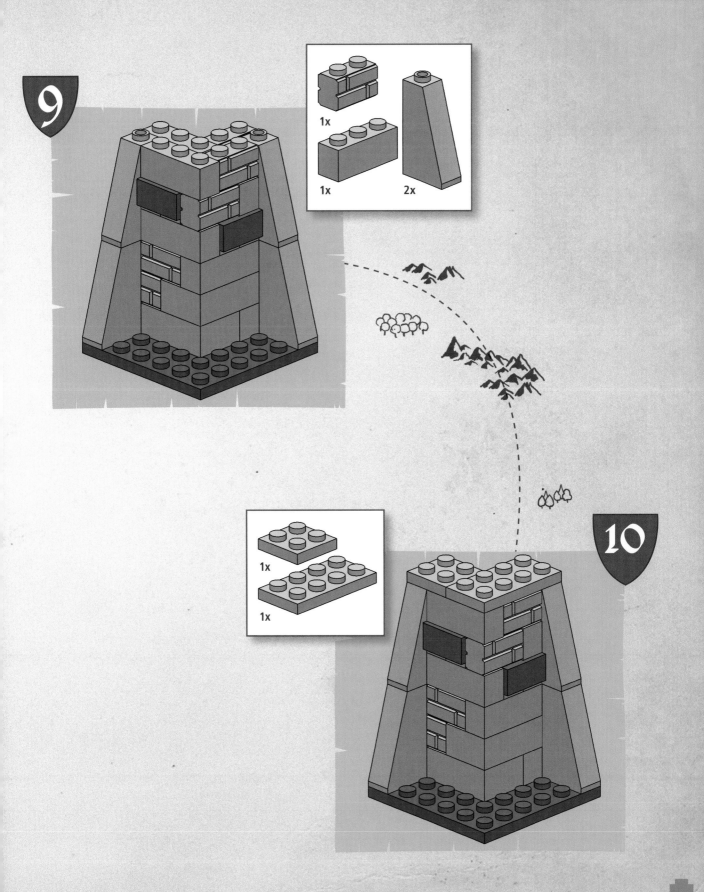

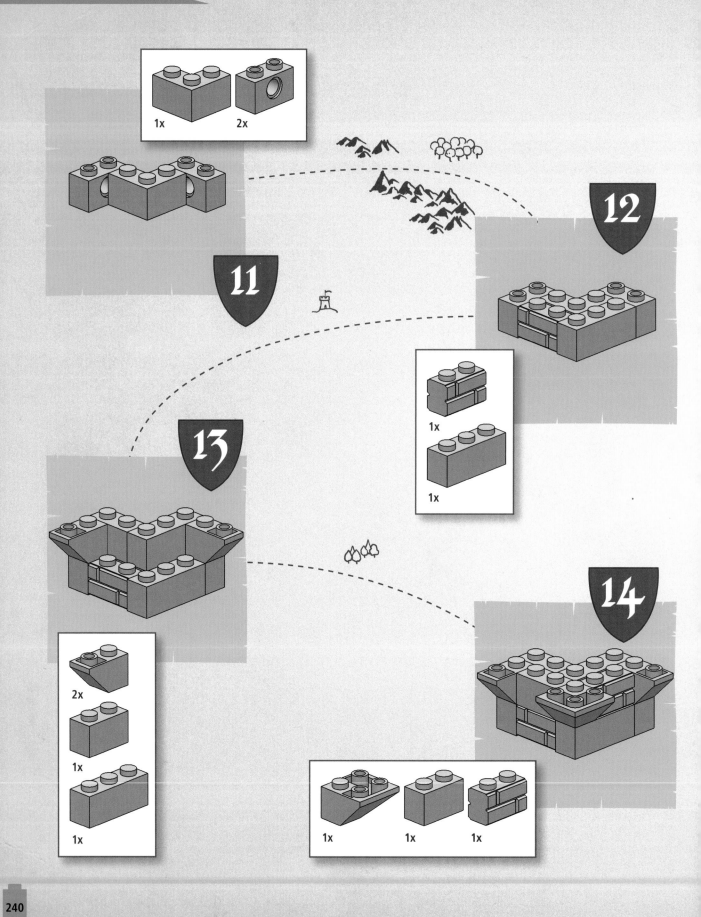

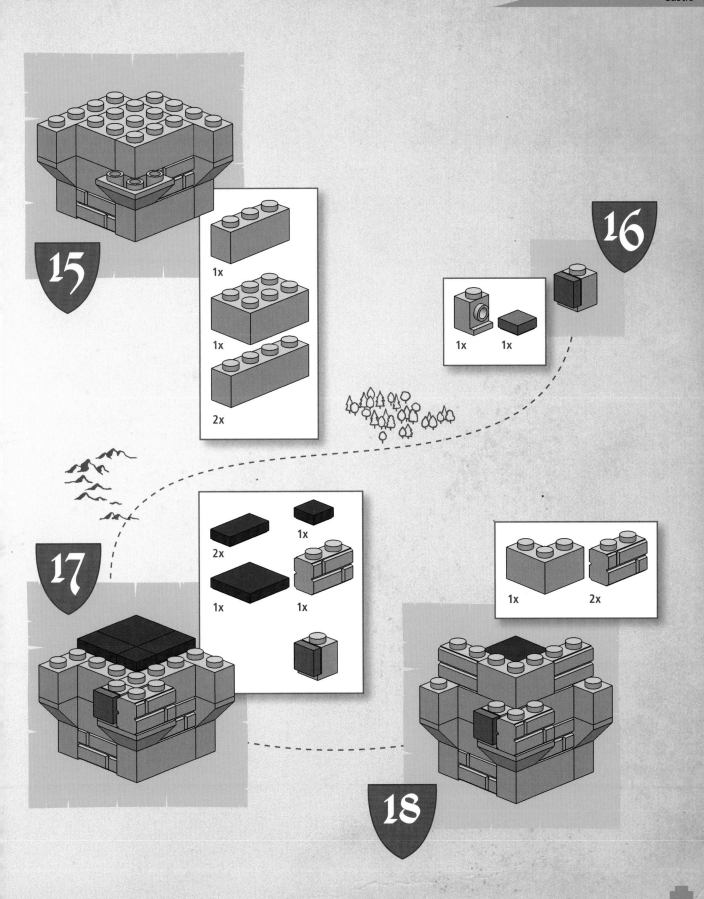

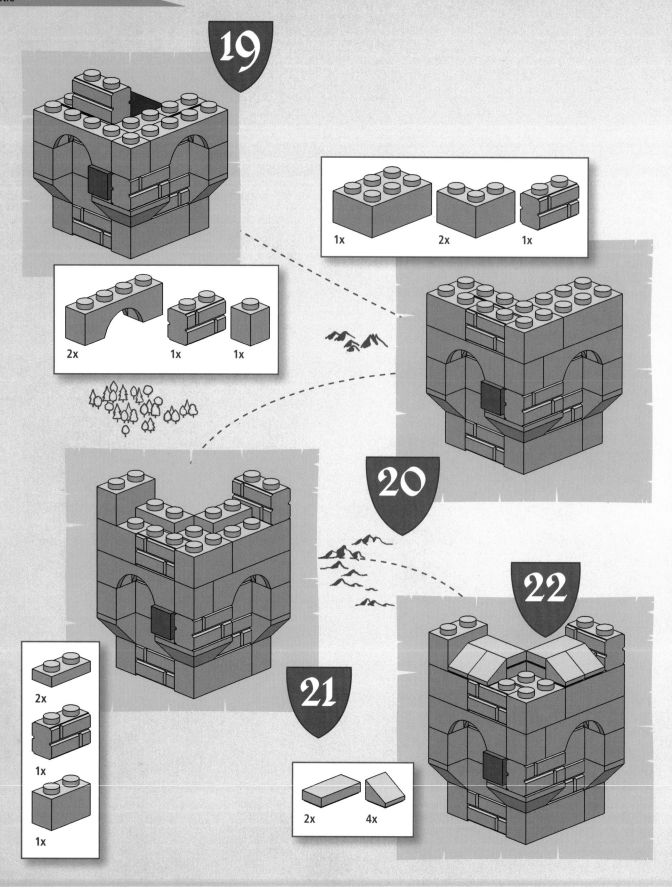

19

1x   2x   1x

2x   1x   1x

20

21

2x

1x

1x

2x   4x

22

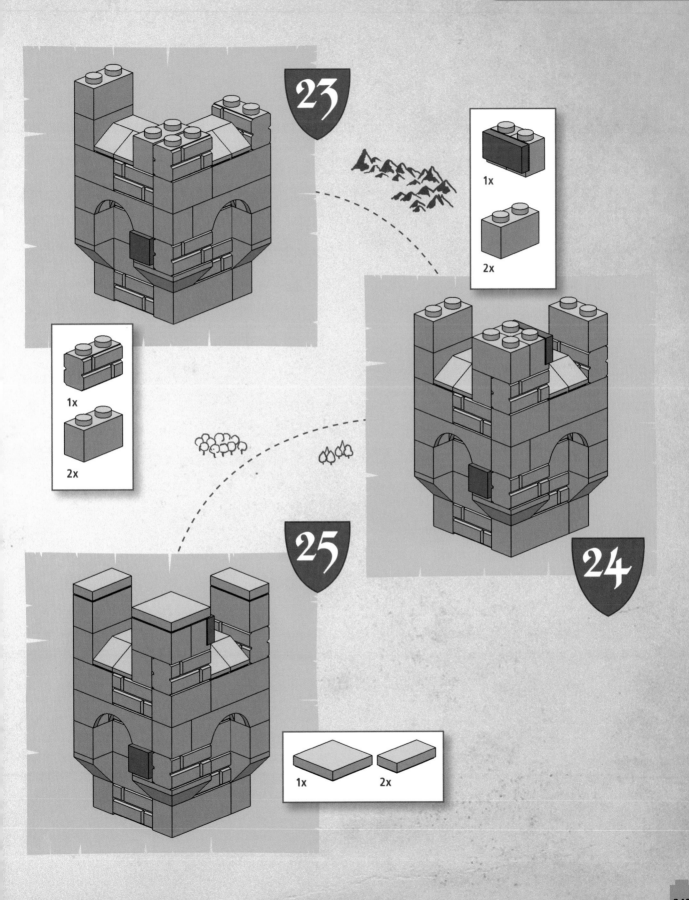

23

1x
2x

1x
2x

24

25

1x
2x

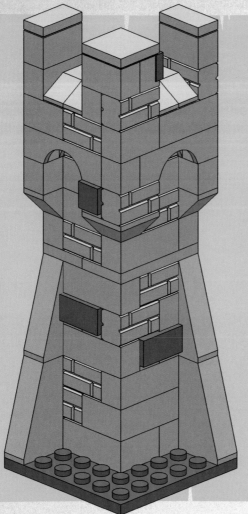

The negative roof tile in the corner of the external wall is very hard to find in new bright gray, so I used old bright gray. But it looks great in this position!

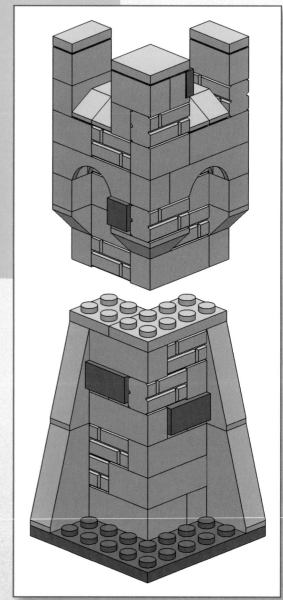

27

2x

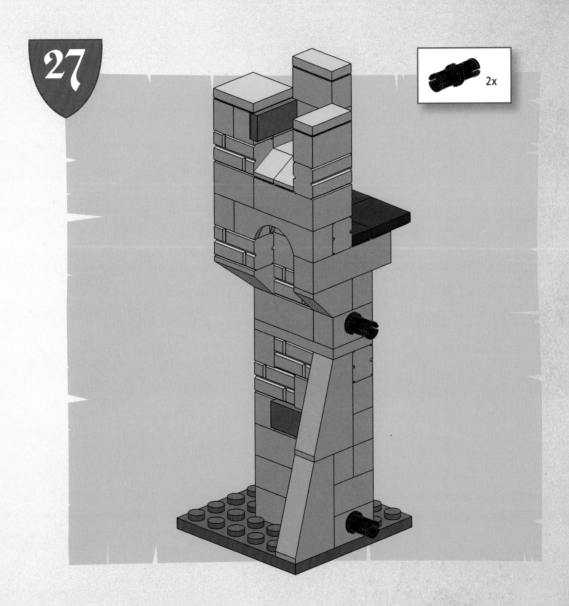

Parts List

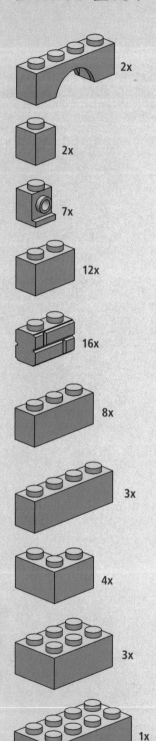

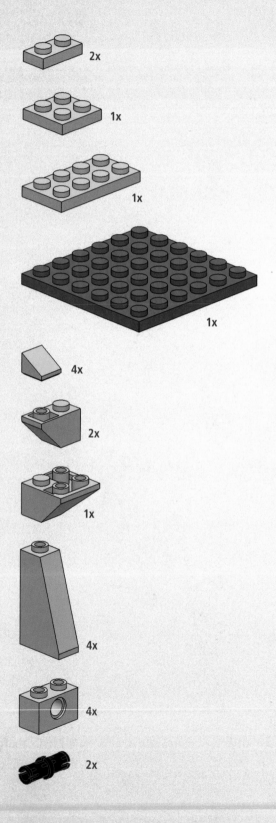

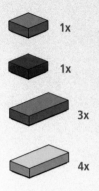

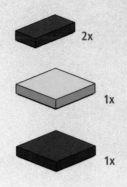

Quantity	Color		Element	Element Name
2		Light Bluish Gray	3659	Arch 1 x 4
2		Light Bluish Gray	3005	Brick 1 x 1
7		Light Bluish Gray	4070	Brick 1 x 1 with Headlight
12		Light Bluish Gray	3004	Brick 1 x 2
16		Light Bluish Gray	98283	Brick 1 x 2 with Embossed Bricks
8		Light Bluish Gray	3622	Brick 1 x 3
3		Light Bluish Gray	3010	Brick 1 x 4
4		Light Bluish Gray	2357	Brick 2 x 2 Corner
3		Light Bluish Gray	3002	Brick 2 x 3
1		Light Bluish Gray	3001	Brick 2 x 4
2		Light Bluish Gray	3023	Plate 1 x 2
1		Light Bluish Gray	3022	Plate 2 x 2
1		Light Bluish Gray	3020	Plate 2 x 4
1		Green	3958	Plate 6 x 6
4		Light Bluish Gray	54200	Slope Brick 31 1 x 1 x 2/3
2		Light Bluish Gray	3665	Slope Brick 45 2 x 1 Inverted
1		Light Bluish Gray	3676	Slope Brick 45 2 x 2 Inverted Double Convex
4		Light Bluish Gray	4460	Slope Brick 75 2 x 1 x 3
4		Light Bluish Gray	3700	Technic Brick 1 x 2 with Hole
2		Black	2780	Technic Pin with Friction and Slots
1		Dark Bluish Gray	3070b	Tile 1 x 1 with Groove
1		Reddish Brown	3070b	Tile 1 x 1 with Groove
3		Dark Bluish Gray	3069b	Tile 1 x 2 with Groove
4		Light Bluish Gray	3069b	Tile 1 x 2 with Groove
2		Reddish Brown	3069b	Tile 1 x 2 with Groove
1		Light Bluish Gray	3068b	Tile 2 x 2 with Groove
1		Reddish Brown	3068b	Tile 2 x 2 with Groove

Wall connection

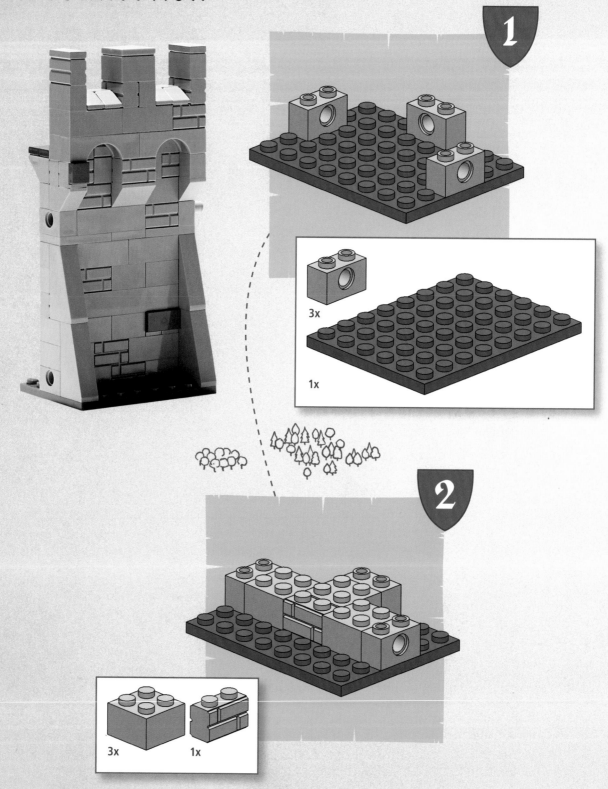

1

3x

1x

2

3x   1x

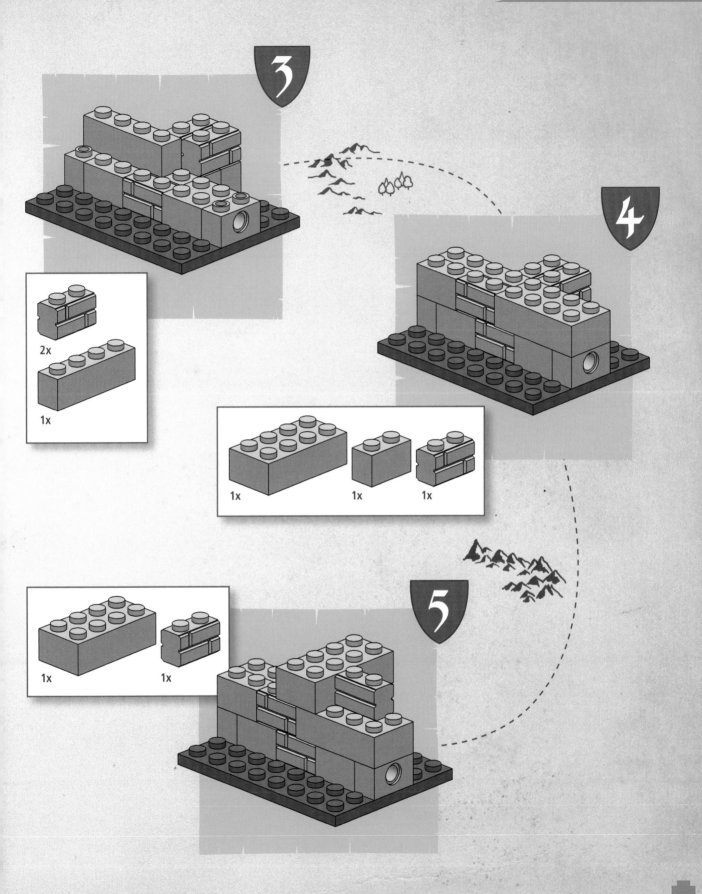

3

2x

1x

1x

1x

1x

4

1x

1x

5

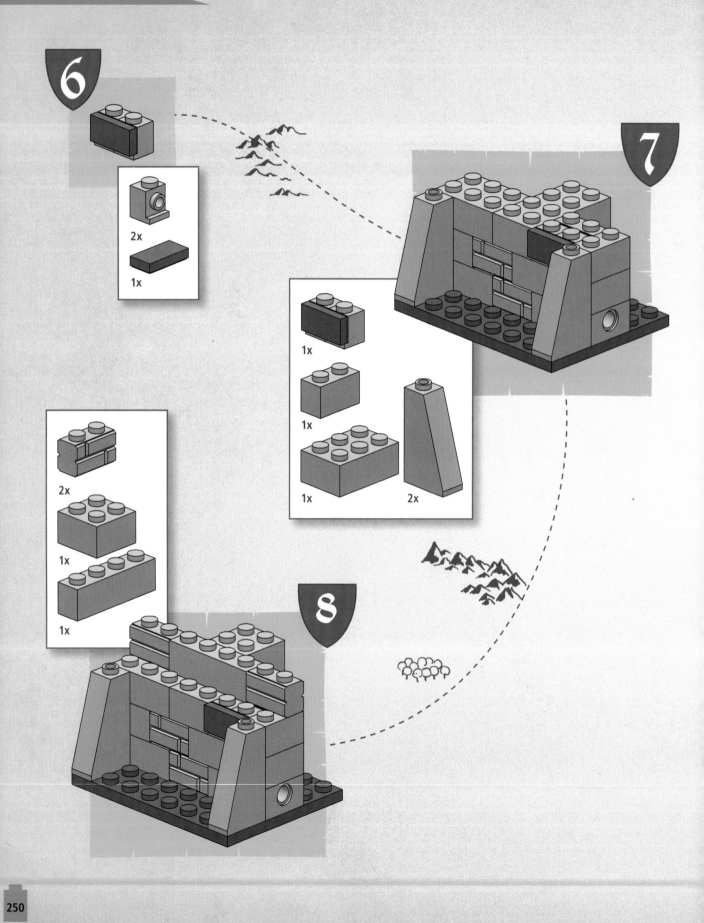

6

2x

1x

7

1x

1x

1x

2x

2x

1x

1x

8

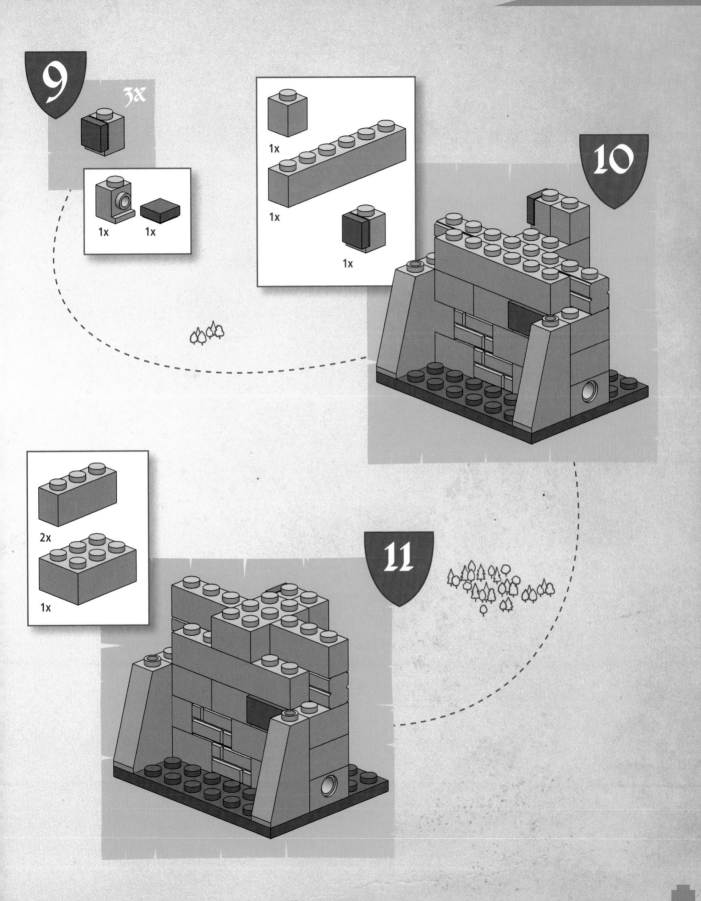

9

3x

1x   1x

1x

1x

1x

10

2x

1x

11

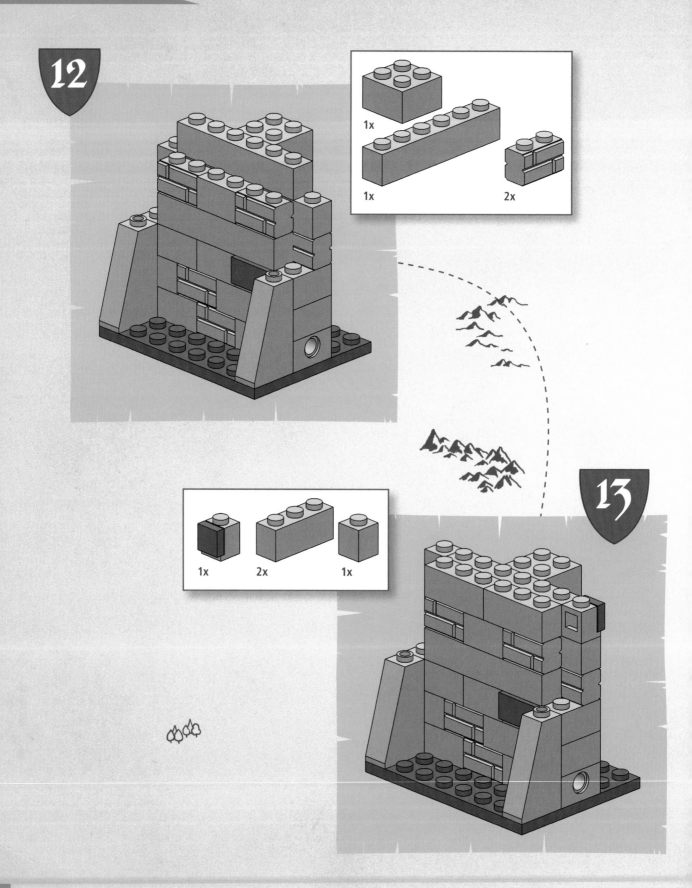

12

1x

1x

2x

13

1x

2x

1x

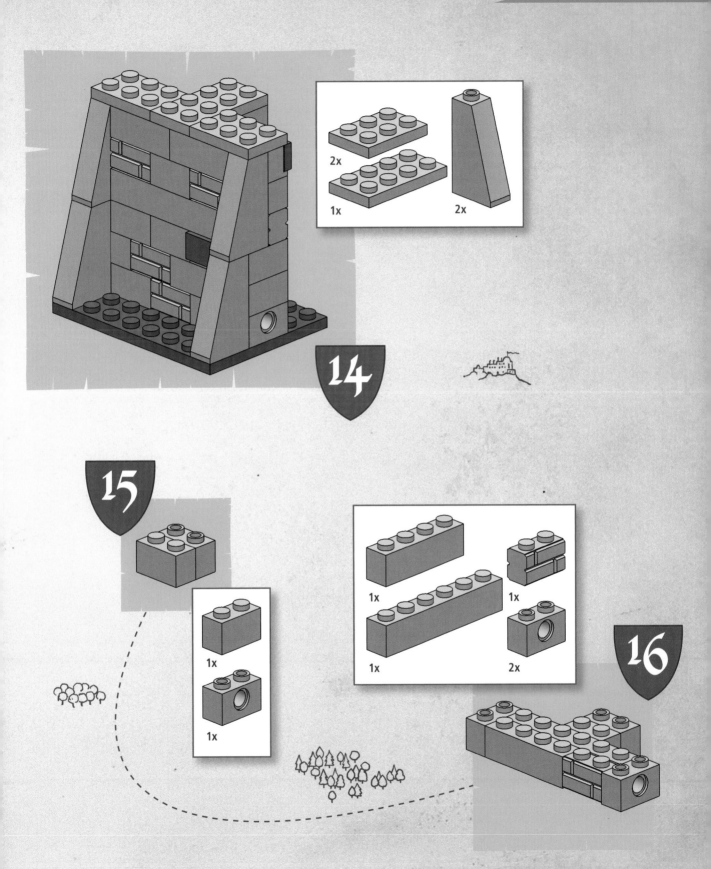

14

15

16

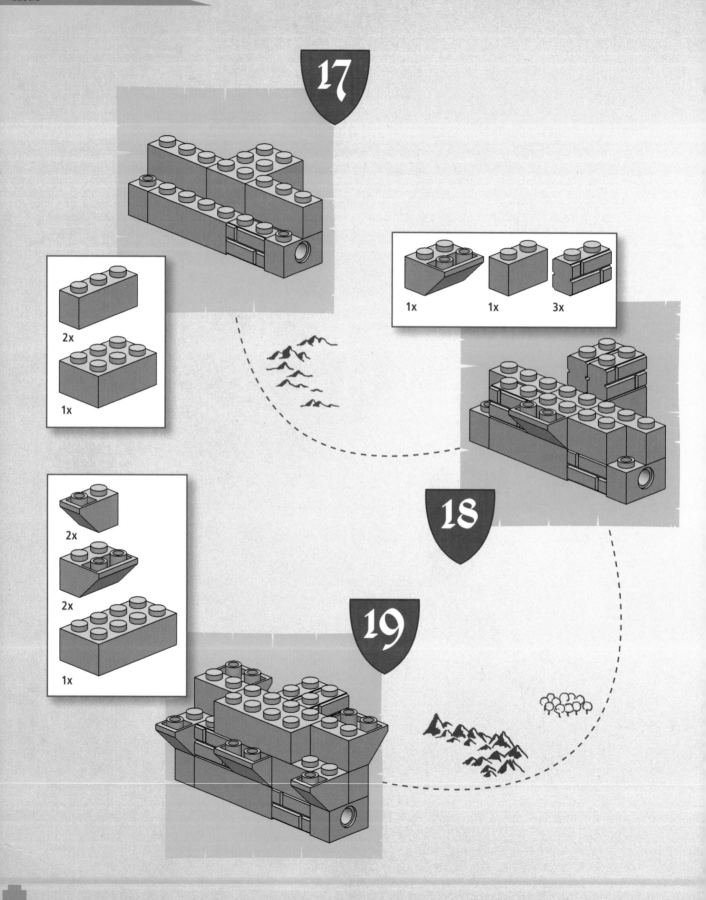

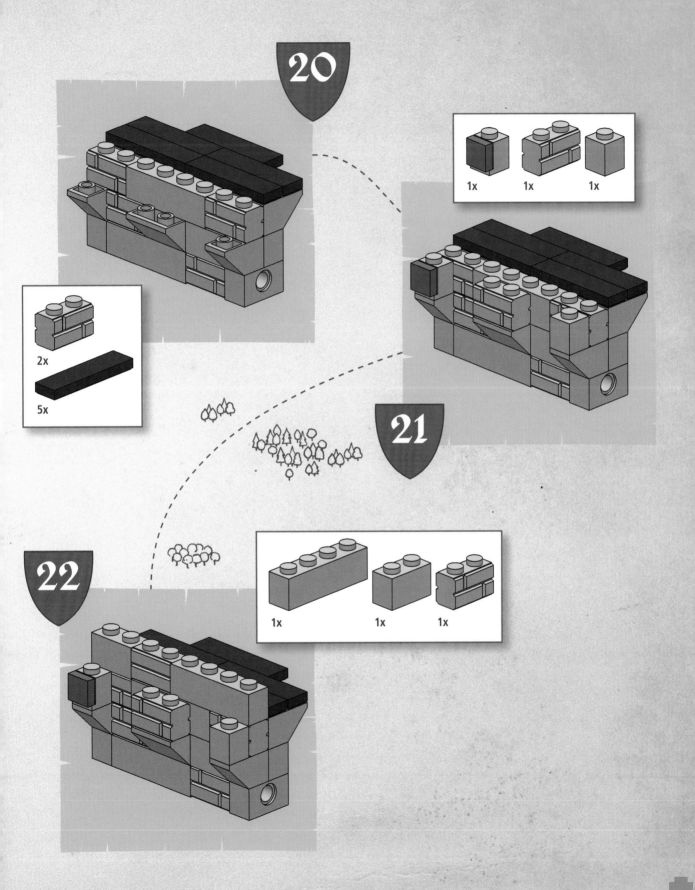

20

2x

5x

1x   1x   1x

21

22

1x   1x   1x

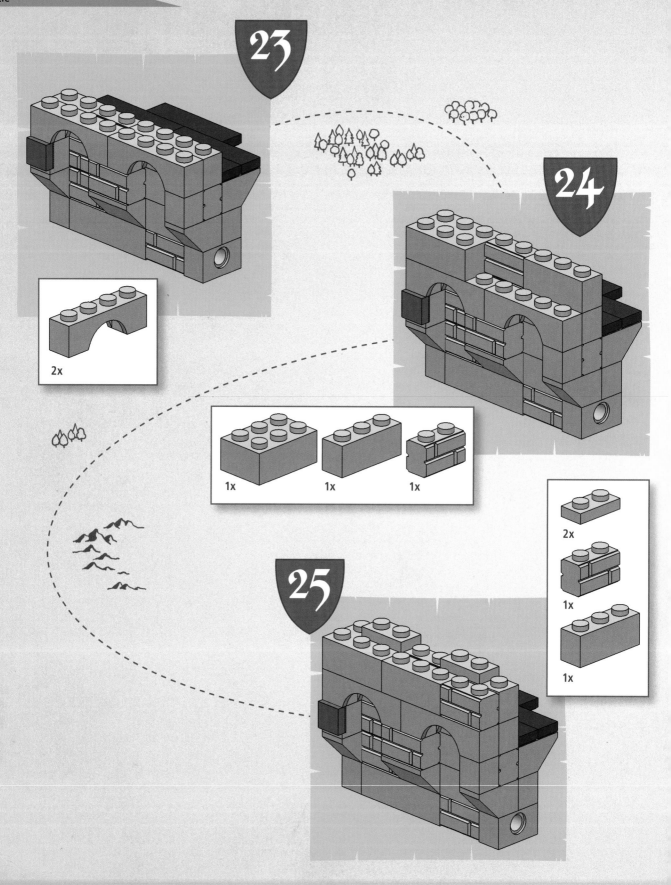

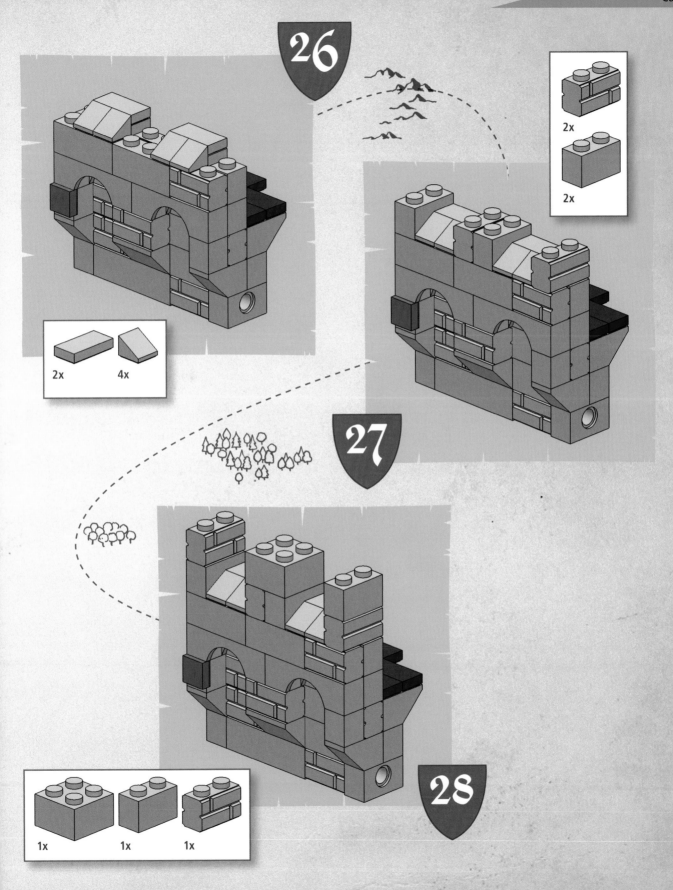

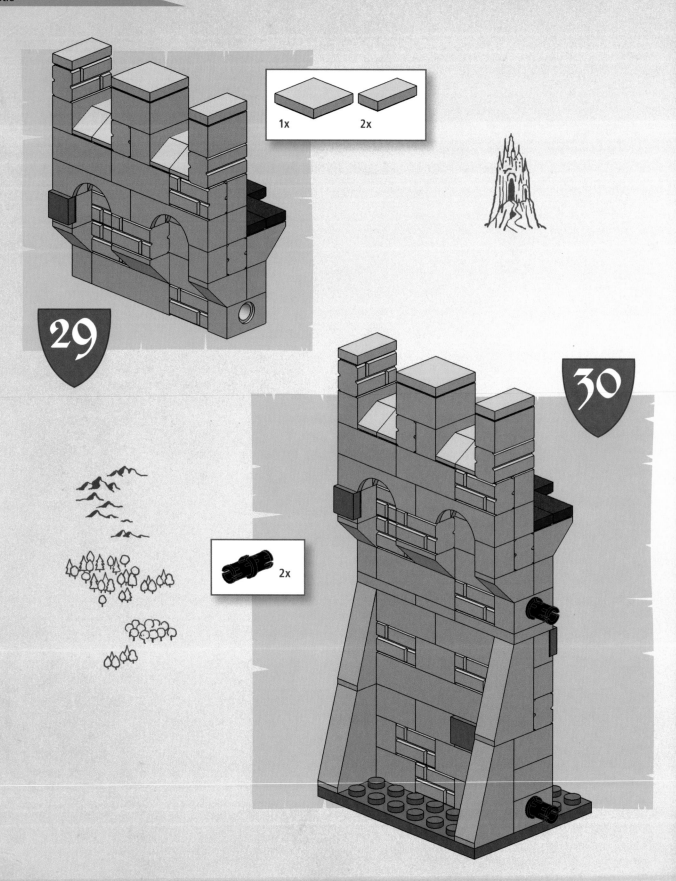

1x   2x

2x

29

30

Parts List

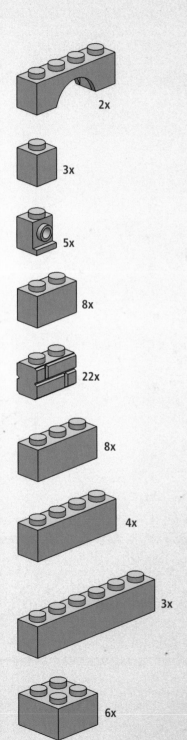

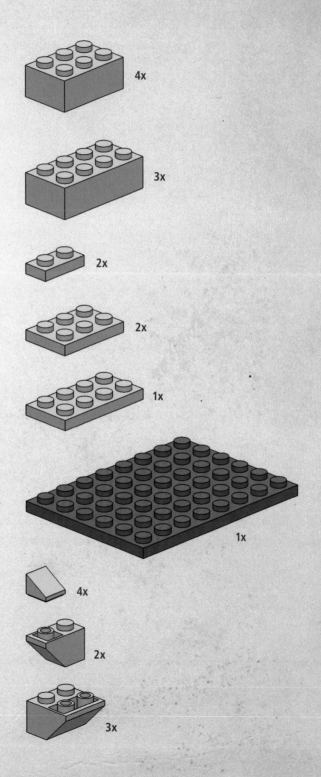

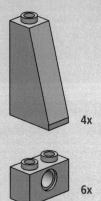

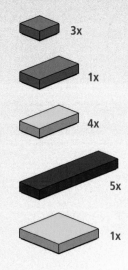

Quantity		Color	Element	Element Name
2		Light Bluish Gray	3659	Arch 1 x 4
3		Light Bluish Gray	3005	Brick 1 x 1
5		Light Bluish Gray	4070	Brick 1 x 1 with Headlight
8		Light Bluish Gray	3004	Brick 1 x 2
22		Light Bluish Gray	98283	Brick 1 x 2 with Embossed Bricks
8		Light Bluish Gray	3622	Brick 1 x 3
4		Light Bluish Gray	3010	Brick 1 x 4
3		Light Bluish Gray	3009	Brick 1 x 6
6		Light Bluish Gray	3003	Brick 2 x 2
4		Light Bluish Gray	3002	Brick 2 x 3
3		Light Bluish Gray	3001	Brick 2 x 4
2		Light Bluish Gray	3023	Plate 1 x 2
2		Light Bluish Gray	3021	Plate 2 x 3
1		Light Bluish Gray	3020	Plate 2 x 4
1		Green	3036	Plate 6 x 8
4		Light Bluish Gray	54200	Slope Brick 31 1 x 1 x 2/3
2		Light Bluish Gray	3665	Slope Brick 45 2 x 1 Inverted
3		Light Bluish Gray	3660	Slope Brick 45 2 x 2 Inverted
4		Light Bluish Gray	4460	Slope Brick 75 2 x 1 x 3
6		Light Bluish Gray	3700	Technic Brick 1 x 2 with Hole
2		Black	2780	Technic Pin with Friction and Slots
3		Dark Bluish Gray	3070b	Tile 1 x 1 with Groove
1		Dark Bluish Gray	3069b	Tile 1 x 2 with Groove
4		Light Bluish Gray	3069b	Tile 1 x 2 with Groove
5		Reddish Brown	2431	Tile 1 x 4 with Groove
1		Light Bluish Gray	3068b	Tile 2 x 2 with Groove

Pillar

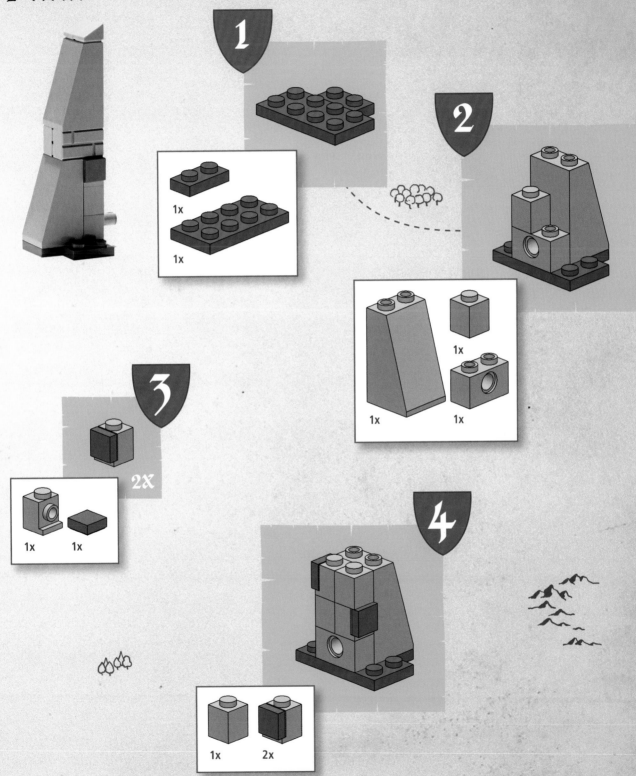

1

1x

1x

2

1x

1x

1x

1x

3

2x

1x

1x

4

1x

2x

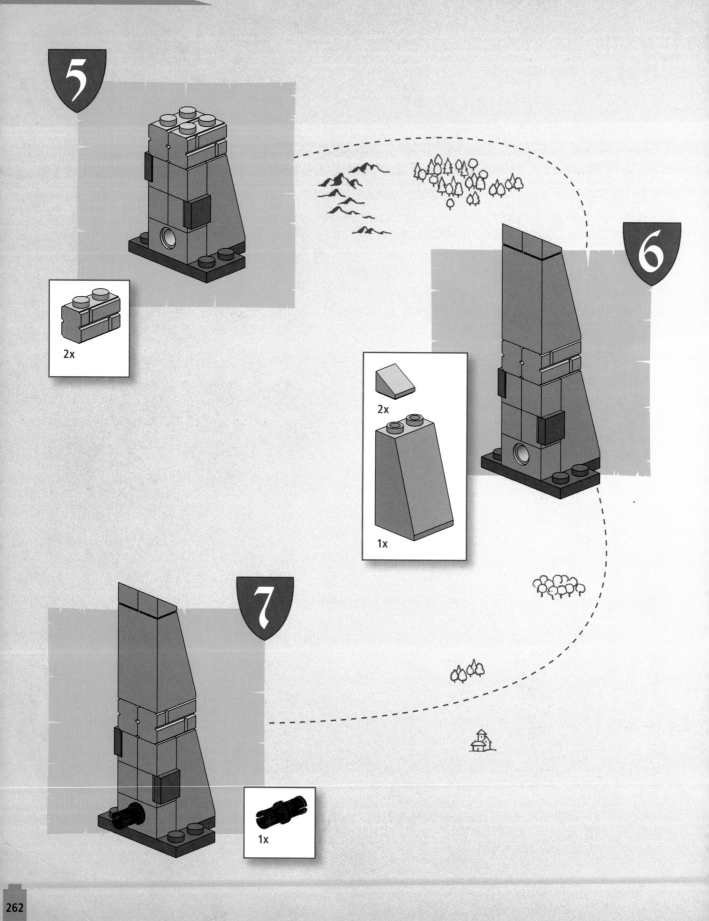

5

2x

6

2x

1x

7

1x

Parts List

 2x

 2x

 2x

 1x

 1x

 2x

 2x

 1x

 1x

 2x

Quantity	Color		Element	Element Name
2		Light_Bluish_Gray	3005	Brick 1 x 1
2		Light_Bluish_Gray	4070	Brick 1 x 1 with Headlight
2		Light_Bluish_Gray	98283	Brick 1 x 2 with Embossed Bricks
1		Green	3023	Plate 1 x 2
1		Green	3020	Plate 2 x 4
2		Light_Bluish_Gray	54200	Slope Brick 31 1 x 1 x 2/3
2		Light_Bluish_Gray	3684	Slope Brick 75 2 x 2 x 3
1		Light_Bluish_Gray	3700	Technic Brick 1 x 2 with Hole
1		Black	2780	Technic Pin with Friction and Slots
2		Dark_Bluish_Gray	3070b	Tile 1 x 1 with Groove

Steps

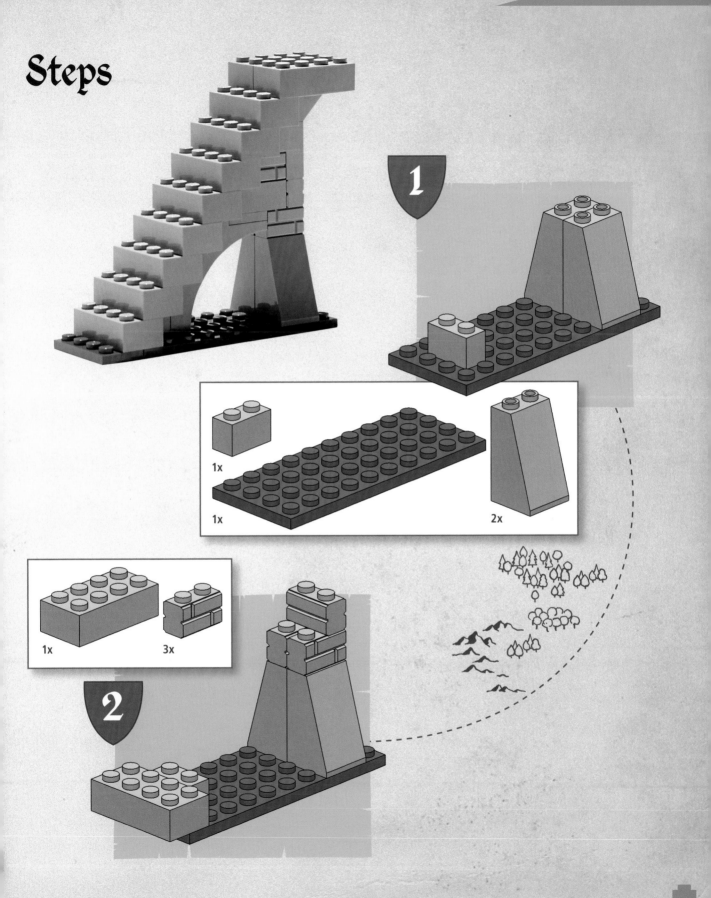

1x
1x
2x

1x
3x

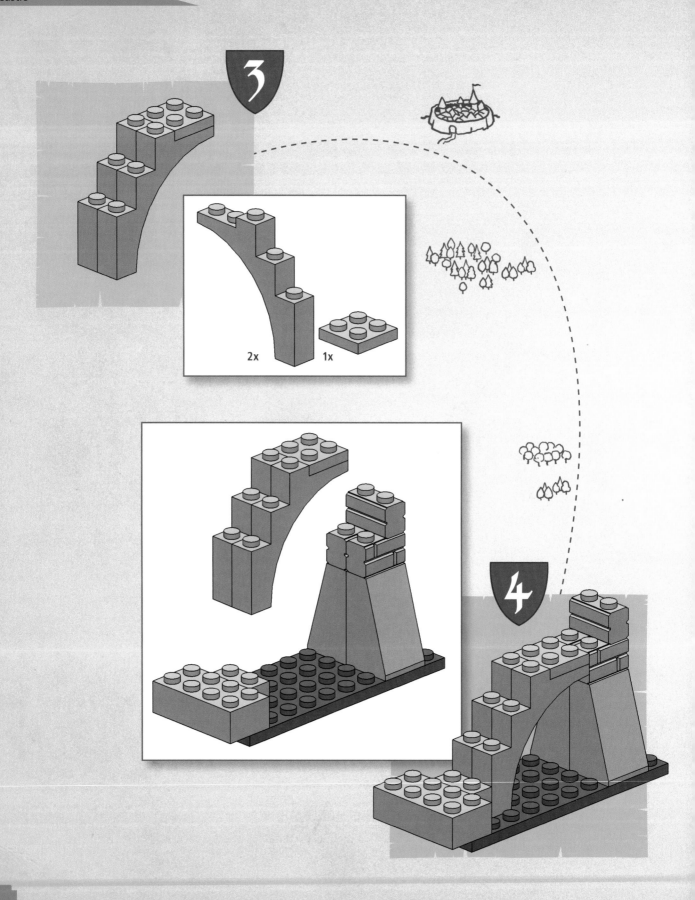

2x   1x

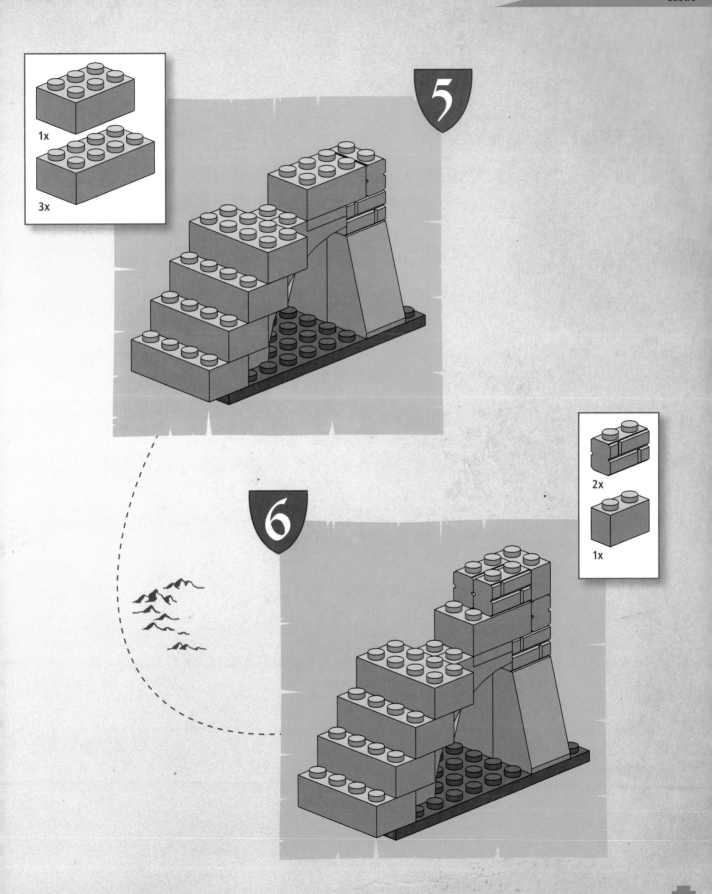

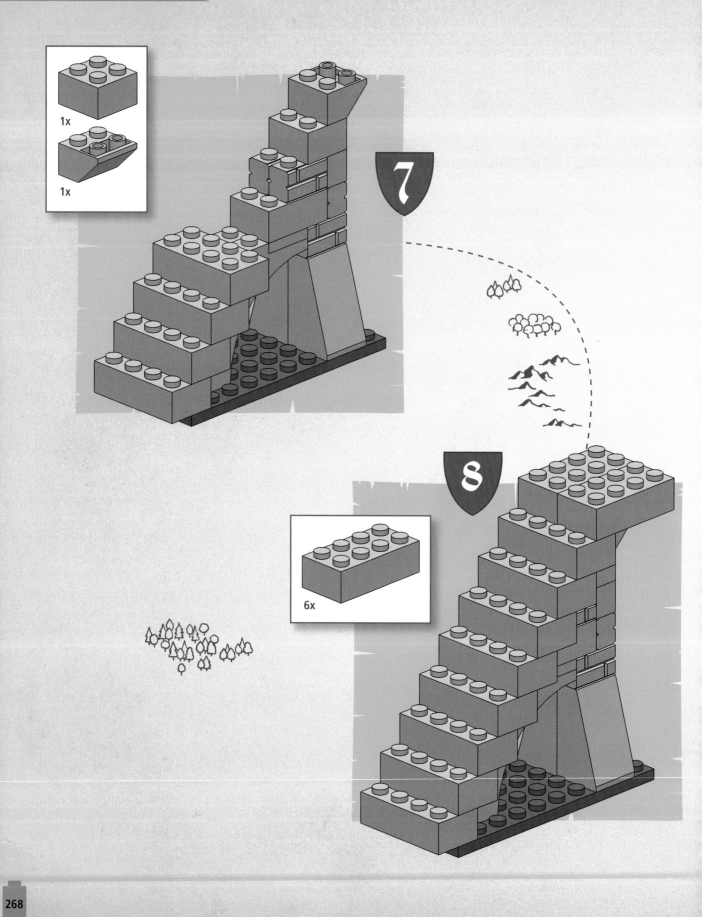

Parts List

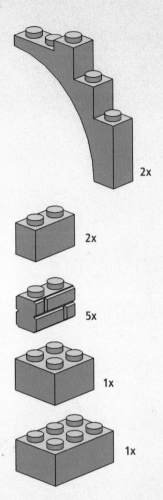

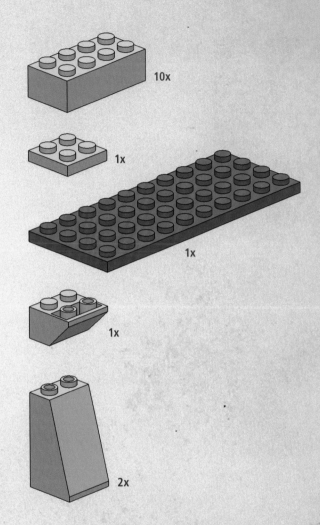

Quantity	Color		Element	Element Name
2		Light_Bluish_Gray	2339	Arch 1 x 5 x 4
2		Light_Bluish_Gray	3004	Brick 1 x 2
5		Light_Bluish_Gray	98283	Brick 1 x 2 with Embossed Bricks
1		Light_Bluish_Gray	3003	Brick 2 x 2
1		Light_Bluish_Gray	3002	Brick 2 x 3
10		Light_Bluish_Gray	3001	Brick 2 x 4
1		Light_Bluish_Gray	3022	Plate 2 x 2
1		Green	3030	Plate 4 x 10
1		Light_Bluish_Gray	3660	Slope Brick 45 2 x 2 Inverted
2		Light_Bluish_Gray	30499	Slope Brick 75 2 x 2 x 3

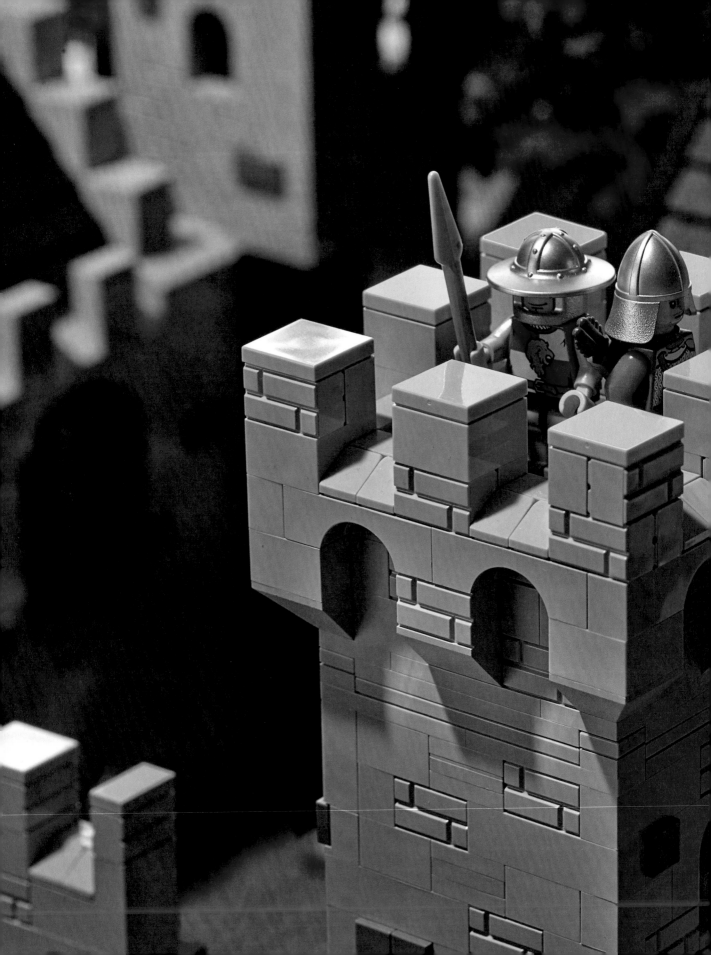

Tower base

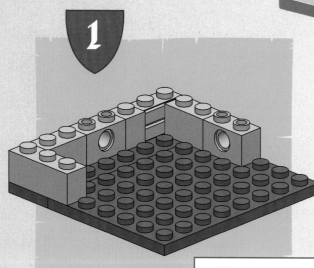

1

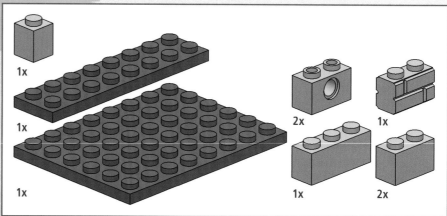

1x

1x

1x

2x

1x

1x

2x

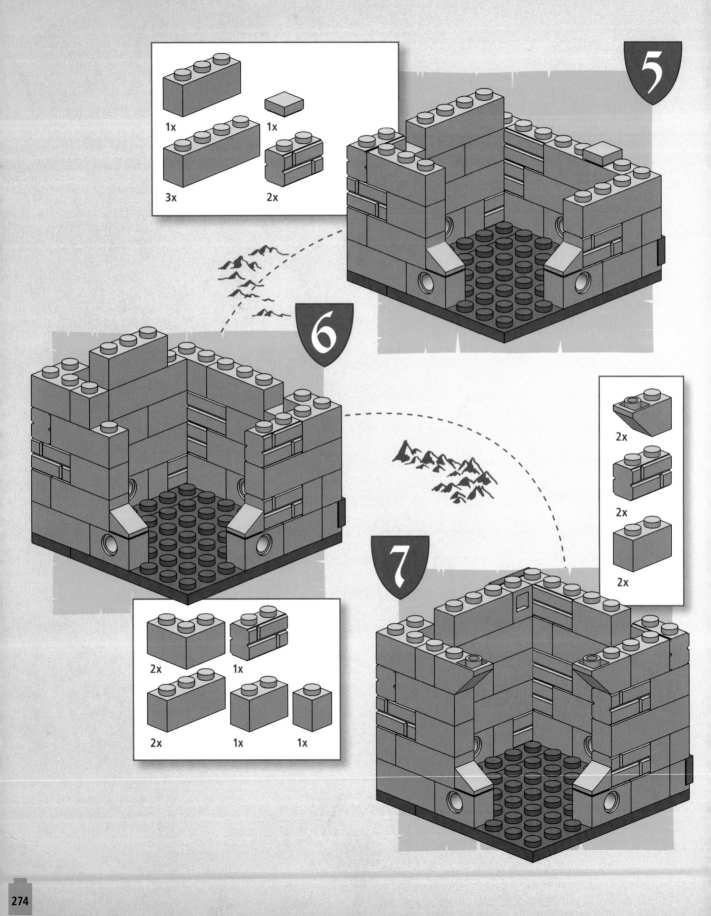

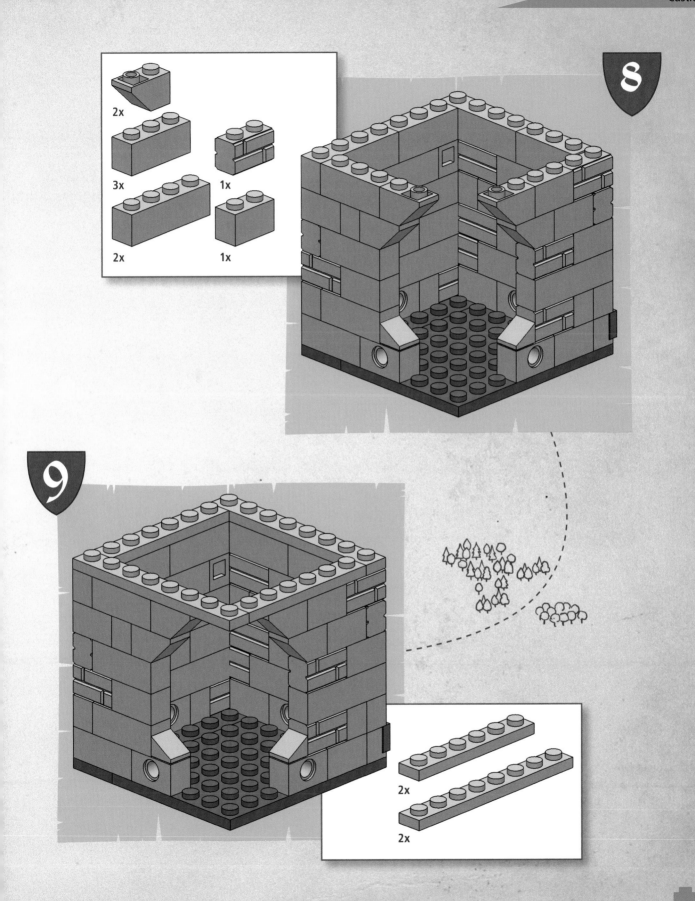

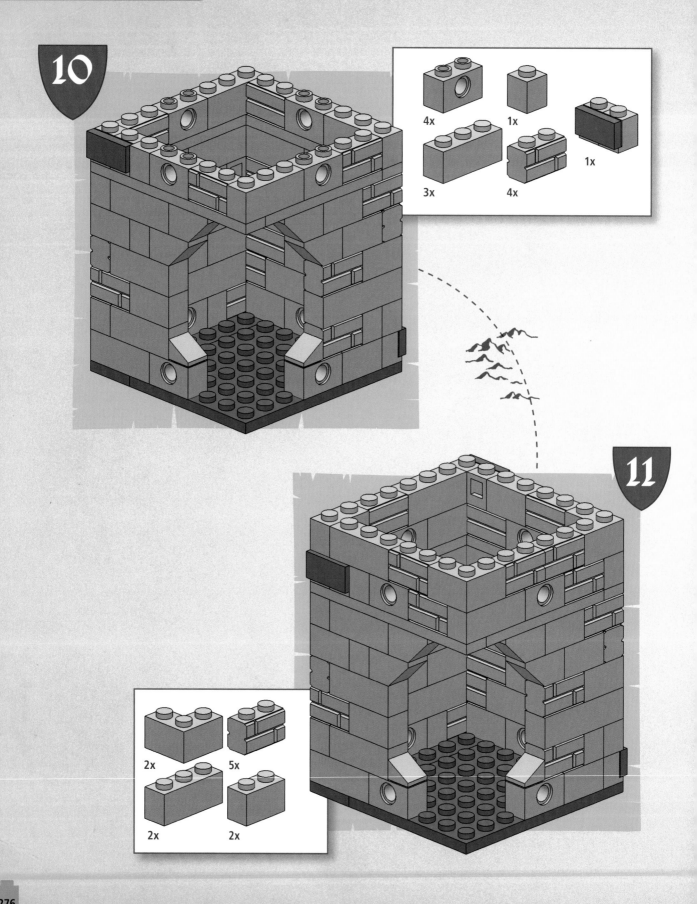

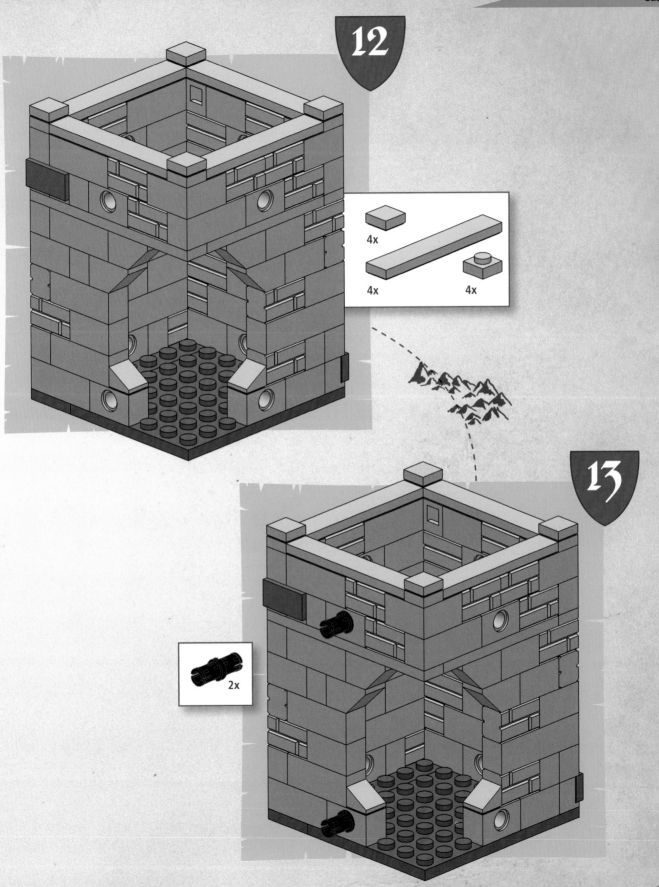

Parts List

Quantity		Color	Element	Element Name
5		Light Bluish Gray	3005	Brick 1 x 1
8		Light Bluish Gray	4070	Brick 1 x 1 with Headlight
11		Light Bluish Gray	3004	Brick 1 x 2
20		Light Bluish Gray	98283	Brick 1 x 2 with Embossed Bricks
15		Light Bluish Gray	3622	Brick 1 x 3
6		Light Bluish Gray	3010	Brick 1 x 4
1		Light Bluish Gray	3009	Brick 1 x 6
4		Light Bluish Gray	2357	Brick 2 x 2 Corner
4		Light Bluish Gray	3024	Plate 1 x 1
2		Light Bluish Gray	3666	Plate 1 x 6
2		Light Bluish Gray	3460	Plate 1 x 8
1		Green	3034	Plate 2 x 8
1		Green	3036	Plate 6 x 8
2		Light Bluish Gray	54200	Slope Brick 31 1 x 1 x 2/3
4		Light Bluish Gray	3665	Slope Brick 45 2 x 1 Inverted
8		Light Bluish Gray	3700	Technic Brick 1 x 2 with Hole
2		Black	2780	Technic Pin with Friction and Slots
6		Light Bluish Gray	3070b	Tile 1 x 1 with Groove
4		Dark Bluish Gray	3069b	Tile 1 x 2 with Groove
4		Light Bluish Gray	6636	Tile 1 x 6

Tower, middle segment

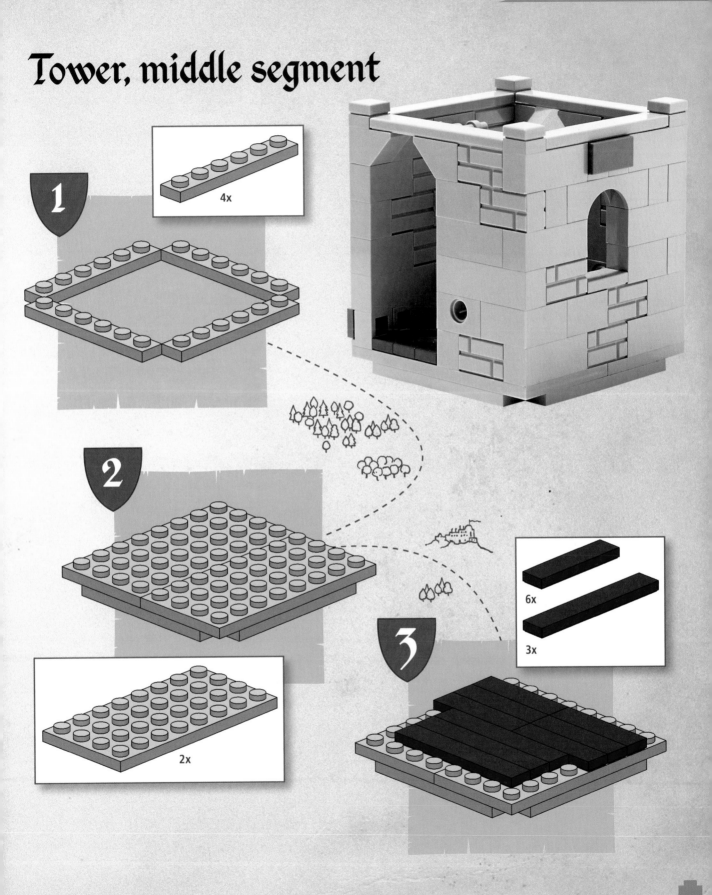

1 4x

2 2x

3 6x
3x

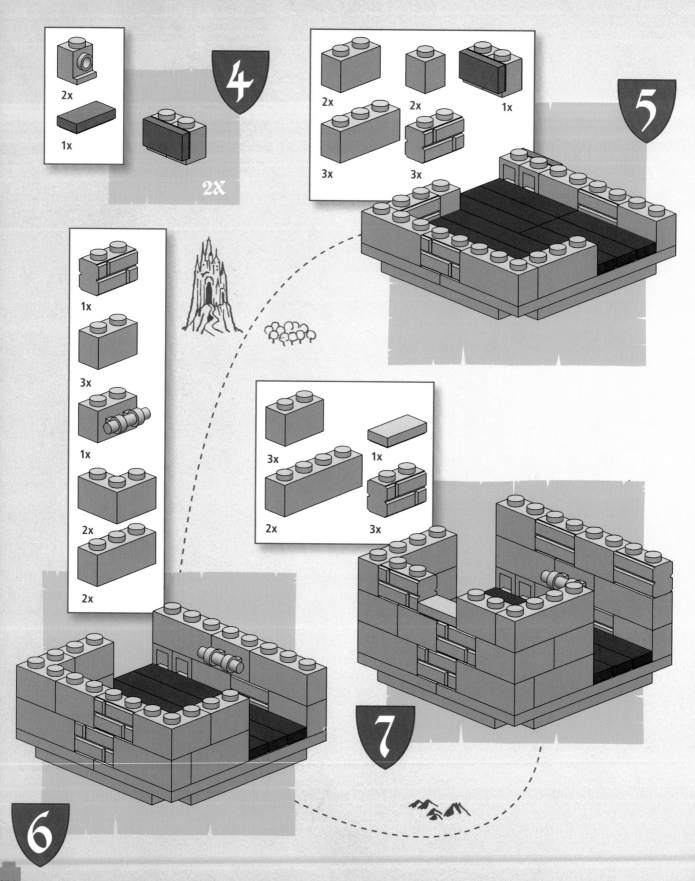

2x

1x

4

2x

2x

2x

1x

3x

3x

5

1x

3x

1x

2x

2x

3x

1x

2x

3x

6

7

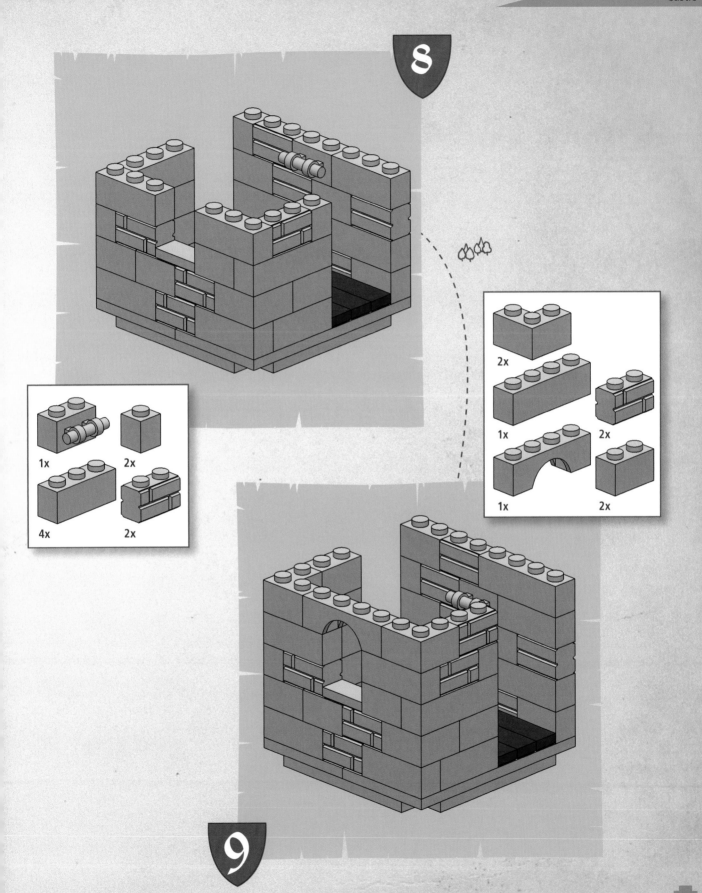

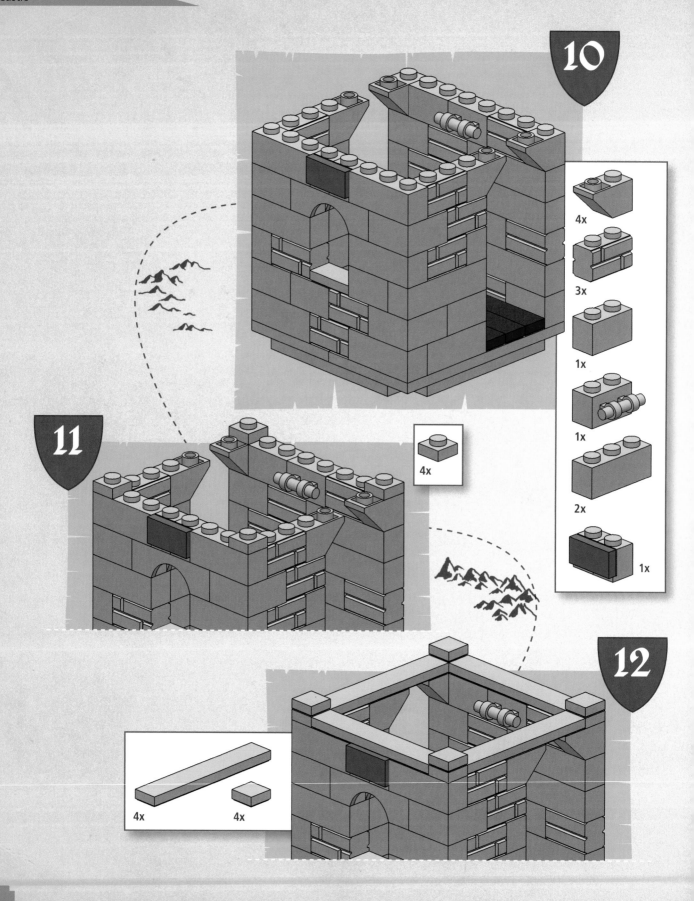

10

4x

3x

1x

1x

2x

1x

4x

11

12

4x 4x

Parts List

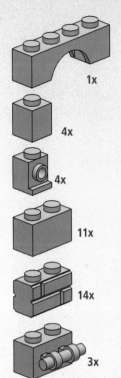

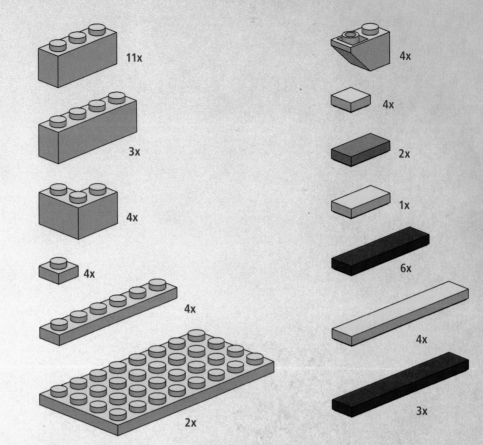

Quantity	Color		Element	Element Name
1		Light Bluish Gray	3659	Arch 1 x 4
4		Light Bluish Gray	3005	Brick 1 x 1
4		Light Bluish Gray	4070	Brick 1 x 1 with Headlight
11		Light Bluish Gray	3004	Brick 1 x 2
14		Light Bluish Gray	98283	Brick 1 x 2 with Embossed Bricks
3		Light Bluish Gray	30236	Brick 1 x 2 with Handle
11		Light Bluish Gray	3622	Brick 1 x 3
3		Light Bluish Gray	3010	Brick 1 x 4
4		Light Bluish Gray	2357	Brick 2 x 2 Corner
4		Light Bluish Gray	3024	Plate 1 x 1
4		Light Bluish Gray	3666	Plate 1 x 6
2		Light Bluish Gray	3035	Plate 4 x 8
4		Light Bluish Gray	3665	Slope Brick 45 2 x 1 Inverted
4		Light Bluish Gray	3070b	Tile 1 x 1 with Groove
2		Dark Bluish Gray	3069b	Tile 1 x 2 with Groove
1		Light Bluish Gray	3069b	Tile 1 x 2 with Groove
6		Reddish Brown	2431	Tile 1 x 4 with Groove
4		Light Bluish Gray	6636	Tile 1 x 6
3		Reddish Brown	6636	Tile 1 x 6

Turret

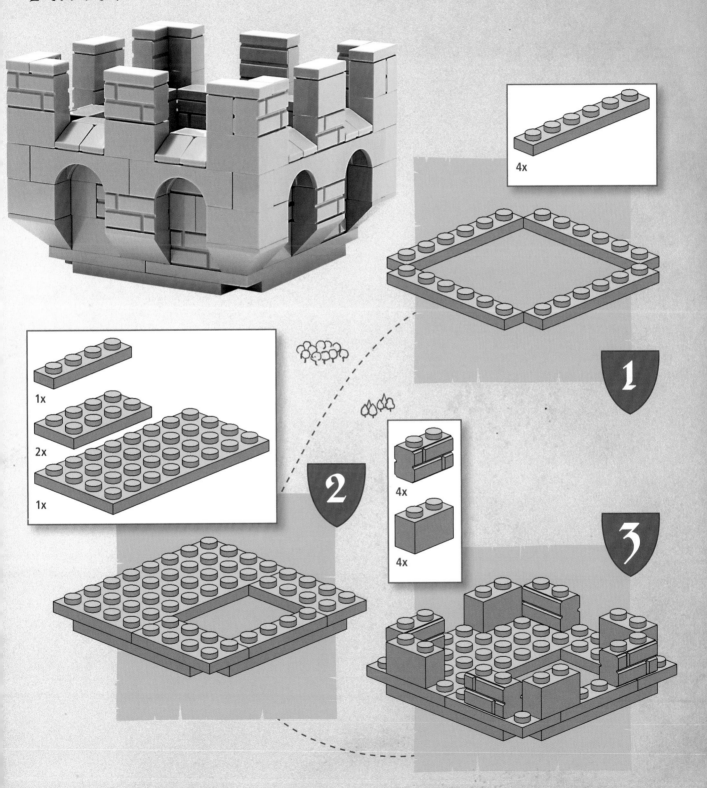

4x

1x

2x

1x

1

2

3

4x

4x

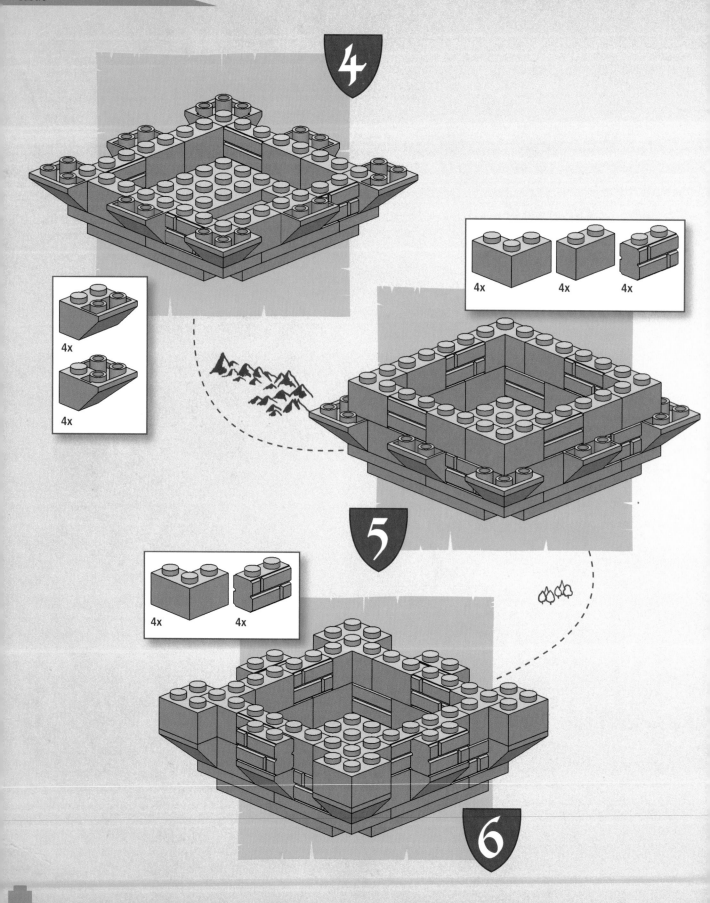

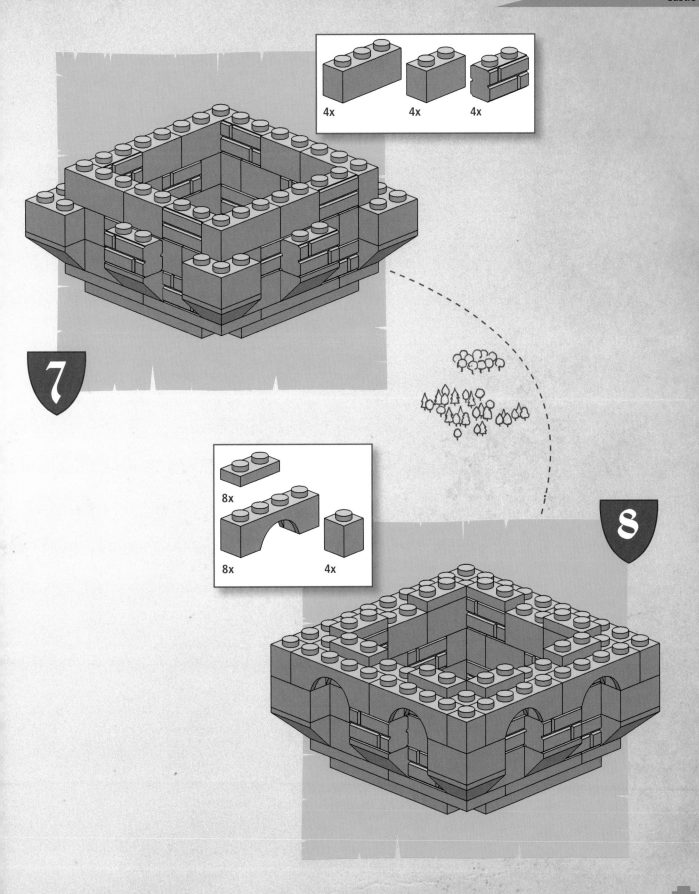

4x 4x 4x

7

8x

8x 4x

8

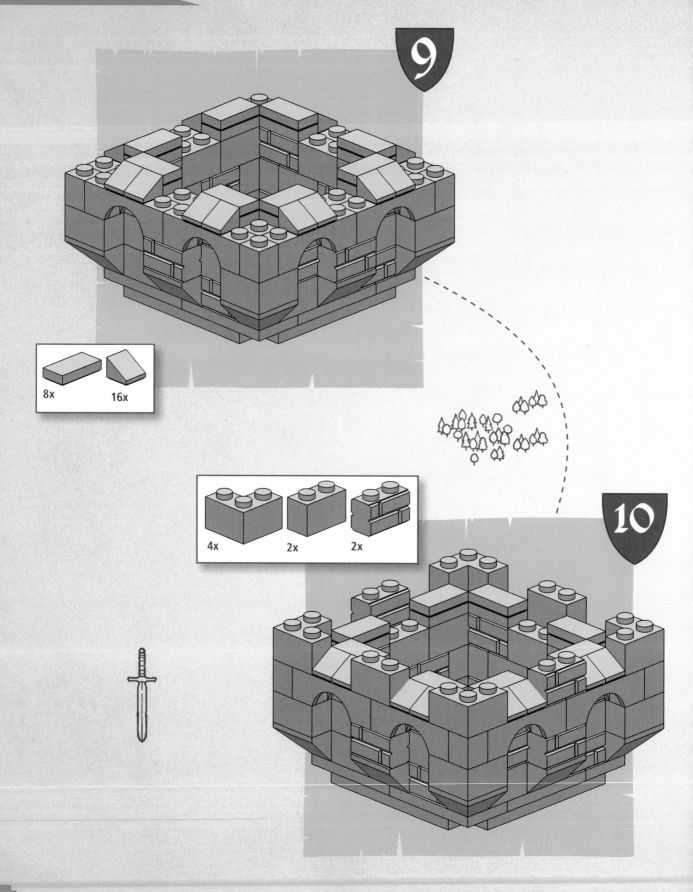

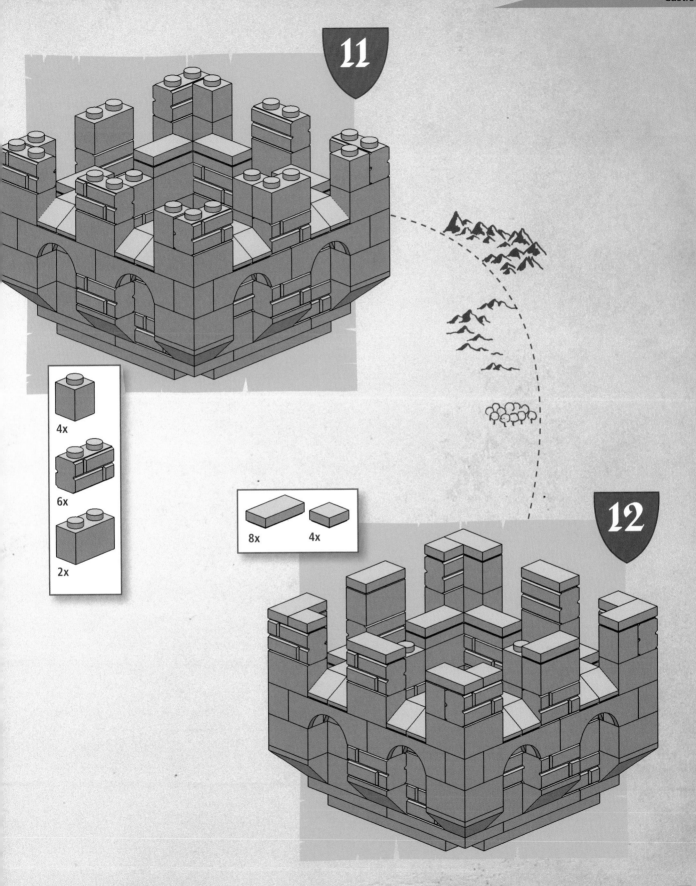

Parts List

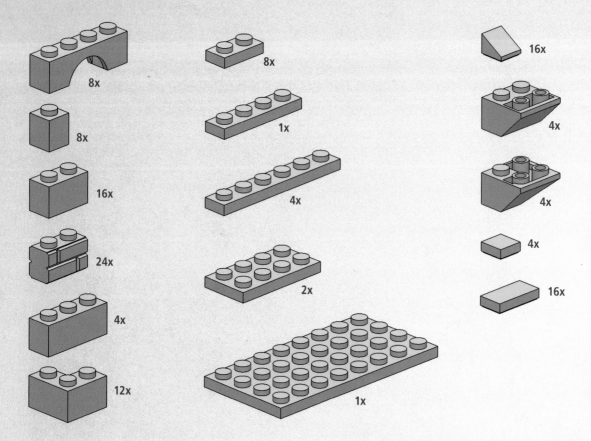

Quantity		Color	Element	Element Name
8		Light Bluish Gray	3659	Arch 1 x 4
8		Light Bluish Gray	3005	Brick 1 x 1
16		Light Bluish Gray	3004	Brick 1 x 2
24		Light Bluish Gray	98283	Brick 1 x 2 with Embossed Bricks
4		Light Bluish Gray	3622	Brick 1 x 3
12		Light Bluish Gray	2357	Brick 2 x 2 Corner
8		Light Bluish Gray	3023	Plate 1 x 2
1		Light Bluish Gray	3710	Plate 1 x 4
4		Light Bluish Gray	3666	Plate 1 x 6
2		Light Bluish Gray	3020	Plate 2 x 4
1		Light Bluish Gray	3035	Plate 4 x 8
16		Light Bluish Gray	54200	Slope Brick 31 1 x 1 x 2/3
4		Light Bluish Gray	3660	Slope Brick 45 2 x 2 Inverted
4		Light Bluish Gray	3676	Slope Brick 45 2 x 2 Inverted Double Convex
4		Light Bluish Gray	3070b	Tile 1 x 1 with Groove
16		Light Bluish Gray	3069b	Tile 1 x 2 with Groove

Tower pinnacle

1

4x

1x

4x

8x

4x

4x

2

3

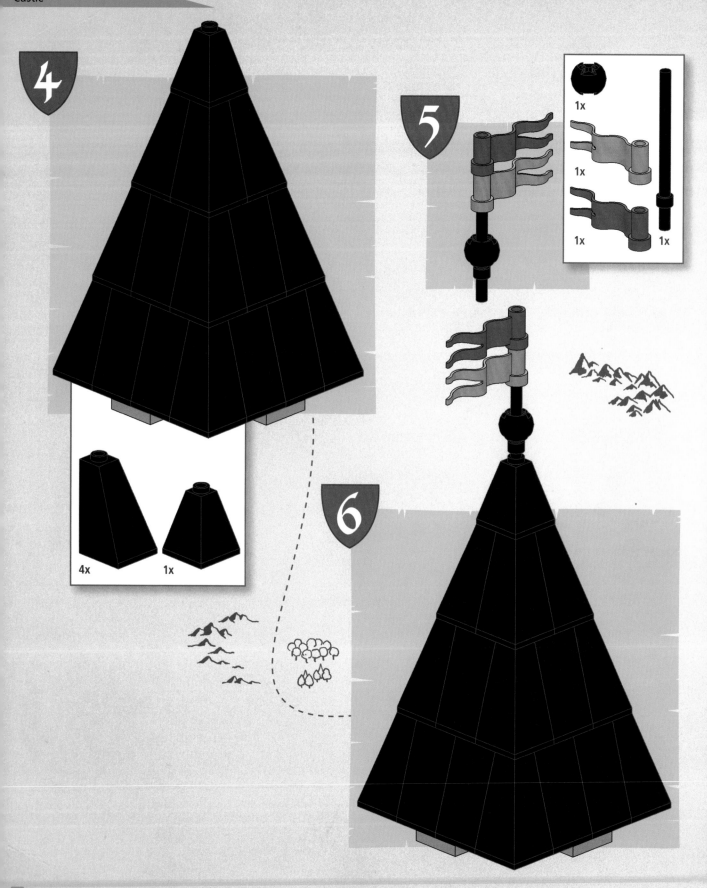

4

4x   1x

5

1x

1x

1x   1x

6

Parts List

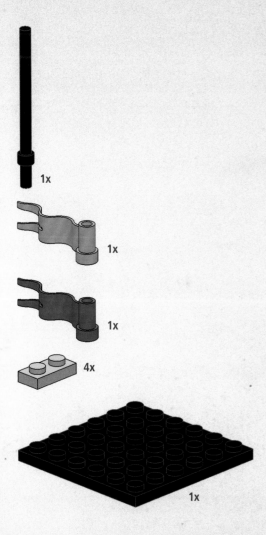

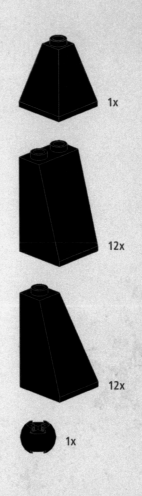

Quantity		Color	Element	Element Name
1		Black	63965	Bar 6L with Thick Stop
1		Pearl Gold	4495b	Flag 4 x 1 with First Wave Right
1		Red	4495b	Flag 4 x 1 with First Wave Right
4		Light Bluish Gray	3023	Plate 1 x 2
1		Black	3958	Plate 6 x 6
1		Black	3688	Slope Brick 75 2 x 2 x 2 Quadruple Convex
12		Black	3684	Slope Brick 75 2 x 2 x 3
12		Black	3685	Slope Brick 75 2 x 2 x 3 Double Convex
1		Black	53585	Technic Ball Joint with Axlehole Open

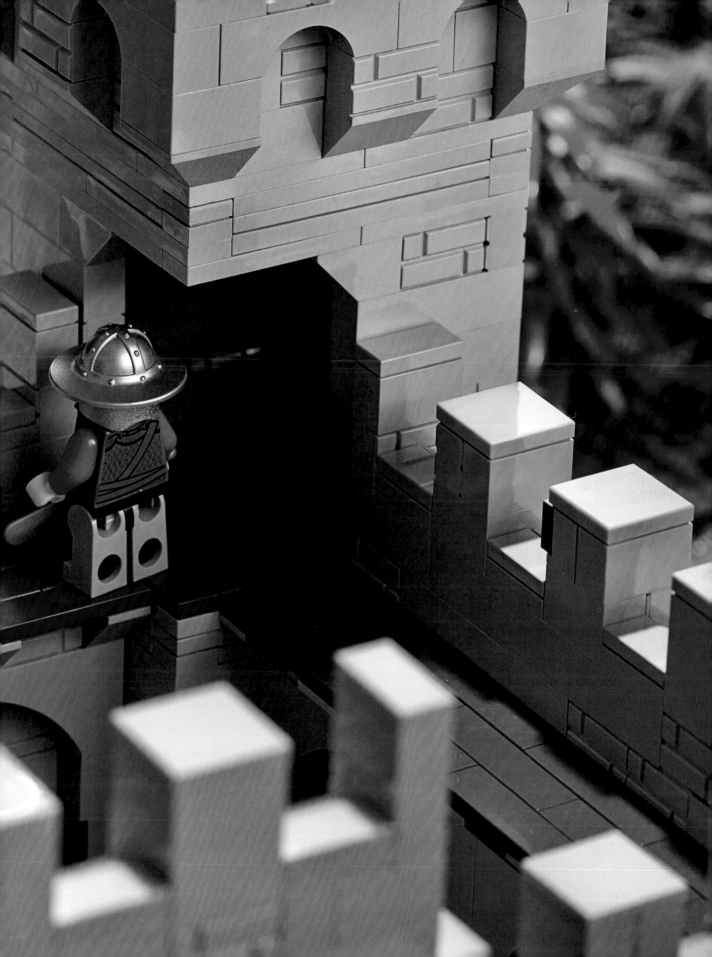

Tower gate

1

2x

1x

2x

2x

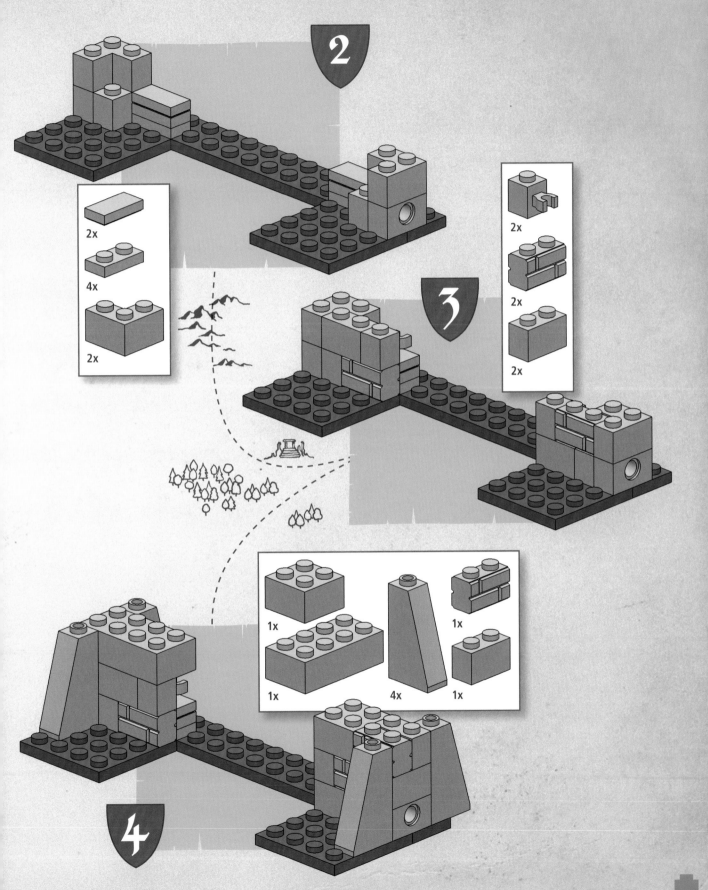

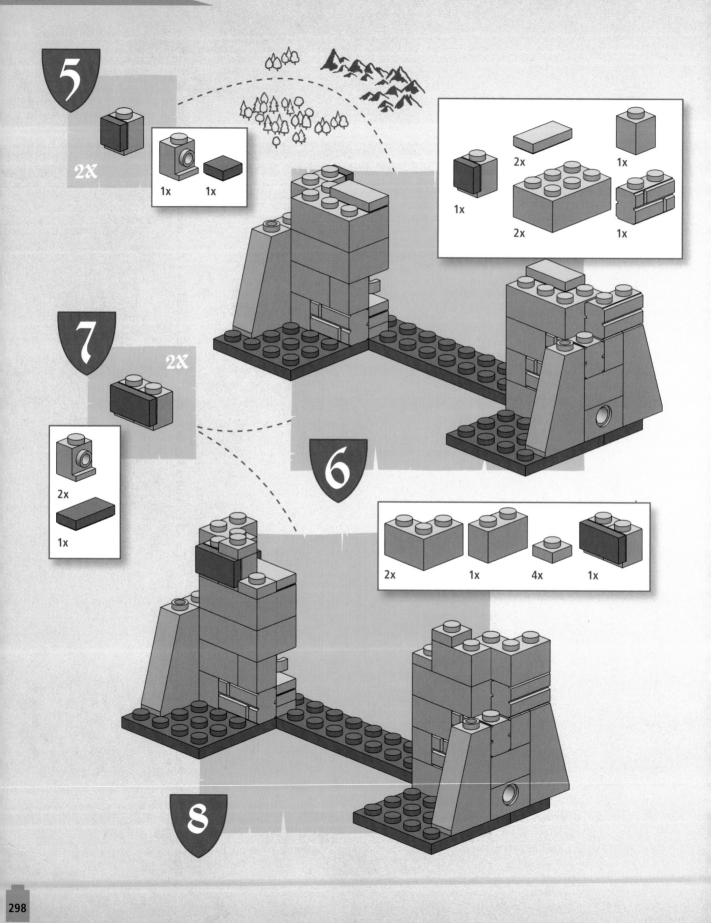

5

2x

1x 1x

1x

2x 1x

2x 1x

7

2x

2x

1x

6

2x 1x 4x 1x

8

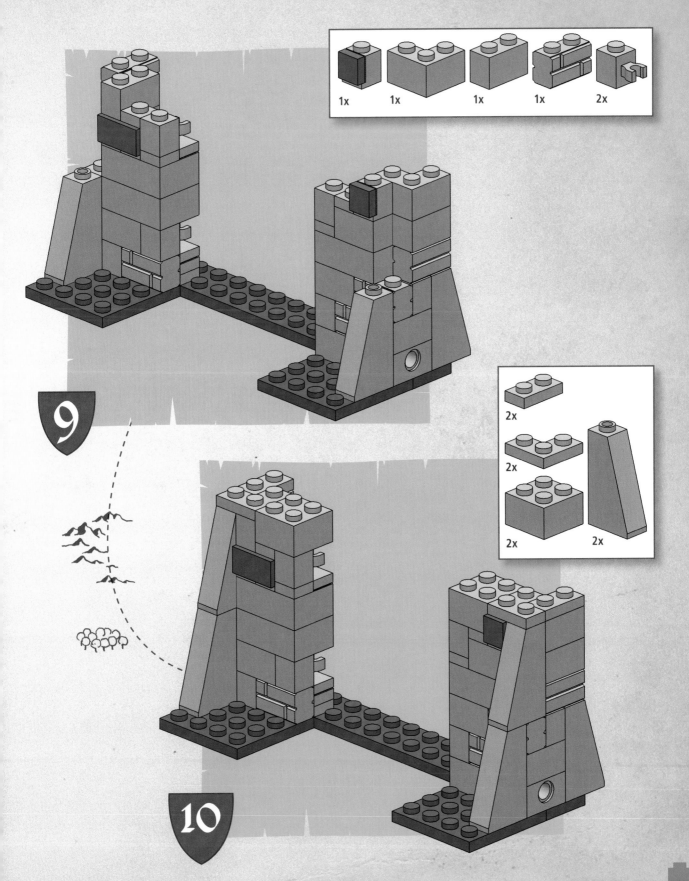

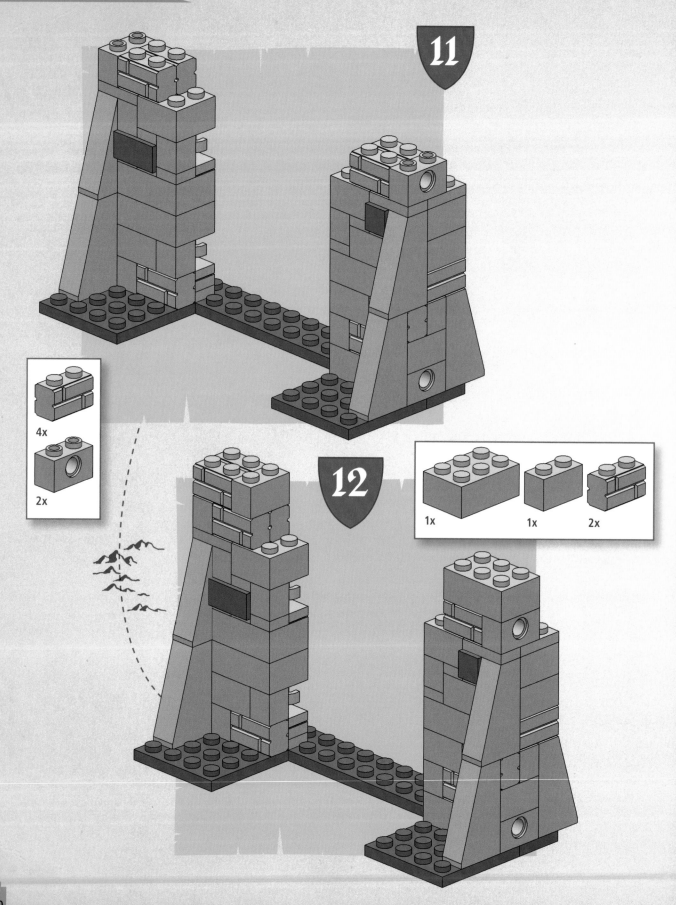

11

4x

2x

12

1x   1x   2x

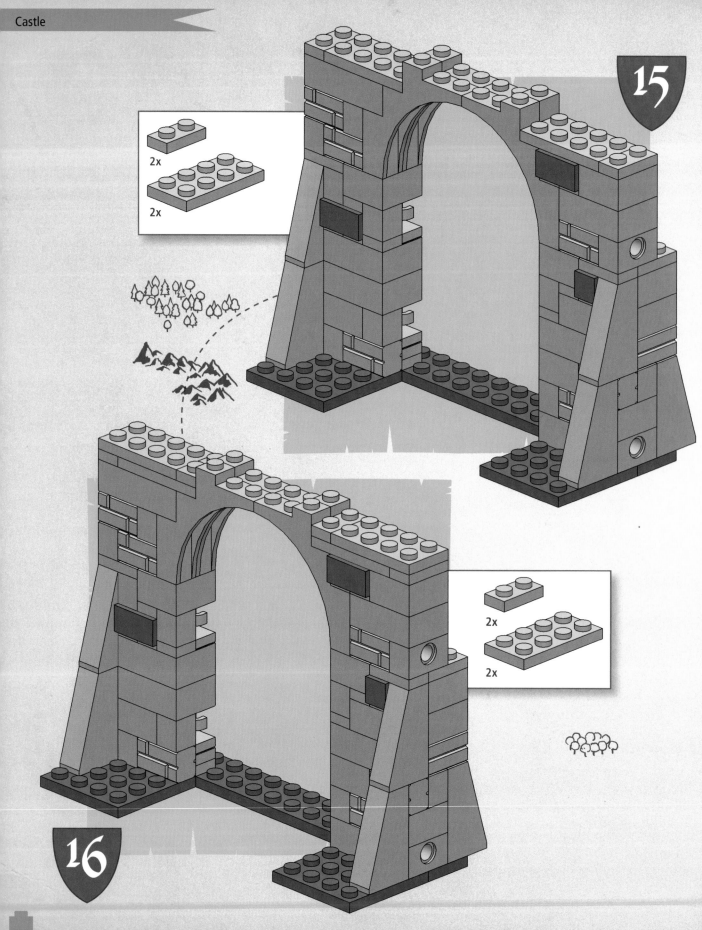

15

2x
2x

2x
2x

16

17

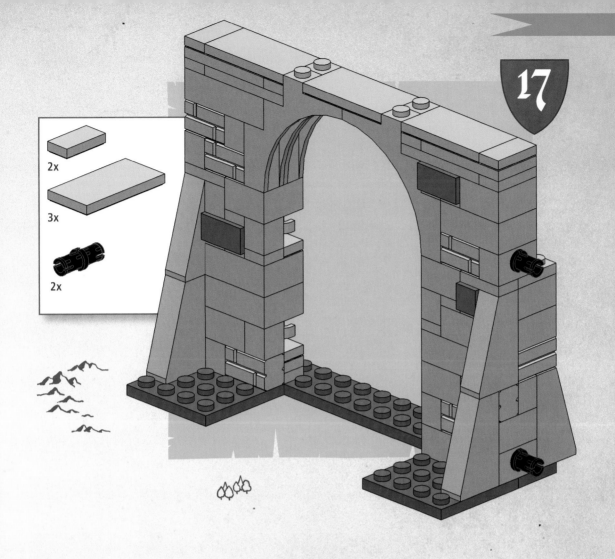

2x

3x

2x

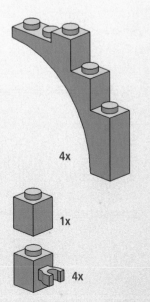

Parts List

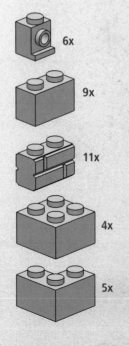

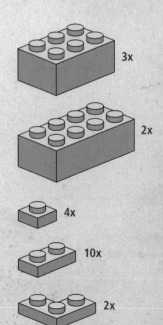

4x

1x

4x

6x

9x

11x

4x

5x

3x

2x

4x

10x

2x

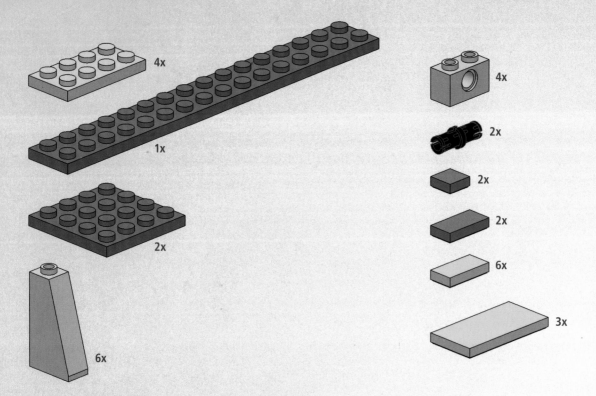

Quantity	Color		Element	Element Name
4		Light Bluish Gray	2339	Arch 1 x 5 x 4
1		Light Bluish Gray	3005	Brick 1 x 1
4		Light Bluish Gray	60475	Brick 1 x 1 with Clip Vertical
6		Light Bluish Gray	4070	Brick 1 x 1 with Headlight
9		Light Bluish Gray	3004	Brick 1 x 2
11		Light Bluish Gray	98283	Brick 1 x 2 with Embossed Bricks
4		Light Bluish Gray	3003	Brick 2 x 2
5		Light Bluish Gray	2357	Brick 2 x 2 Corner
3		Light Bluish Gray	3002	Brick 2 x 3
2		Light Bluish Gray	3001	Brick 2 x 4
4		Light Bluish Gray	3024	Plate 1 x 1
10		Light Bluish Gray	3023	Plate 1 x 2
2		Light Bluish Gray	2420	Plate 2 x 2 Corner
4		Light Bluish Gray	3020	Plate 2 x 4
1		Green	4282	Plate 2 x 16
2		Green	3031	Plate 4 x 4
6		Light Bluish Gray	4460	Slope Brick 75 2 x 1 x 3
4		Light Bluish Gray	3700	Technic Brick 1 x 2 with Hole
2		Black	2780	Technic Pin with Friction and Slots
2		Dark Bluish Gray	3070b	Tile 1 x 1 with Groove
2		Dark Bluish Gray	3069b	Tile 1 x 2 with Groove
6		Light Bluish Gray	3069b	Tile 1 x 2 with Groove
3		Light Bluish Gray	87079	Tile 2 x 4 with Groove

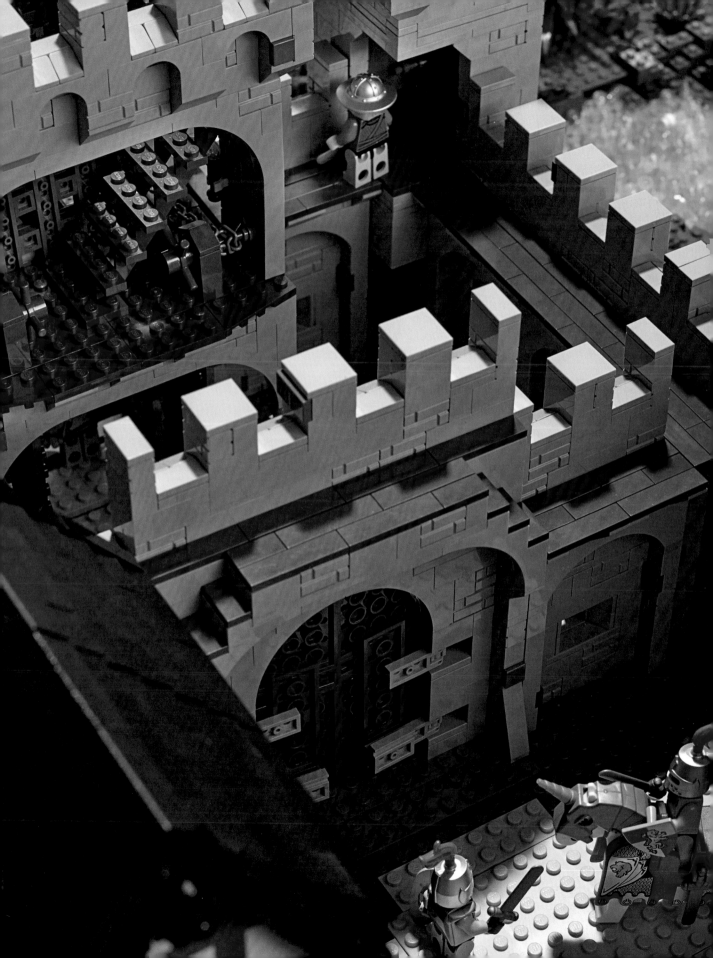

Draw-bridge

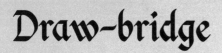

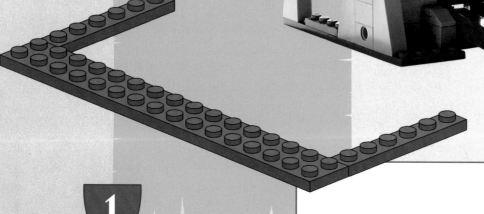

1

1x   2x

2x

2x

2x   4x

Here, step 17 of the arch-way is to be included.

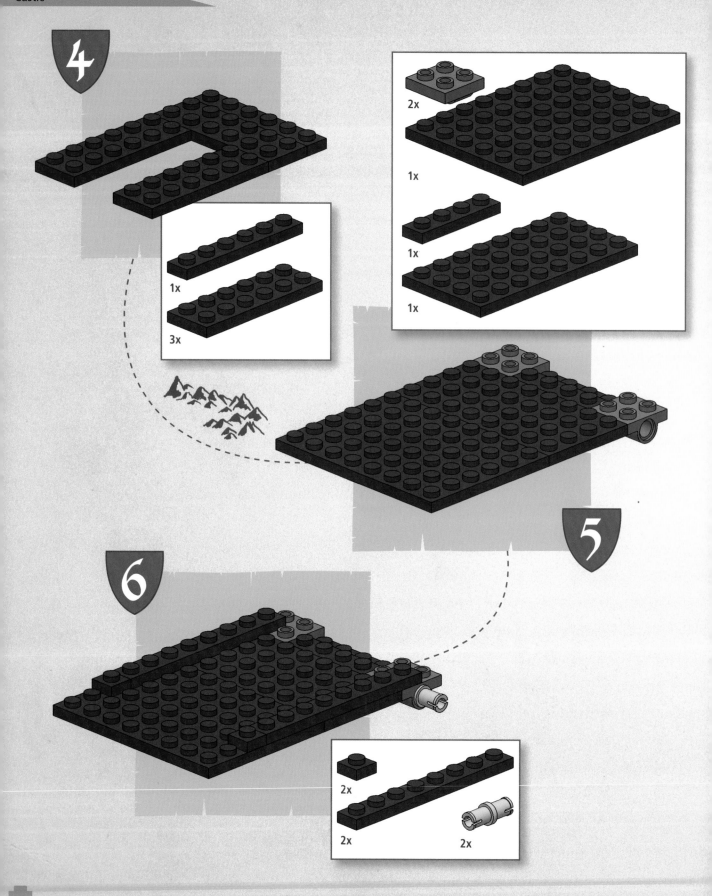

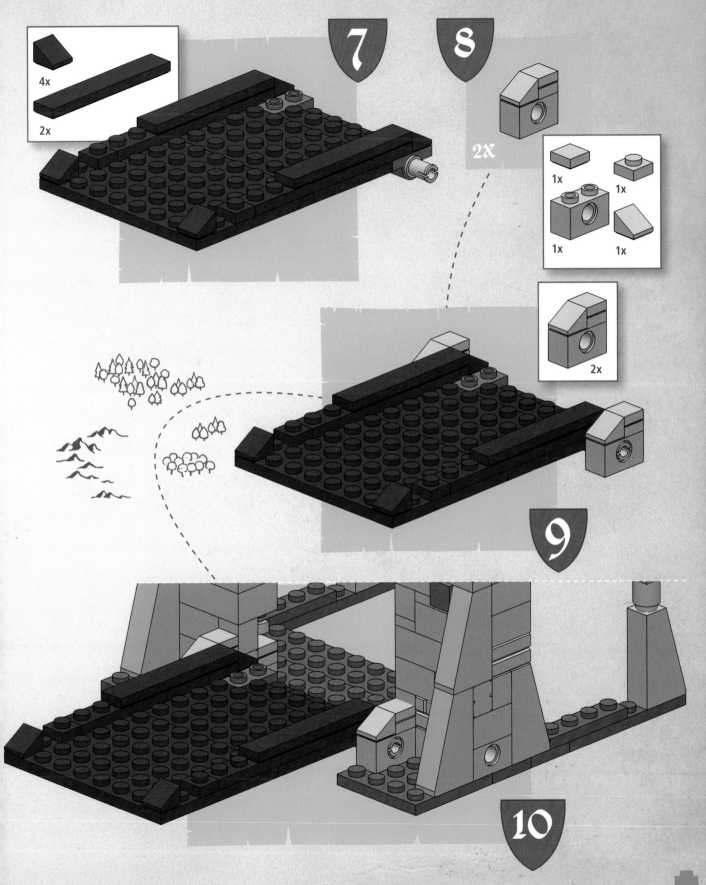

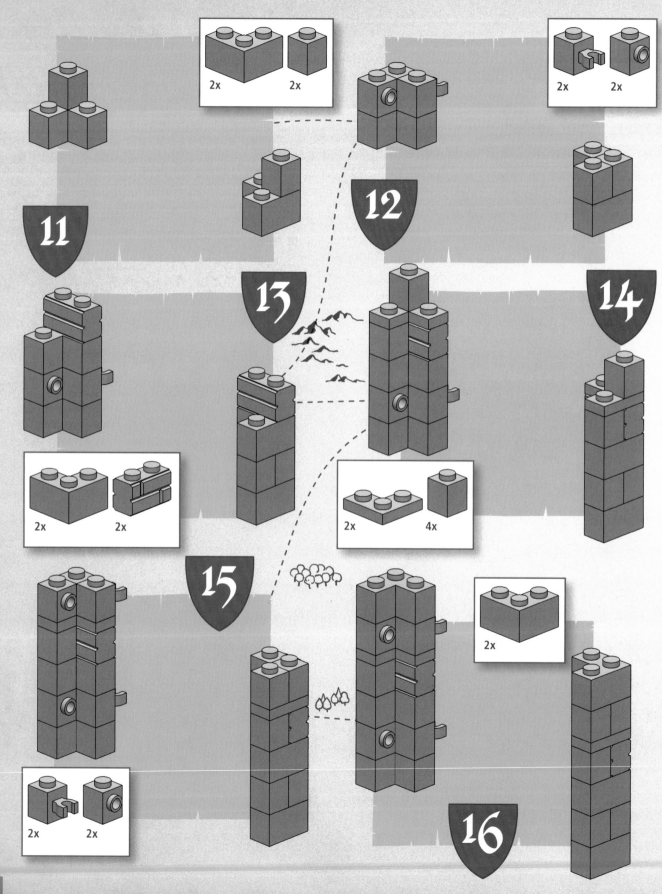

17

2x

2x

18

2x

2x

1x

19

4x

2x

20

21

2x

2x   2x

22

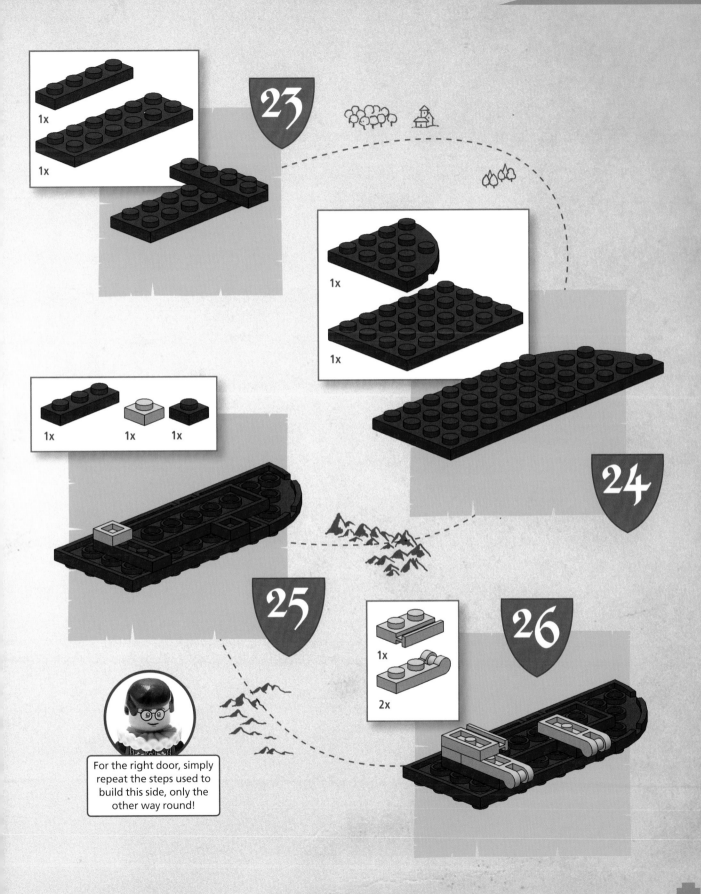

23

24

25

26

1x

1x

1x

1x

1x

1x

1x

1x

2x

For the right door, simply repeat the steps used to build this side, only the other way round!

27

28

2x

3x

29

1x

1x

2x

30

5x

2x

2x

2x

1x

1x

31

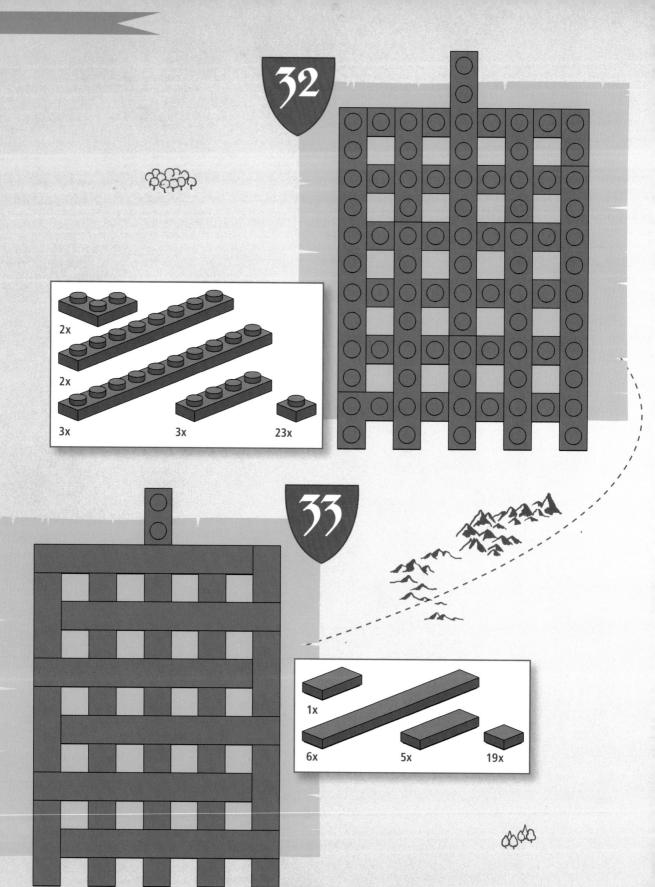

32

2x
2x
3x   3x   23x

33

1x
6x   5x   19x

34

35

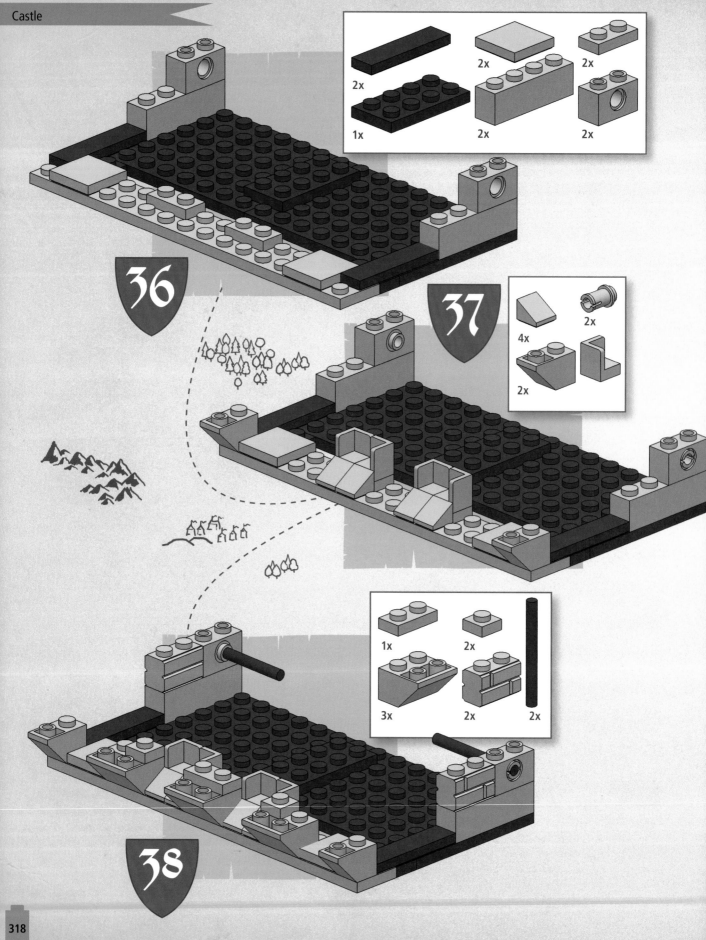

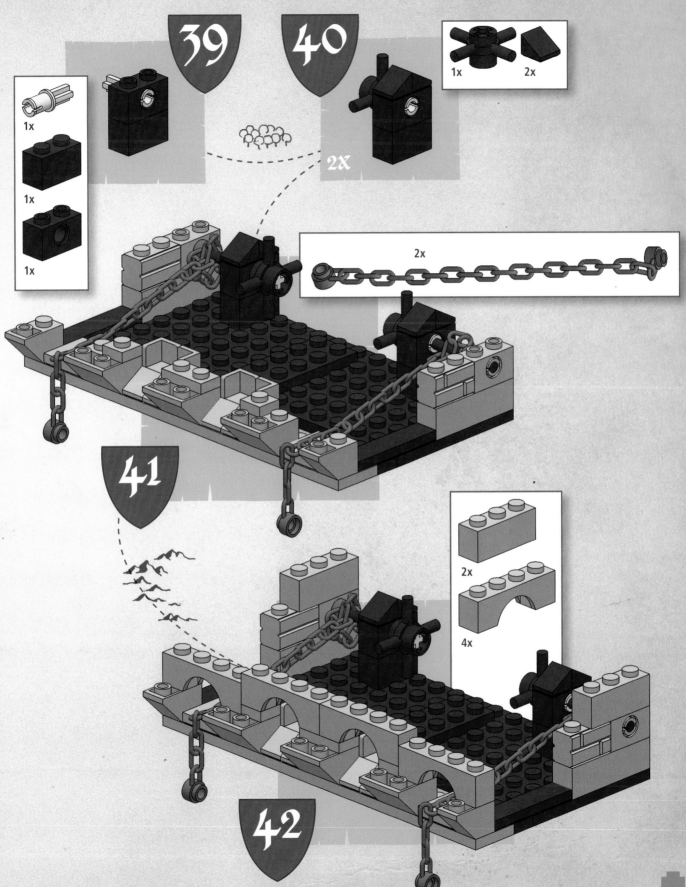

39

40

1x 2x

2x

1x

1x

1x

2x

41

2x

2x

4x

42

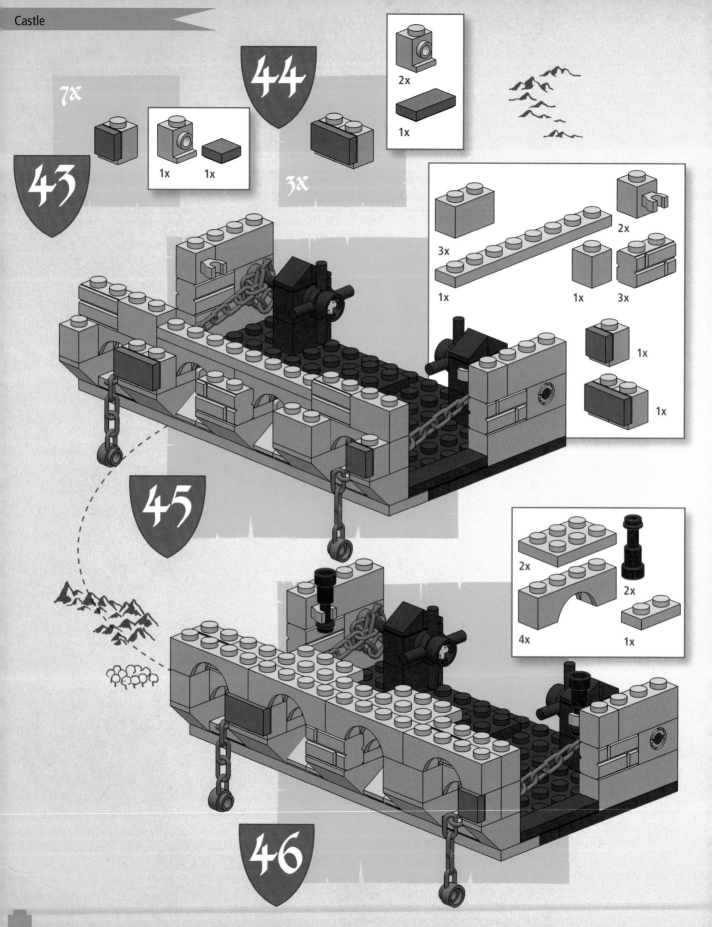

44

2x
1x

7x

43

1x   1x

3x

3x
1x
2x
1x   3x
1x
1x

45

2x
2x
4x   1x

46

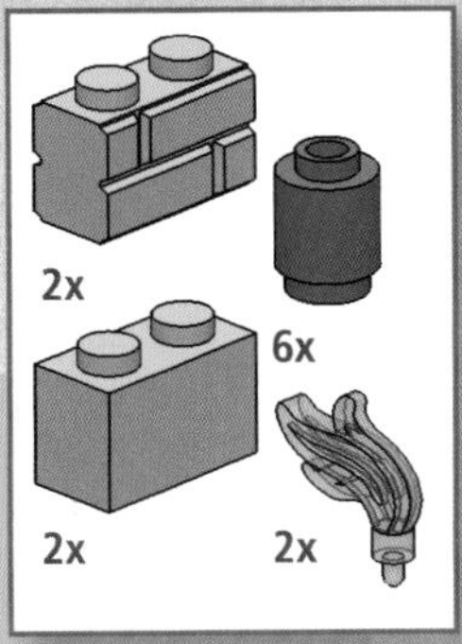

2x

6x

2x

2x

47

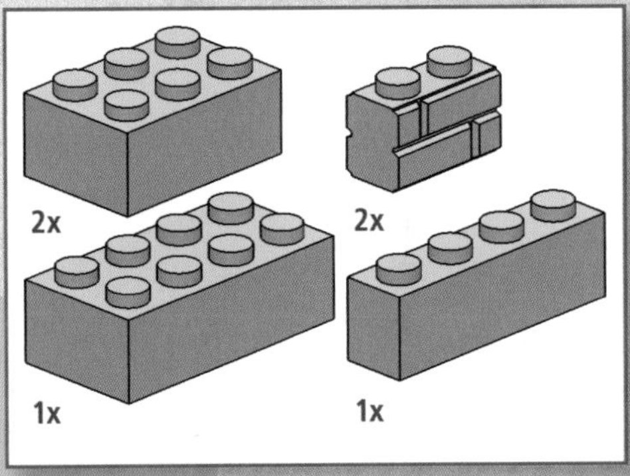

2x

2x

1x

1x

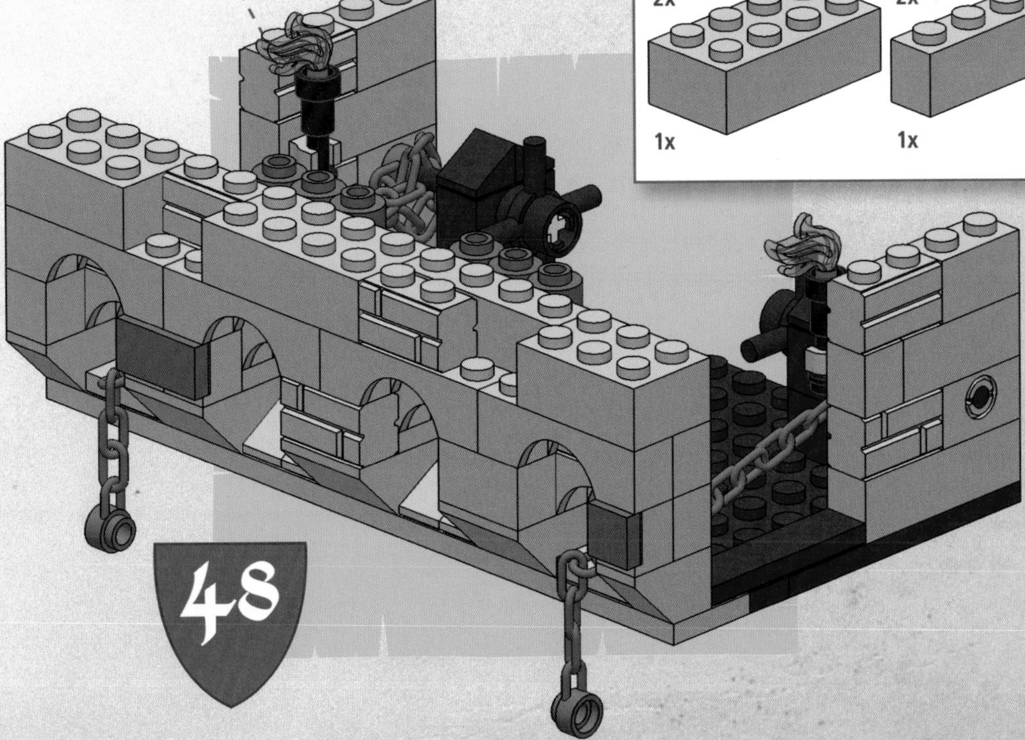

48

49

50

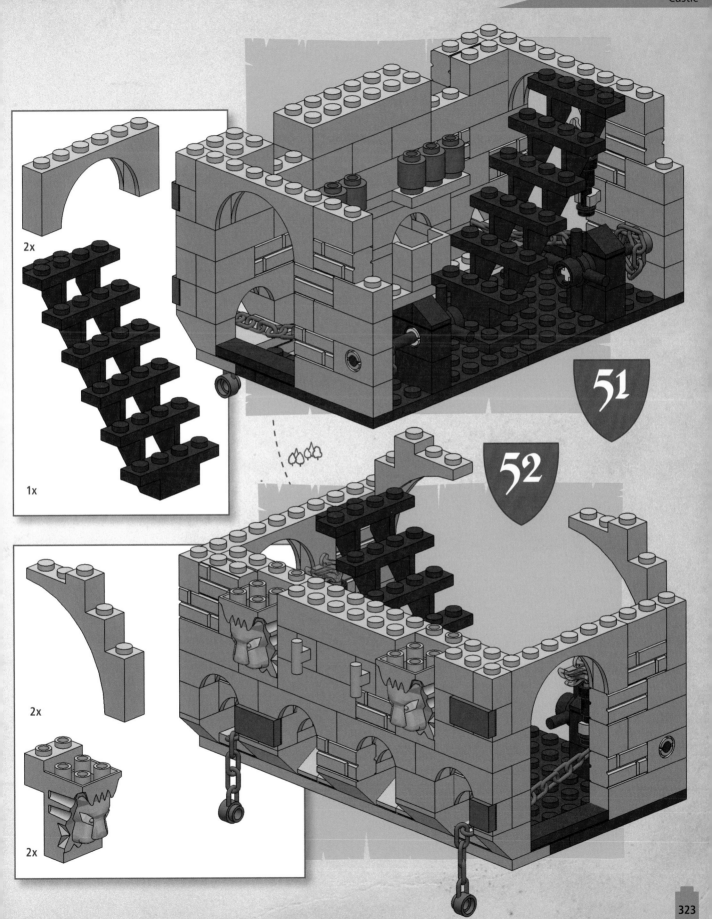

2x

1x

2x

2x

51

52

53

1x
1x

2x
2x

2x
2x

1x

54

2x
2x
2x

5x

1x

1x

1x

4x

1x

1x

1x

1x

2x

2x

3x

1x

56

3x   3x

1x   6x

1x   5x

2x

2x

57

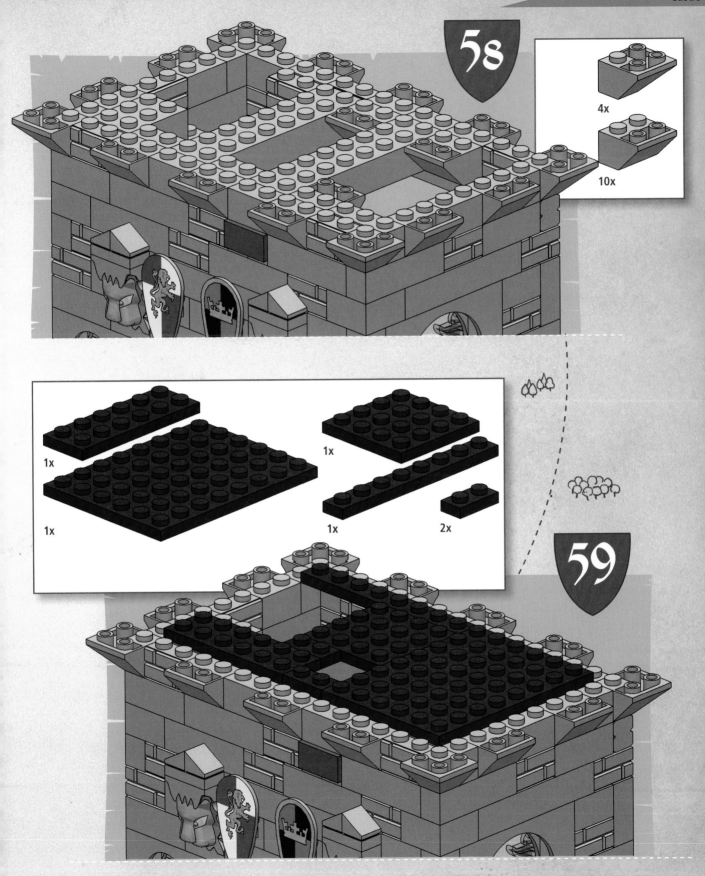

58

4x

10x

1x

1x

1x

1x

2x

59

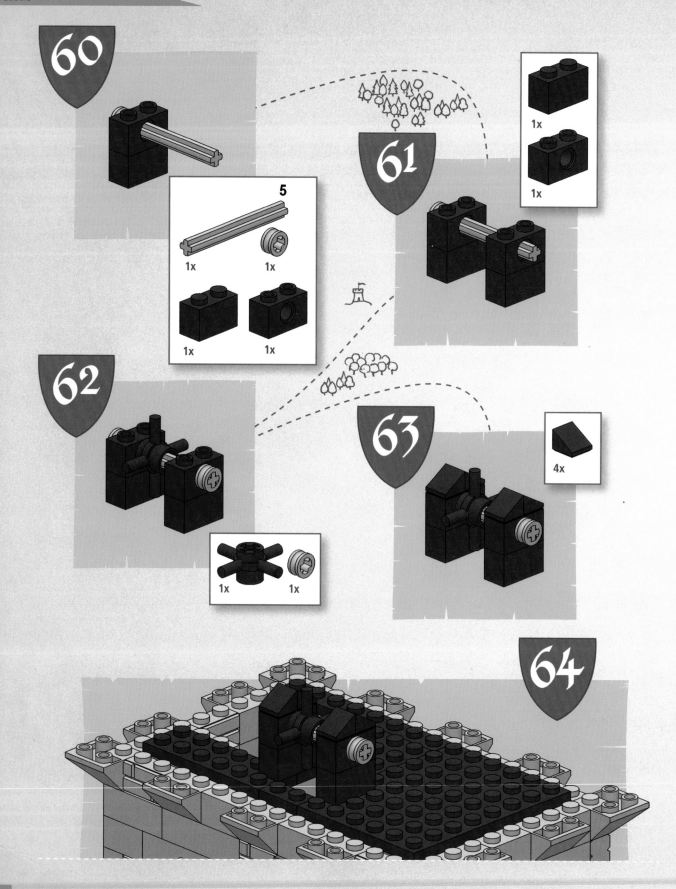

60

61

1x

1x

5

1x   1x

1x   1x

62

63

4x

1x   1x

64

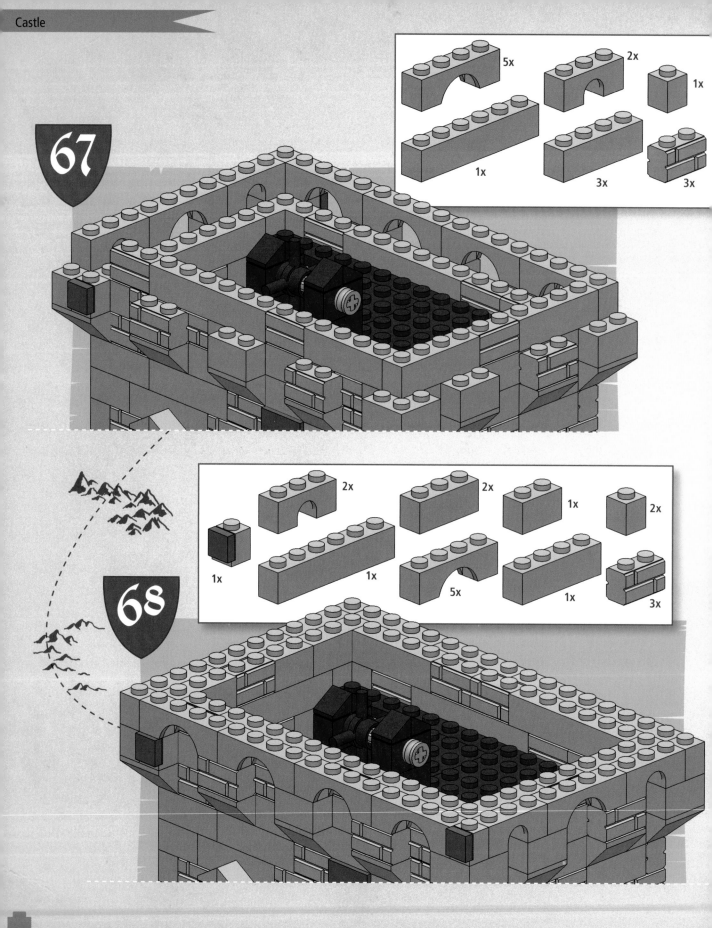

67

5x
2x
1x
1x
3x
3x

68

1x
2x
2x
1x
2x
1x
5x
1x
3x

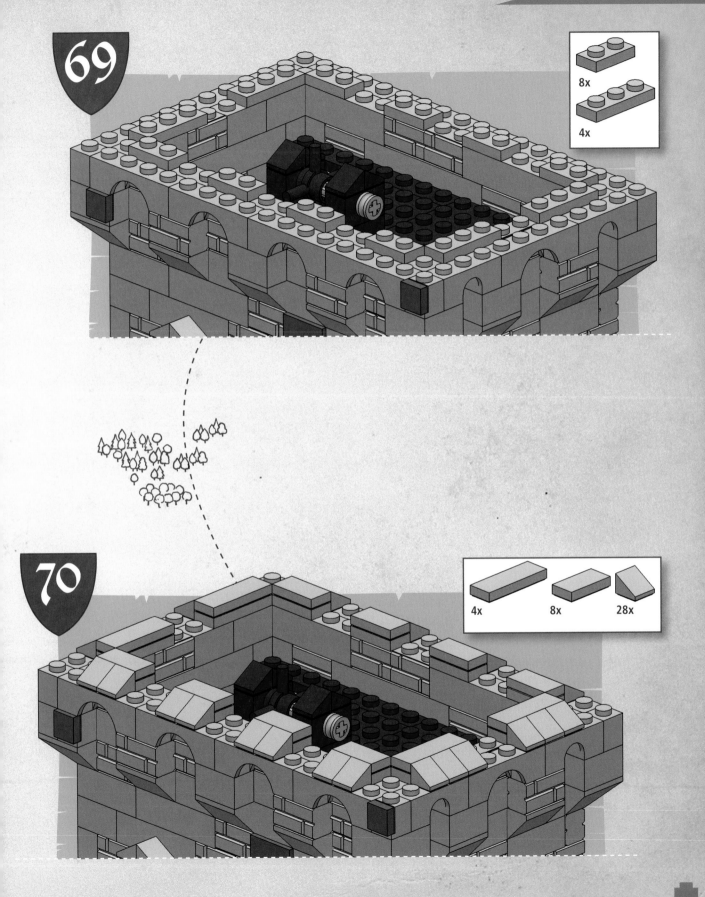

69

8x
4x

70

4x
8x
28x

71

1x 4x
3x 2x

72

1x 2x 4x 2x

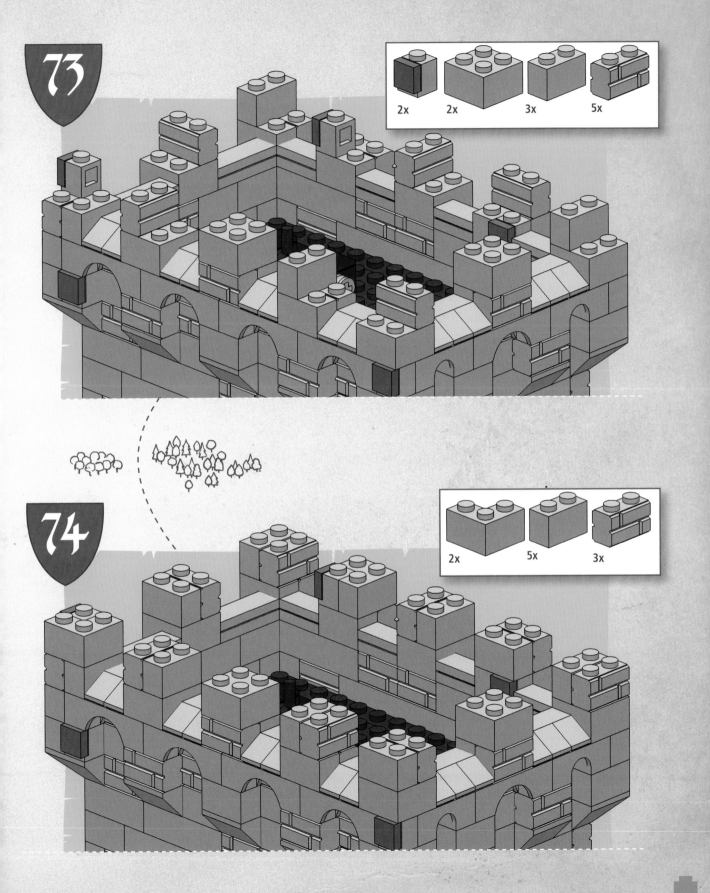

75

12x

76

1:2

1x

77

1:1,43

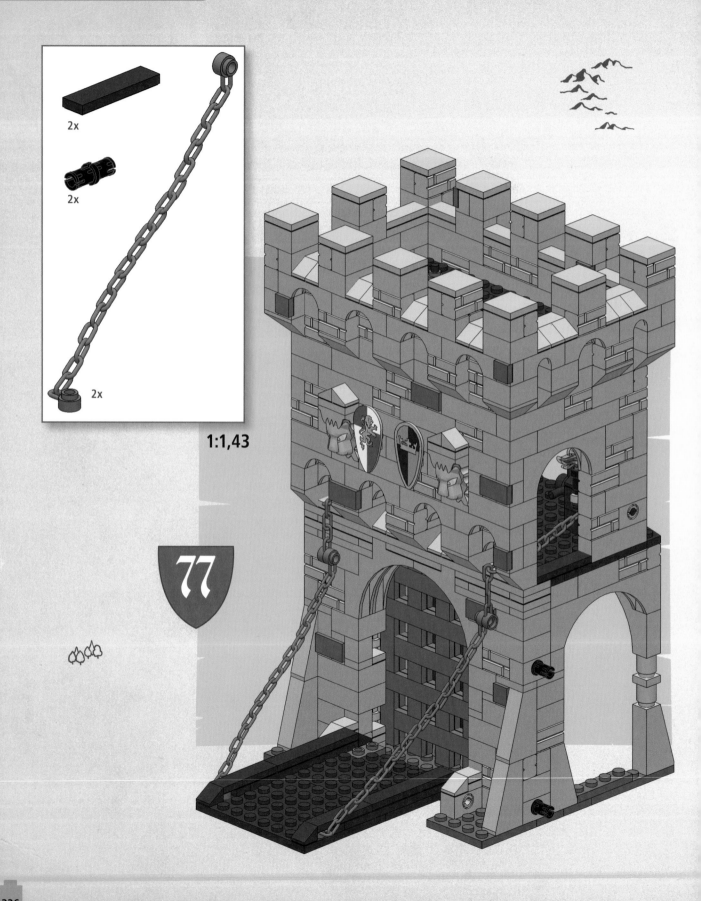

2x

2x

2x

1:1,43

77

Parts List

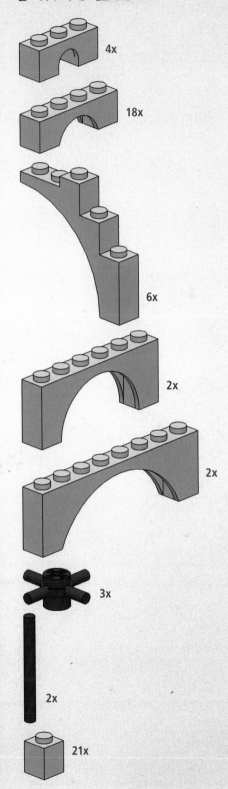

4x

18x

6x

2x

2x

3x

2x

21x

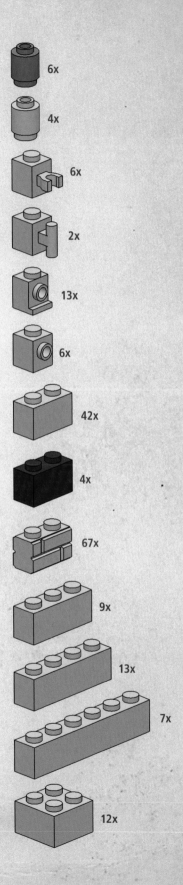

6x

4x

6x

2x

13x

6x

42x

4x

67x

9x

13x

7x

12x

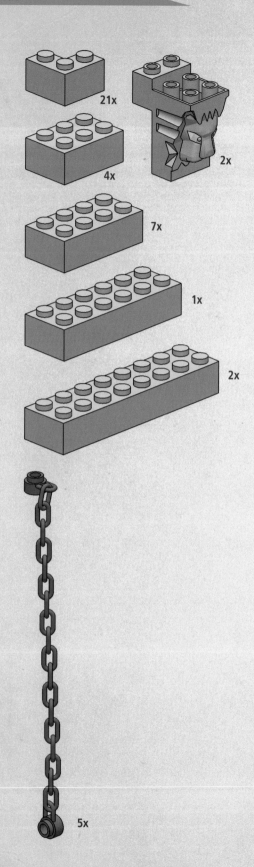

21x

4x

2x

7x

1x

2x

5x

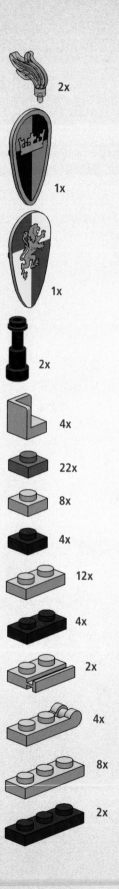

2x

1x

1x

2x

4x

22x

8x

4x

12x

4x

2x

4x

8x

2x

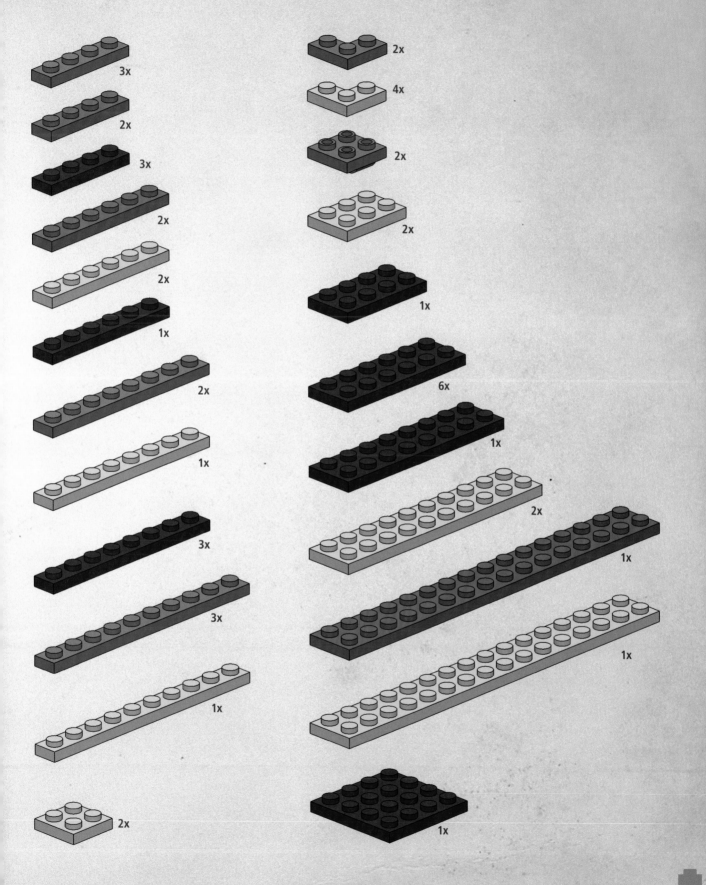

3x
2x
3x
2x
2x
1x
2x
1x
3x
3x
1x
2x

2x
4x
2x
2x
1x
6x
1x
2x
1x
1x
1x

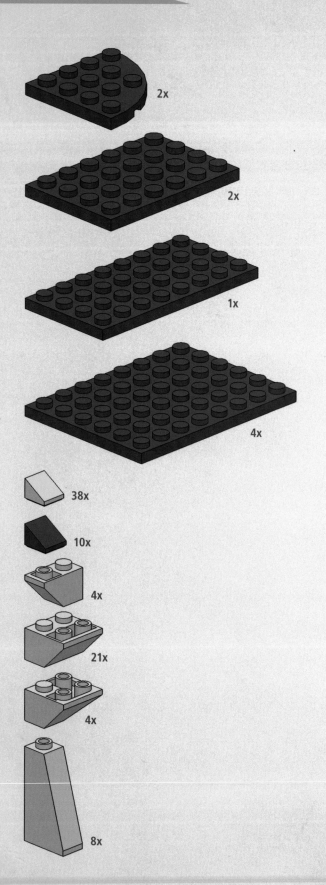

2x

2x

1x

4x

38x

10x

4x

21x

4x

8x

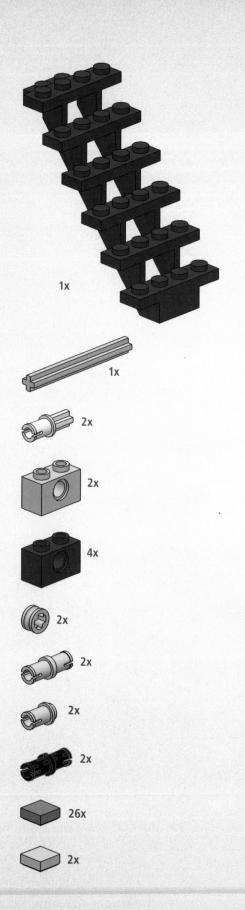

1x

1x

2x

2x

4x

2x

2x

2x

2x

26x

2x

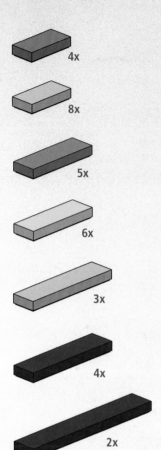

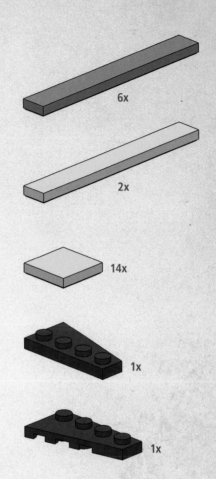

Quantity		Color	Element	Element Name
4		Light Bluish Gray	4490	Arch 1 x 3
18		Light Bluish Gray	3659	Arch 1 x 4
6		Light Bluish Gray	2339	Arch 1 x 5 x 4
2		Light Bluish Gray	3307	Arch 1 x 6 x 2
2		Light Bluish Gray	3308	Arch 1 x 8 x 2
3		Reddish Brown	48723	Bar 1L Quadruple with Axlehole Hub
2		Reddish Brown	30374	Bar 4L Light Sabre Blade
21		Light Bluish Gray	3005	Brick 1 x 1
6		Dark Bluish Gray	3062b	Brick 1 x 1 Round with Hollow Stud
4		Light Bluish Gray	3062b	Brick 1 x 1 Round with Hollow Stud
6		Light Bluish Gray	60475	Brick 1 x 1 with Clip Vertical
2		Light Bluish Gray	2921	Brick 1 x 1 with Handle

13	Light Bluish Gray	4070	Brick 1 x 1 with Headlight
6	Light Bluish Gray	87087	Brick 1 x 1 with Stud on 1 Side
42	Light Bluish Gray	3004	Brick 1 x 2
4	Reddish_Brown	3004	Brick 1 x 2
67	Light Bluish Gray	98283	Brick 1 x 2 with Embossed Bricks
9	Light Bluish Gray	3622	Brick 1 x 3
13	Light Bluish Gray	3010	Brick 1 x 4
7	Light Bluish Gray	3009	Brick 1 x 6
12	Light Bluish Gray	3003	Brick 2 x 2
21	Light Bluish Gray	2357	Brick 2 x 2 Corner
7	Light Bluish Gray	3002	Brick 2 x 3
2	Light Bluish Gray	30274	Brick 2 x 3 x 3 with Lion's Head Carving and Cutout
4	Light Bluish Gray	3001	Brick 2 x 4
1	Light Bluish Gray	2456	Brick 2 x 6
2	Light Bluish Gray	3007	Brick 2 x 8
5	Dark Bluish Gray	30104	Minifig Chain 21 Links
2	Trans Neon Orange	64647	Minifig Plume/Flame Triple
1	Light Bluish Gray	2586p4j	Minifig Shield Ovoid w/ Crown on Dark/Med Blue Quarters Pattern
1	Light Bluish Gray	2586p4l	Minifig Shield Ovoid with Gold Lion on Red/White Quart. Pattern
2	Dark Brown	64644	Minifig Telescope
4	Light Bluish Gray	6231	Panel 1 x 1 x 1 Corner with Rounded Corners
23	Dark Bluish Gray	3024	Plate 1 x 1
8	Light Bluish Gray	3024	Plate 1 x 1
4	Reddish Brown	3024	Plate 1 x 1
12	Light Bluish Gray	3023	Plate 1 x 2
4	Reddish Brown	3023	Plate 1 x 2
2	Light Bluish Gray	32028	Plate 1 x 2 with Door Rail
4	Light Bluish Gray	60478	Plate 1 x 2 with Handle on End
8	Light Bluish Gray	3623	Plate 1 x 3
2	Reddish Brown	3623	Plate 1 x 3
3	Dark Bluish Gray	3710	Plate 1 x 4
2	Green	3710	Plate 1 x 4
3	Reddish Brown	3710	Plate 1 x 4
2	Green	3666	Plate 1 x 6
2	Light Bluish Gray	3666	Plate 1 x 6
1	Reddish Brown	3666	Plate 1 x 6
2	Dark Bluish Gray	3460	Plate 1 x 8
1	Light Bluish Gray	3460	Plate 1 x 8
3	Reddish_Brown	3460	Plate 1 x 8
3	Dark Bluish Gray	4477	Plate 1 x 10
1	Light Bluish Gray	4477	Plate 1 x 10
2	Light Bluish Gray	3022	Plate 2 x 2
2	Dark Bluish Gray	2420	Plate 2 x 2 Corner

4	Light Bluish Gray	2420	Plate 2 x 2 Corner
2	Dark Bluish Gray	2444	Plate 2 x 2 with Hole
2	Light Bluish Gray	3021	Plate 2 x 3
1	Reddish Brown	3020	Plate 2 x 4
6	Reddish Brown	3795	Plate 2 x 6
1	Reddish Brown	3034	Plate 2 x 8
2	Light Bluish Gray	3832	Plate 2 x 10
1	Green	4282	Plate 2 x 16
1	Light Bluish Gray	4282	Plate 2 x 16
1	Reddish Brown	3031	Plate 4 x 4
2	Reddish Brown	30565	Plate 4 x 4 Corner Round
2	Reddish Brown	3032	Plate 4 x 6
1	Reddish Brown	3035	Plate 4 x 8
4	Reddish Brown	3036	Plate 6 x 8
38	Light Bluish Gray	54200	Slope Brick 31 1 x 1 x 2/3
10	Reddish Brown	54200	Slope Brick 31 1 x 1 x 2/3
4	Light Bluish Gray	3665	Slope Brick 45 2 x 1 Inverted
21	Light Bluish Gray	3660	Slope Brick 45 2 x 2 Inverted
4	Light Bluish Gray	3676	Slope Brick 45 2 x 2 Inverted Double Convex
2	Light Bluish Gray	4460	Slope Brick 75 2 x 1 x 3
1	Reddish Brown	30134	Staircase 7 x 4 x 6 Open
1	Light Bluish Gray	32073	Technic Axle 5
2	Tan	3749	Technic Axle Pin
4	Light Bluish Gray	3700	Technic Brick 1 x 2 with Hole
4	Reddish Brown	3700	Technic Brick 1 x 2 with Hole
2	Light Bluish Gray	32123a	Technic Bush 1/2 Smooth with Axle Hole Reduced
2	Light Bluish Gray	3673	Technic Pin
2	Light Bluish Gray	4274	Technic Pin 1/2
2	Black	2780	Technic Pin with Friction and Slots
26	Dark Bluish Gray	3070b	Tile 1 x 1 with Groove
2	Light Bluish Gray	3070b	Tile 1 x 1 with Groove
4	Dark Bluish Gray	3069b	Tile 1 x 2 with Groove
8	Light Bluish Gray	3069b	Tile 1 x 2 with Groove
5	Dark Bluish Gray	63864	Tile 1 x 3 with Groove
6	Light Bluish Gray	63864	Tile 1 x 3 with Groove
3	Light Bluish Gray	2431	Tile 1 x 4 with Groove
4	Reddish Brown	2431	Tile 1 x 4 with Groove
2	Reddish Brown	6636	Tile 1 x 6
6	Dark Bluish Gray	4162	Tile 1 x 8
2	Light Bluish Gray	4162	Tile 1 x 8
14	Light Bluish Gray	3068b	Tile 2 x 2 with Groove
1	Reddish Brown	41770	Wing 2 x 4 Left
1	Reddish Brown	41769	Wing 2 x 4 Right

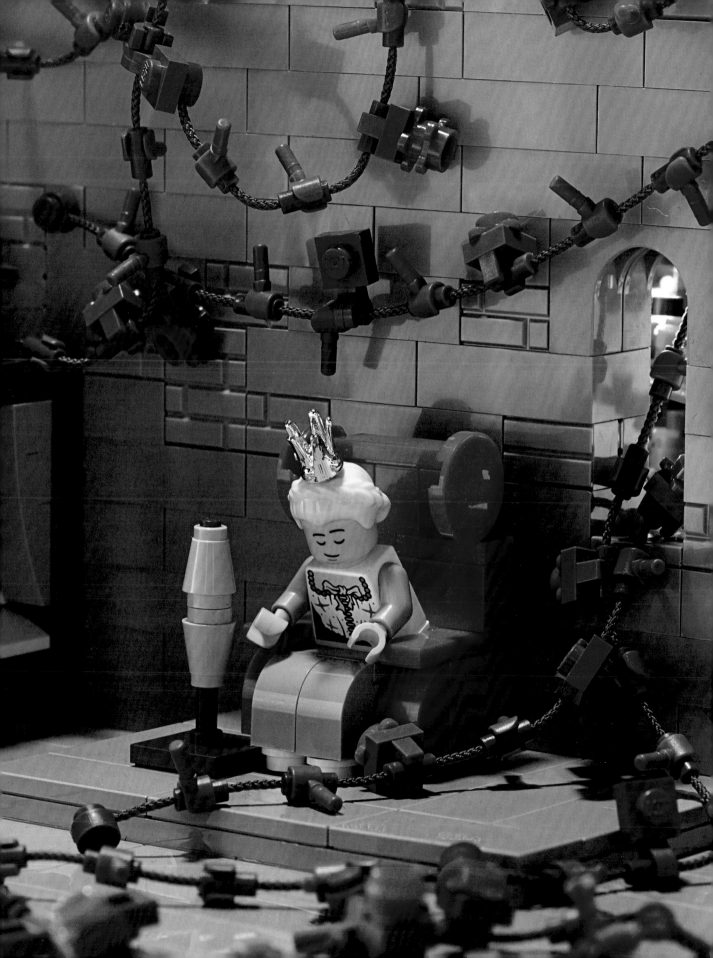

Bed

A four-poster bed for Sleeping Beauty. A pity she's not actually sleeping in it! It looks so snug.

Build the curtains in whatever colors you can find in your LEGO® box.

1

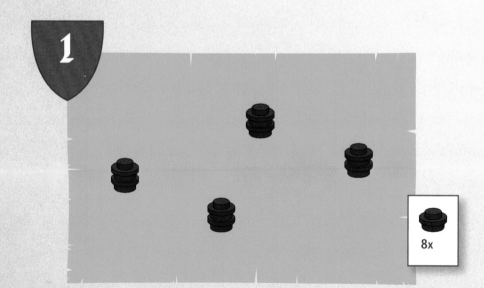

8x

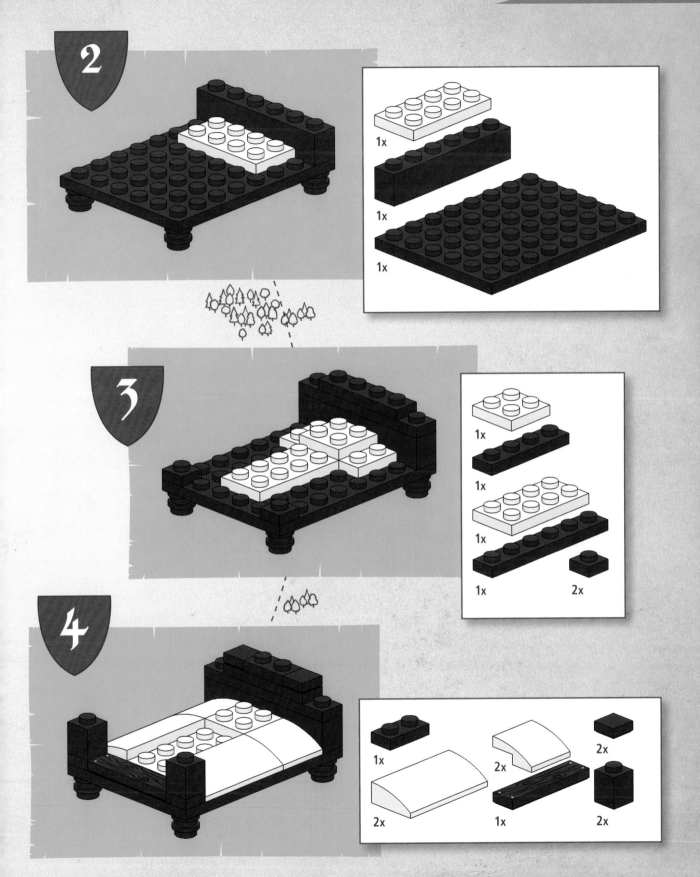

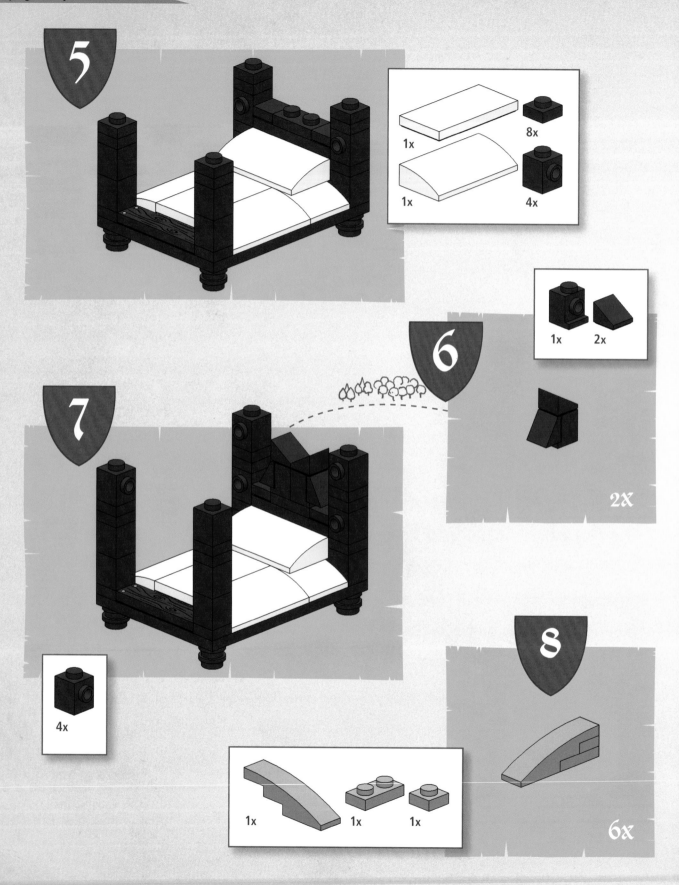

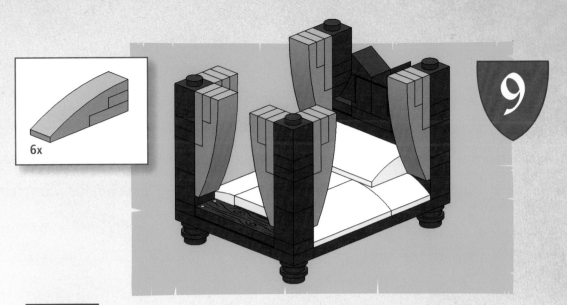

6x

10

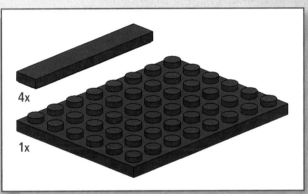

4x

1x

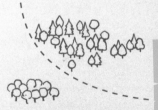

11

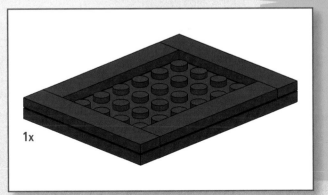

1x

Parts List

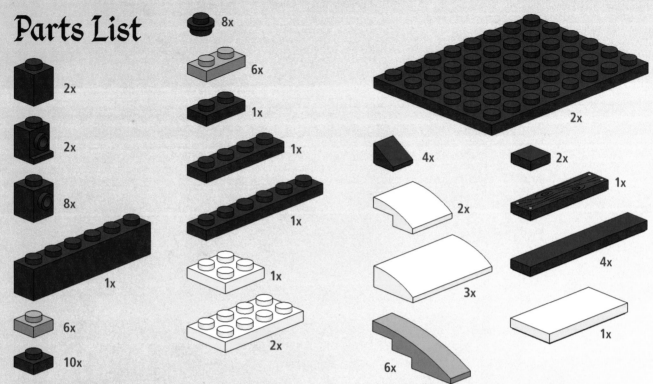

8x

2x

6x

2x

1x

2x

1x

8x

1x

2x

4x

6x

1x

2x

2x

3x

4x

10x

6x

1x

6x

Quantity	Color		Element	Element Name
2		Reddish Brown	3005	Brick 1 x 1
2		Reddish Brown	4070	Brick 1 x 1 with Headlight
8		Reddish Brown	87087	Brick 1 x 1 with Stud on 1 Side
1		Reddish Brown	3009	Brick 1 x 6
6		Medium Blue	3024	Plate 1 x 1
10		Reddish Brown	3024	Plate 1 x 1
8		Reddish Brown	4073	Plate 1 x 1 Round
6		Medium Blue	3023	Plate 1 x 2
1		Reddish Brown	3023	Plate 1 x 2
1		Reddish Brown	3710	Plate 1 x 4
1		Reddish Brown	3666	Plate 1 x 6
1		White	3022	Plate 2 x 2
2		White	3020	Plate 2 x 4
2		Reddish Brown	3036	Plate 6 x 8
4		Reddish Brown	54200	Slope Brick 31 1 x 1 x 2/3
2		White	15068	Slope Brick Curved 2 x 2 x 2/3
3		White	88930	Slope Brick Curved 2 x 4 with Underside Studs
6		Medium Blue	61678	Slope Brick Curved 4 x 1
2		Reddish Brown	3070b	Tile 1 x 1 with Groove
1		Reddish Brown	2431p01	Tile 1 x 4 with Wood Grain and 4 Nails Pattern
4		Reddish Brown	6636	Tile 1 x 6
1		White	87079	Tile 2 x 4 with Groove

Armchair

I t's not so hard to build a wingback chair, with a figure dressed up and sitting in it. The instructions show the basic design, so you can combine the clothes items and their colors as you wish.

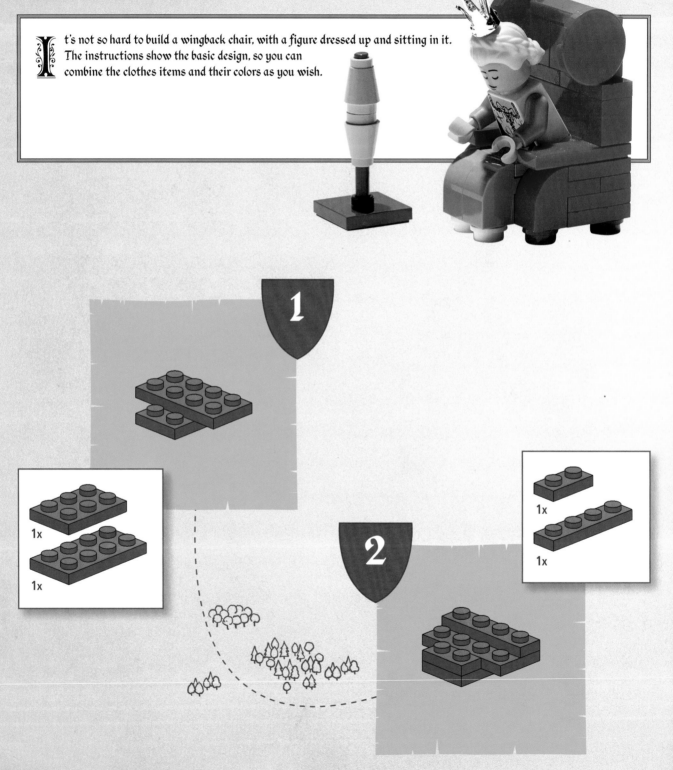

1

1x

1x

1x

1x

2

2x   2x

2x   4x

3

4

1x

2x

5

6

This brick has two facing knobs on opposite sides.

7

2x

1x

1x   2x

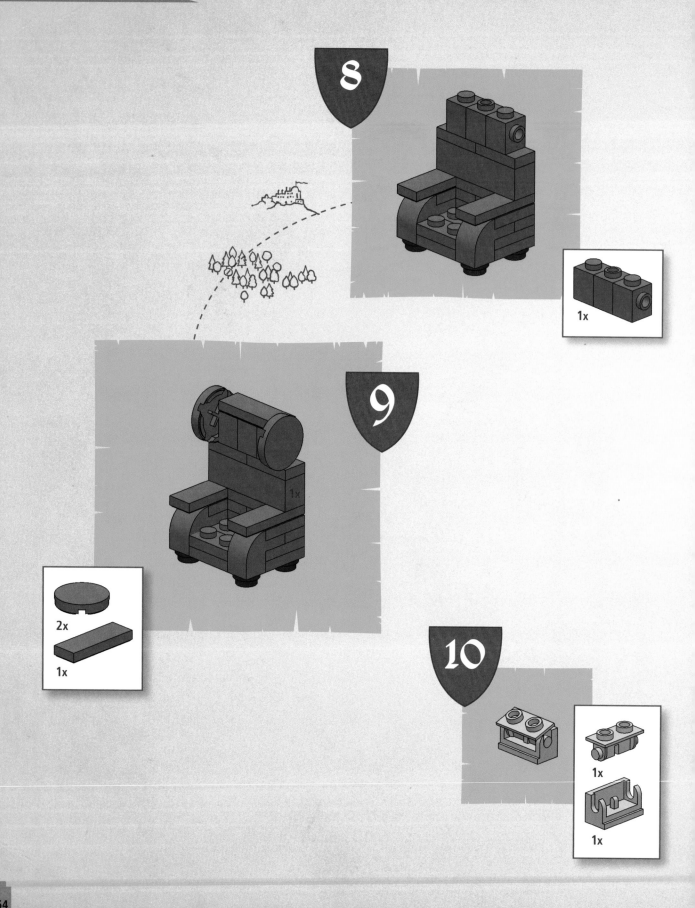

Parts List

 2x

 1x

 2x

 4x

 4x

 2x

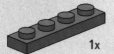 1x

 2x

 1x

 1x

 1x

 3x

 2x

Quantity		Color	Element	Element Name
2		Red	47905	Brick 1 x 1 with Studs on Two Opposite Sides
1		Red	3010	Brick 1 x 4
2		Red	6091	Brick 2 x 1 x 1 & 1/3 with Curved Top
4		Reddish Brown	4073	Plate 1 x 1 Round
4		Red	3023	Plate 1 x 2
2		Red	3794a	Plate 1 x 2 without Groove with 1 Centre Stud
1		Red	3710	Plate 1 x 4
2		Red	2420	Plate 2 x 2 Corner
1		Red	3021	Plate 2 x 3
1		Red	3020	Plate 2 x 4
1		Red	6541	Technic Brick 1 x 1 with Hole
3		Red	63864	Tile 1 x 3 with Groove
2		Red	4150	Tile 2 x 2 Round with Cross Underside Stud

Throne

s can be seen from the picture of the feast, there are several ways to build a throne. As a guide, we've shown you our favorite. Two different designs are provided at the end of the backrests, one for the king's throne, and one for the queen's.

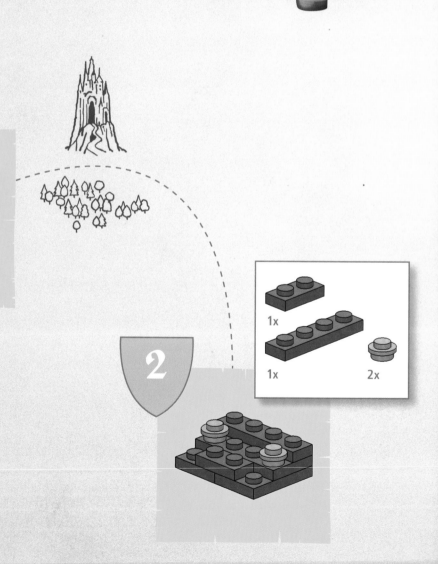

1

2x
1x

2

1x
1x
2x

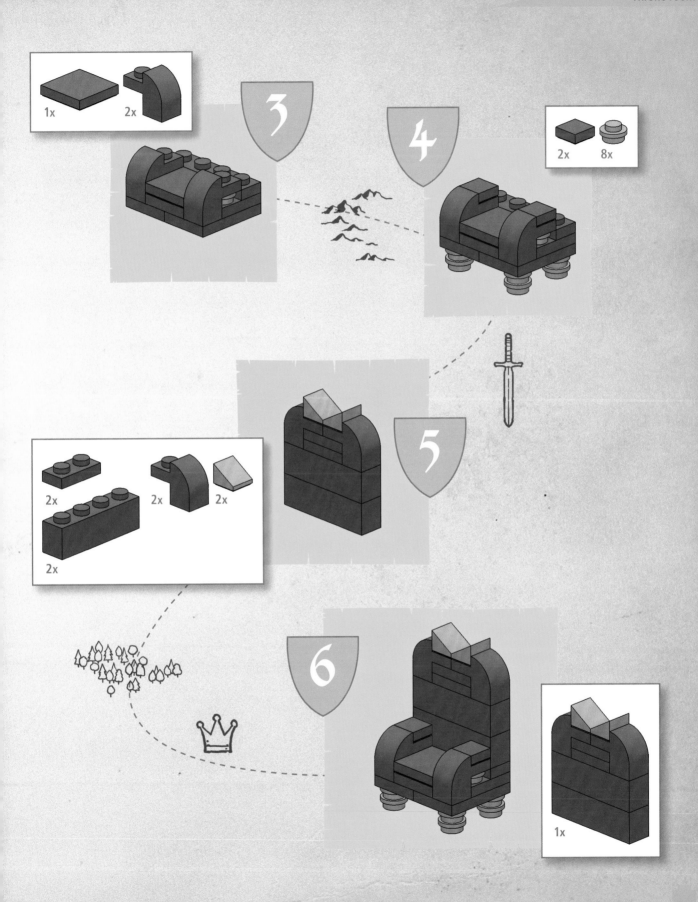

Parts List

 2x

 4x

 10x

 3x

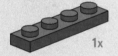 1x

 2x

 1x

 2x

 2x

 1x

Quantity		Color	Element	Element Name
2		Red	3010	Brick 1 x 4
4		Red	6091	Brick 2 x 1 x 1 & 1/3 with Curved Top
10		Pearl Gold	4073	Plate 1 x 1 Round
3		Red	3023	Plate 1 x 2
1		Red	3710	Plate 1 x 4
2		Red	3021	Plate 2 x 3
1		Red	3020	Plate 2 x 4
2		Pearl Gold	54200	Slope Brick 31 1 x 1 x 2/3
2		Red	3070b	Tile 1 x 1 with Groove
1		Red	3068b	Tile 2 x 2 with Groove

Table

You don't have to use printed tiles for the table, but they work well. The size of the table surface and its base can also be varied. The use of miniature legs brings out the wooden carvings to great effect.

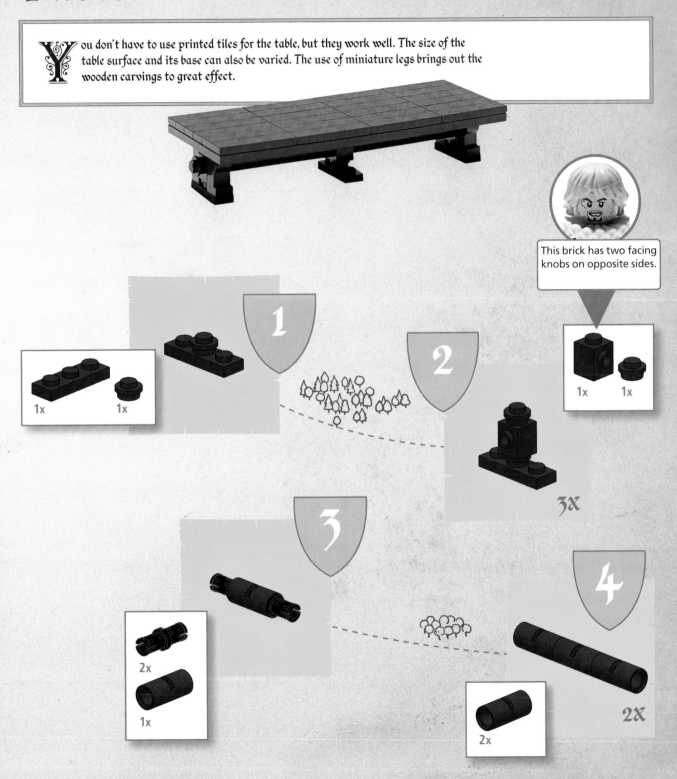

This brick has two facing knobs on opposite sides.

1
1x   1x

2
3x

3
2x
1x

4
2x
2x

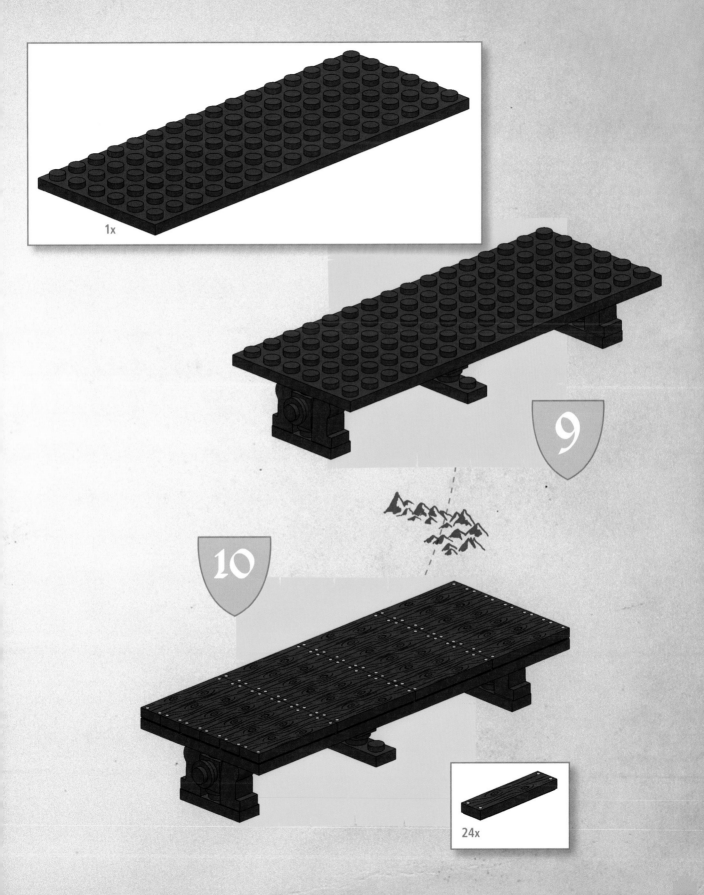

1x

9

10

24x

Parts List

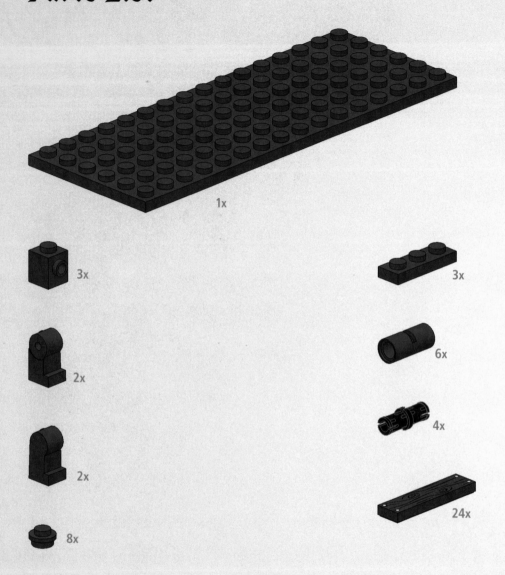

1x

3x

2x

2x

8x

3x

6x

4x

24x

Quantity	Color		Element	Element Name
1		Reddish Brown	3027	Plate 6 x 16
3		Reddish Brown	47905	Brick 1 x 1 with Studs on Two Opposite Sides
2		Reddish Brown	3817	Minifig Leg Left
2		Reddish Brown	3816	Minifig Leg Right
8		Reddish Brown	4073	Plate 1 x 1 Round
3		Reddish Brown	3623	Plate 1 x 3
6		Reddish Brown	62462	Technic Pin Joiner Round with Slot
4		Black	2780	Technic Pin with Friction and Slots
24		Reddish Brown	2431p01	Tile 1 x 4 with Wood Grain and 4 Nails Pattern

Small Table

The small table shows a differing construction of table-legs. Keep an eye on the heights of the seatings to match your table with the chairs.

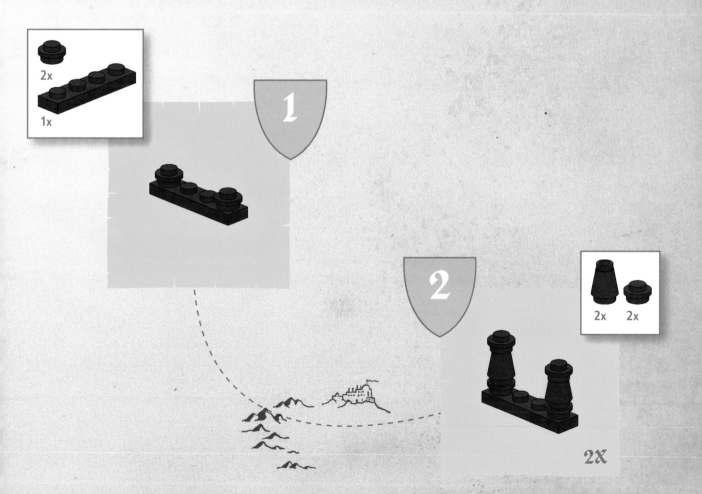

2x
1x

1

2

2x   2x

2X

Parts List

Quantity	Color		Element	Element Name
1		Reddish Brown	3029	Plate 4 x 12
4		Reddish Brown	59900	Cone 1 x 1 with Stop
8		Reddish Brown	4073	Plate 1 x 1 Round
2		Reddish Brown	3710	Plate 1 x 4
12		Reddish Brown	2431p01	Tile 1 x 4 with Wood Grain and 4 Nails Pattern

Chair

I In this model, our most important consideration was the simple shape of the chair. The part used for the legs is quite rare in brown. But you can just build it in another color and modify the shape of the seats accordingly.

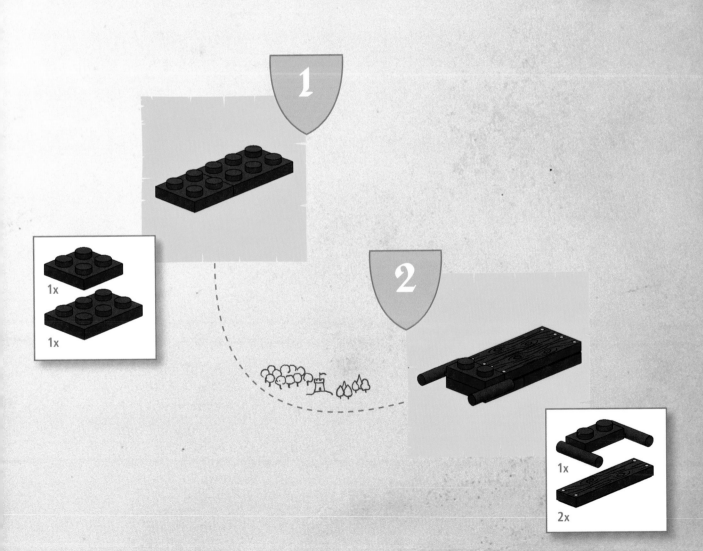

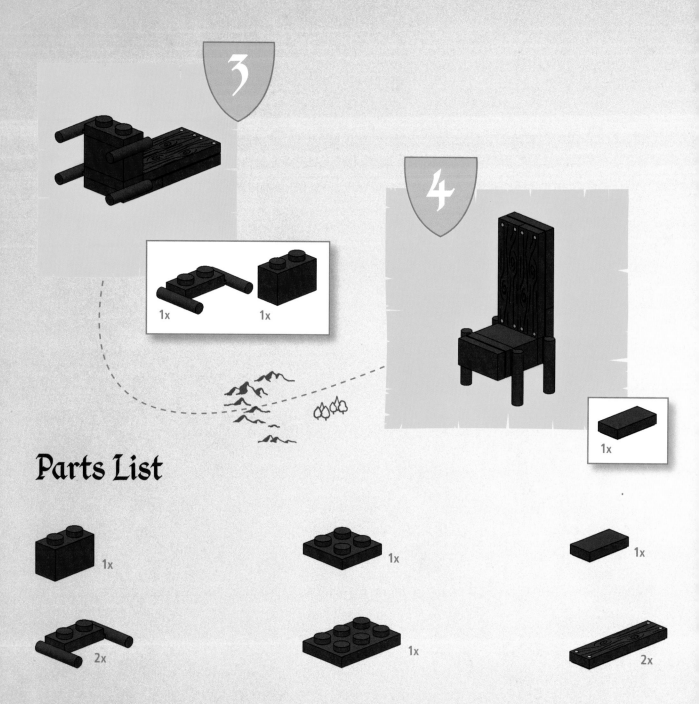

Parts List

Quantity		Color	Element	Element Name
1		Reddish Brown	3004	Brick 1 x 2
2		Reddish Brown	3839b	Plate 1 x 2 with Handles Type 2
1		Reddish Brown	3022	Plate 2 x 2
1		Reddish Brown	3021	Plate 2 x 3
1		Reddish Brown	3069b	Tile 1 x 2 with Groove
2		Reddish Brown	2431p01	Tile 1 x 4 with Wood Grain and 4 Nails Pattern

Fire basket

The fire basket is really easy to build, but has a great effect. On the double-page spread of the entrance you could well believe that somebody's sitting too close to the fire ...

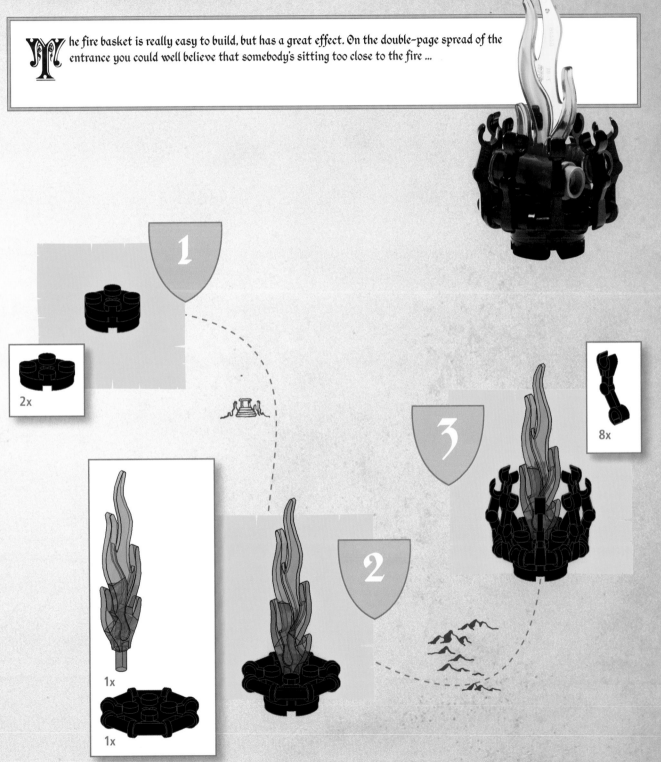

1

2x

2

1x

1x

3

8x

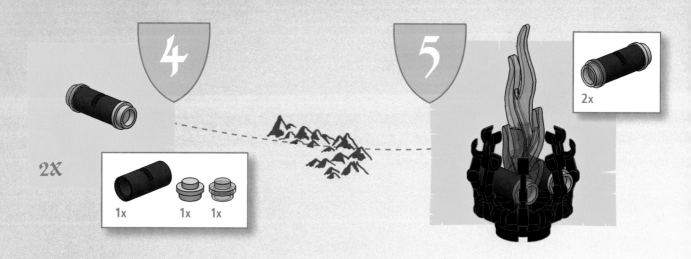

Parts List

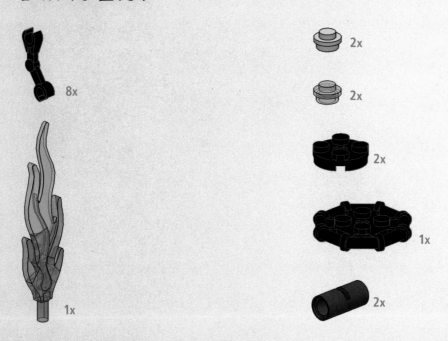

Quantity	Color		Element	Element Name
8		Black	30377	Minifig Mechanical Arm
1		Trans Orange	85959px1	Flame Large Marbled
2		Light Bluish Gray	4073	Plate 1 x 1 Round
2		Trans Orange	4073	Plate 1 x 1 Round
2		Black	4032a	Plate 2 x 2 Round with Axlehole Type 1
1		Black	30033	Plate 2 x 2 with Rod Frame Octagonal
2		Reddish Brown	62462	Technic Pin Joiner Round with Slot

Candlesticks

Y ou also need candlesticks at a banquet, of course. The manacles we have built can be used in several ways, and even the candles and technic pins can be found in several different colors and sizes.

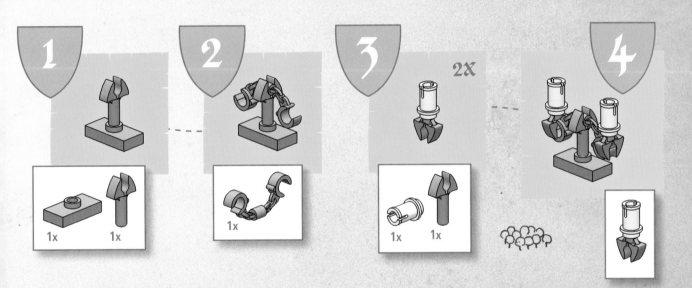

Parts List

Quantity		Color	Element	Element Name
3		Light Bluish Gray	48729	Bar 1.5L with Clip
1		Light Bluish Gray	61482	Minifig Handcuffs
1		Light Bluish Gray	3794a	Plate 1 x 2 without Groove with 1 Centre Stud
2		White	4274	Technic Pin 1/2

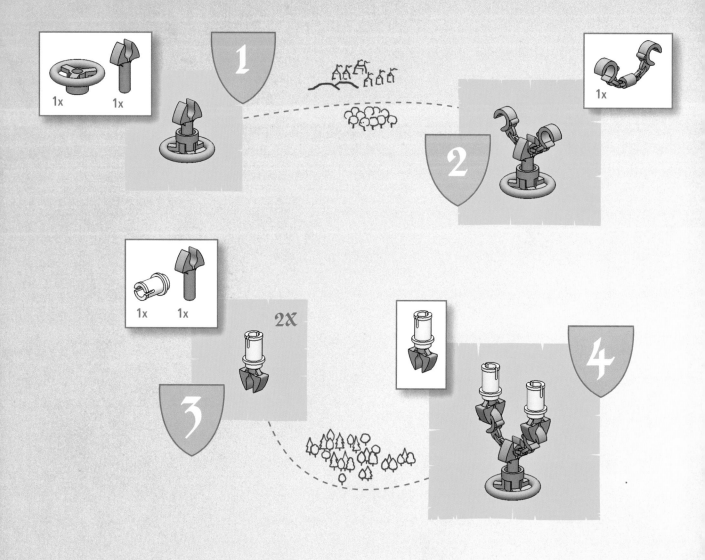

Parts List

 3x

 1x

 1x

 2x

Quantity		Color	Element	Element Name
3		Light Bluish Gray	48729	Bar 1.5L with Clip
1		Light Bluish Gray	30663	Car Steering Wheel Large
1		Light Bluish Gray	61482	Minifig Handcuffs
2		White	4274	Technic Pin 1/2

Crane

With such major port facilities, you also need a loading crane, of course. But the other things you can see pictured are unfortunately too big for us to include in the instructions in this book. Not even 400 pages would be enough for such a ship! But the picture very nicely shows what the many different LEGO® bricks can help you make. For us, it's become a hobby we can't imagine living without. And over time, not only does a LEGO® collection grow; the ability to make things from it also increases. And you don't have to pile things on top of one another – the water, for example, is just scattered in.

1

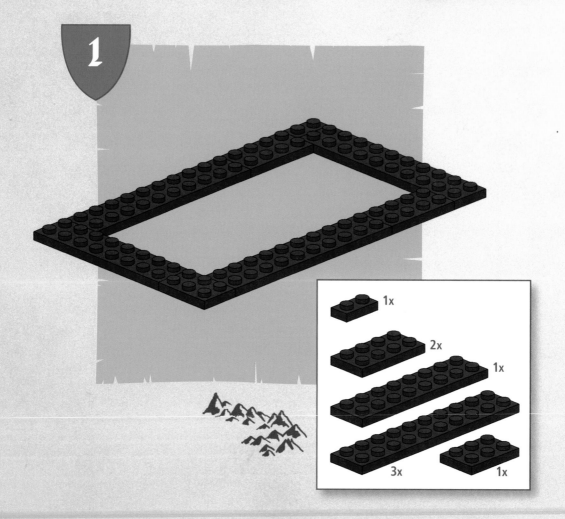

1x

2x

1x

3x

1x

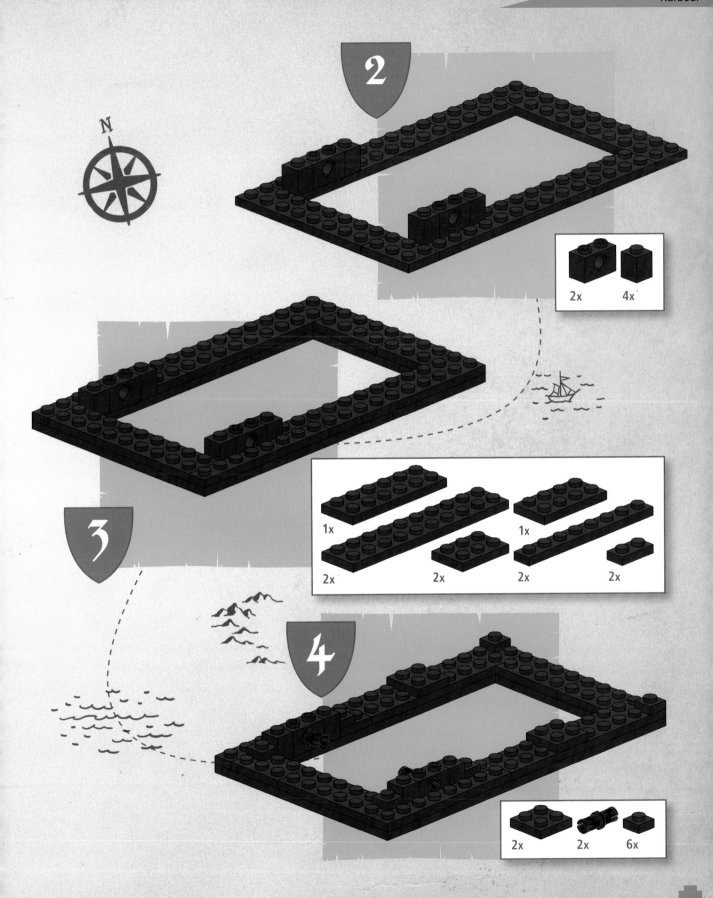

These tiles are with groove, ...

11x

3x

1x

4x

1x

1x

... these are without groove!

5

6

8x

7

1x

6x

2x

1x

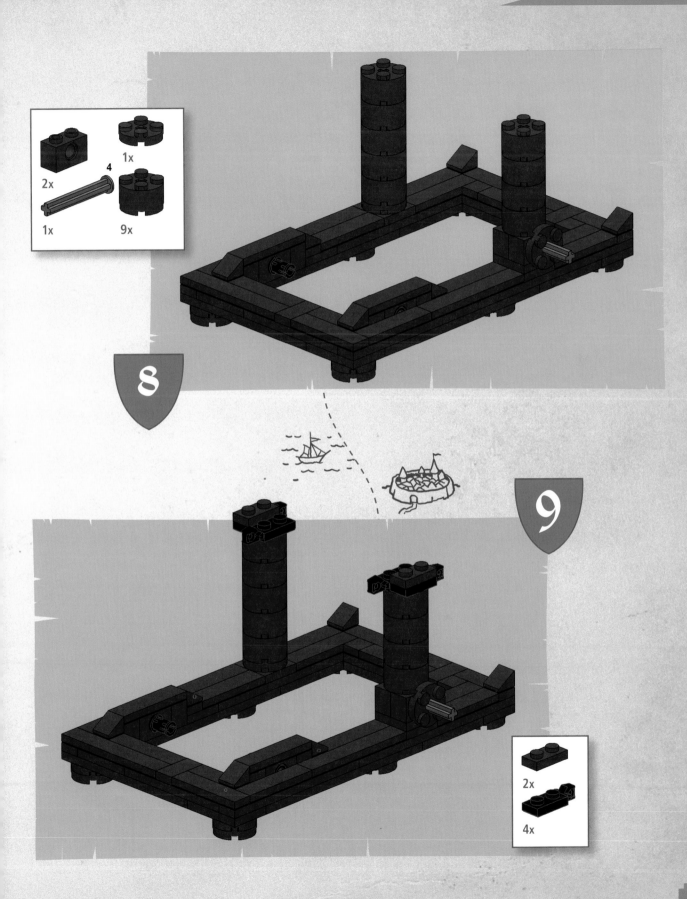

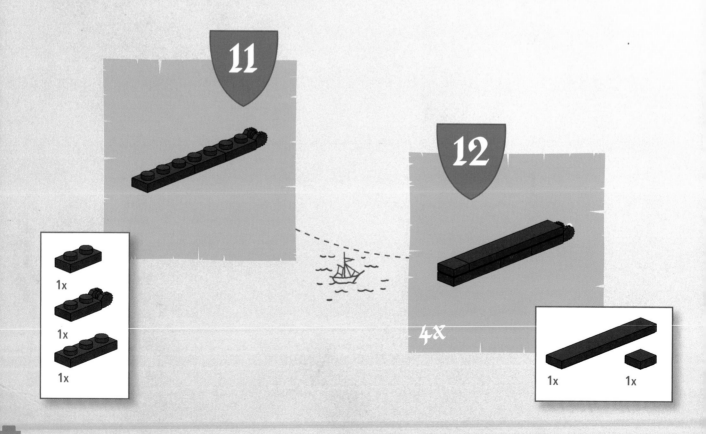

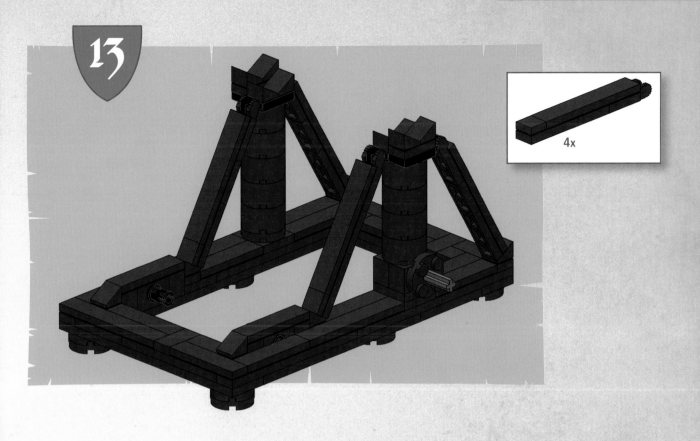

13

4x

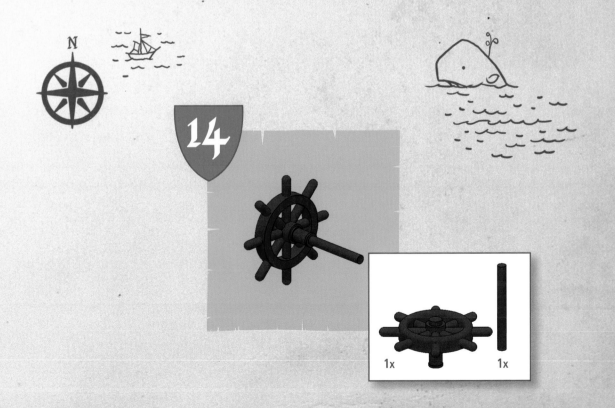

N

14

1x   1x

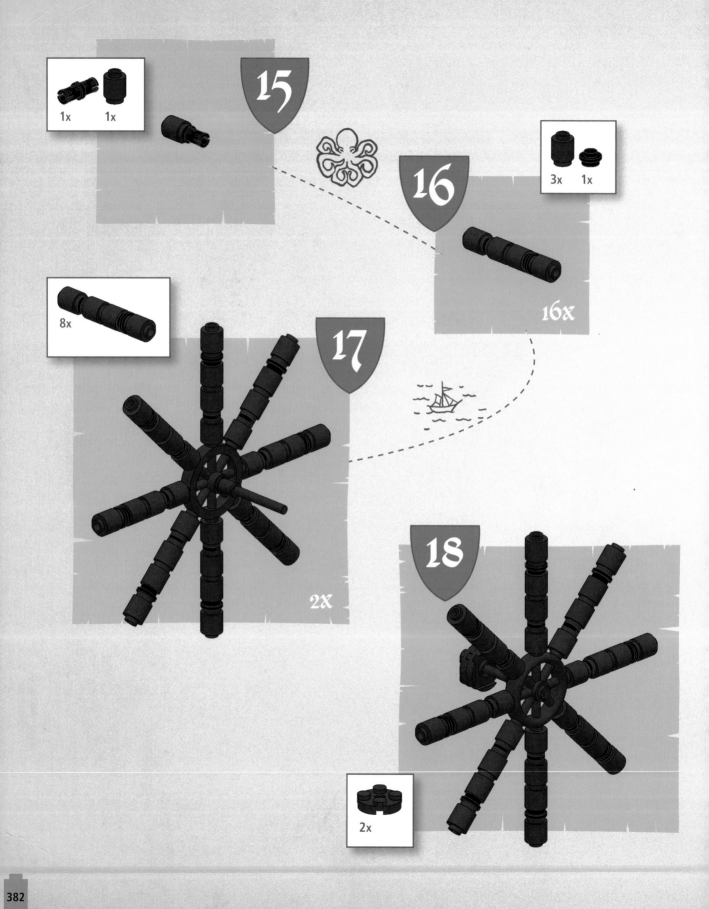

1x 1x

15

16

3x 1x

8x

16x

17

2x

18

2x

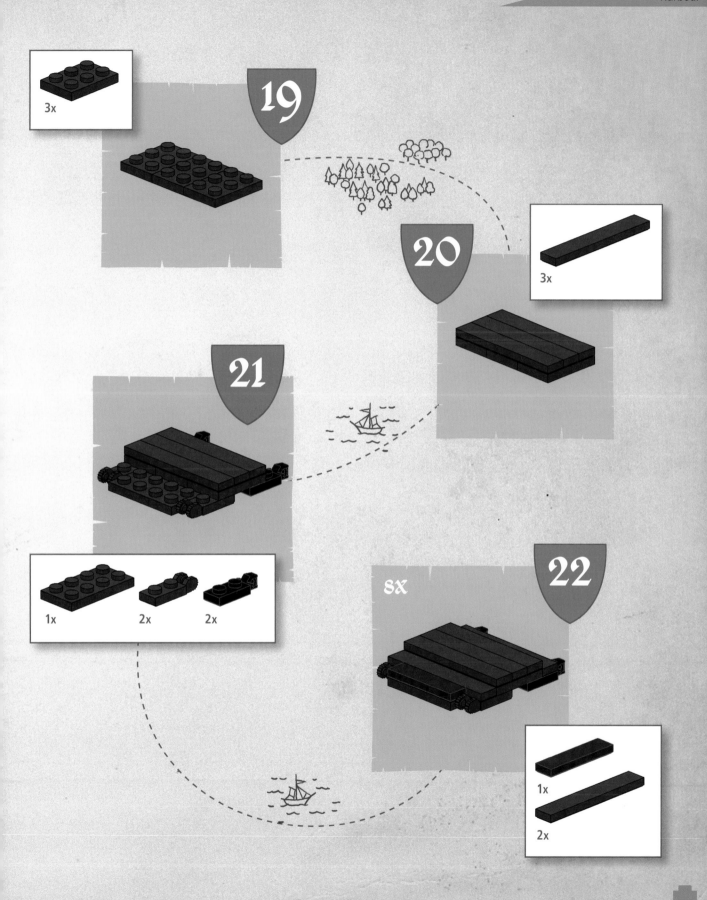

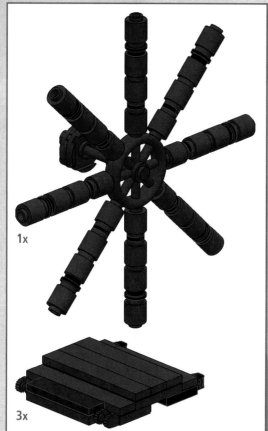

1x

3x

23

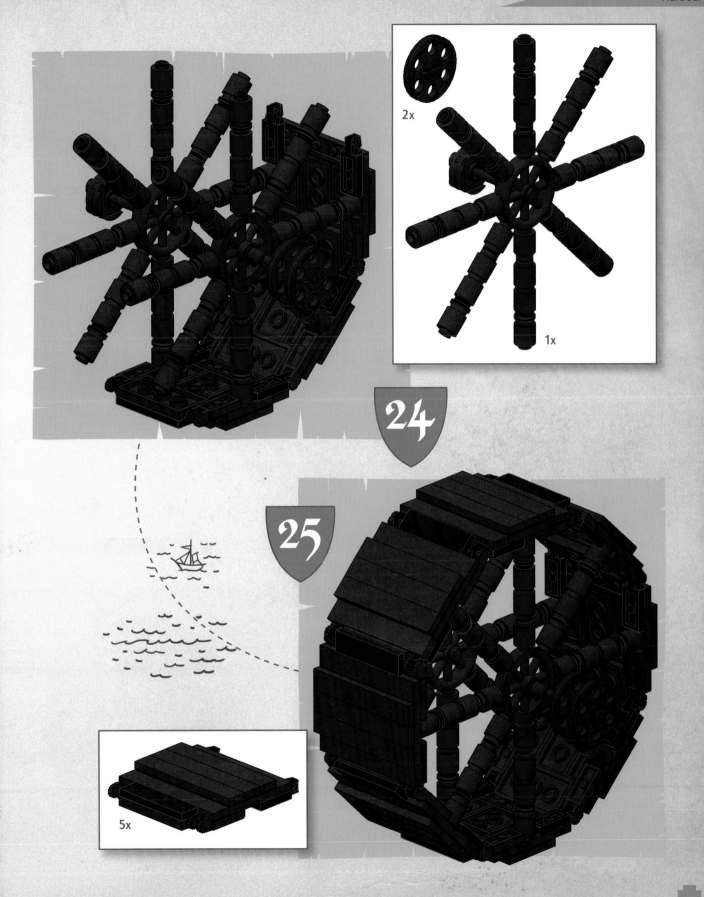

2x

1x

24

25

5x

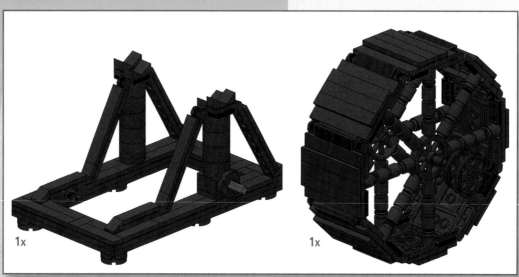

1x

1x

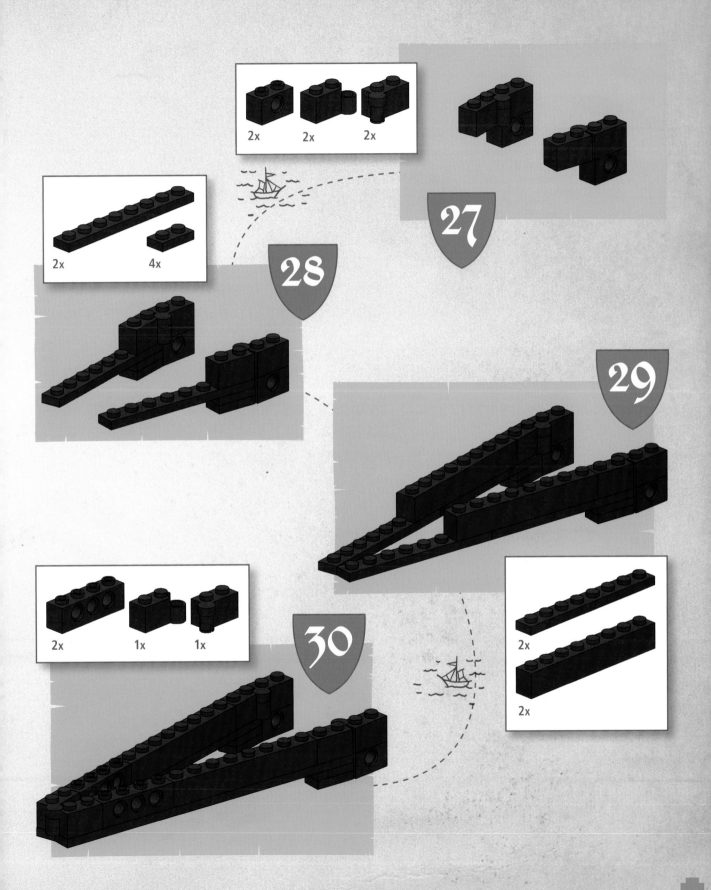

27

28

2x   2x   2x

2x   4x

29

30

2x   1x   1x

2x

2x

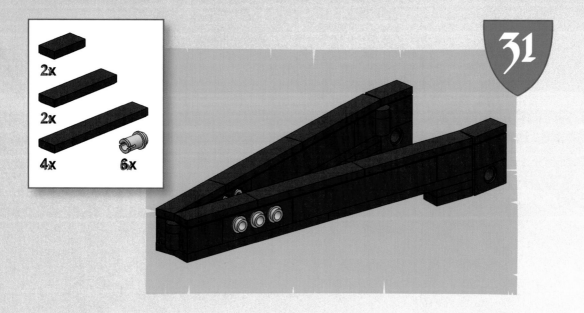

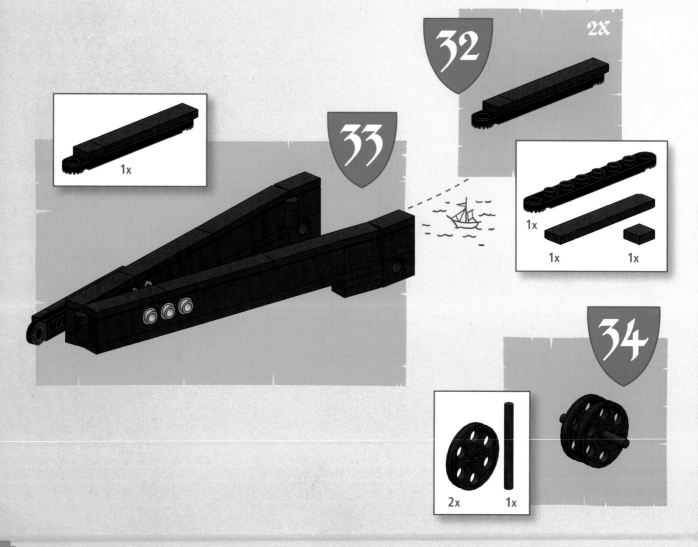

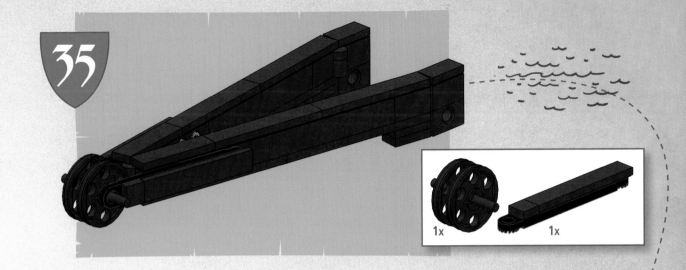

35

36

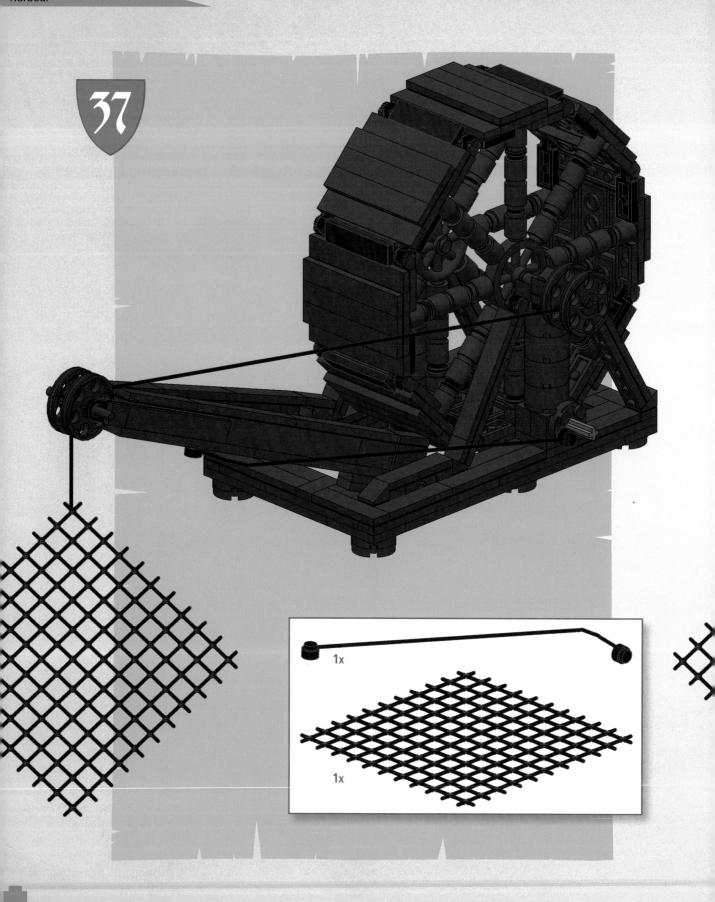

37

1x

1x

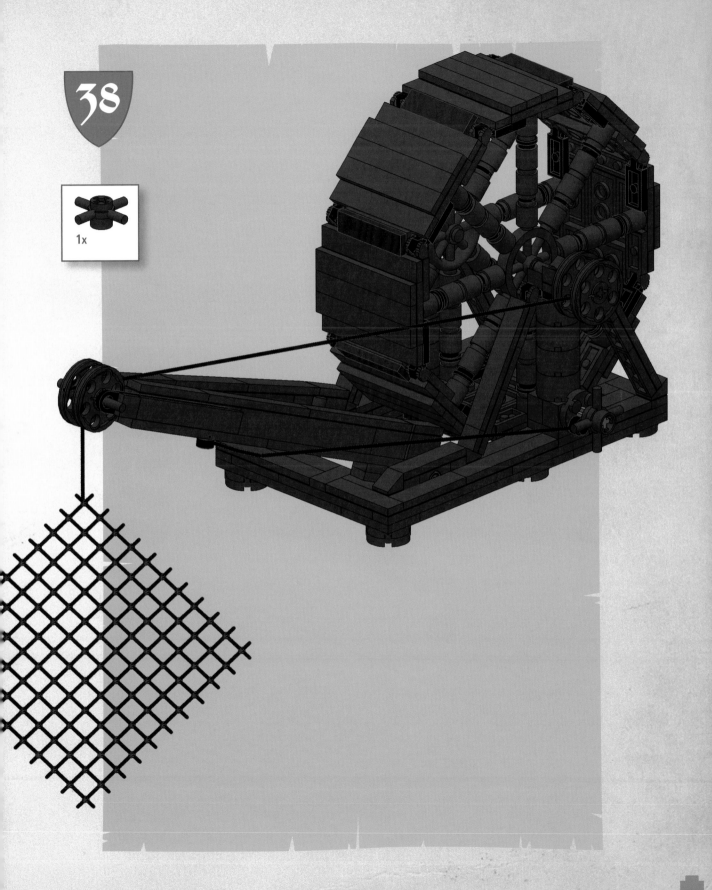

Parts List

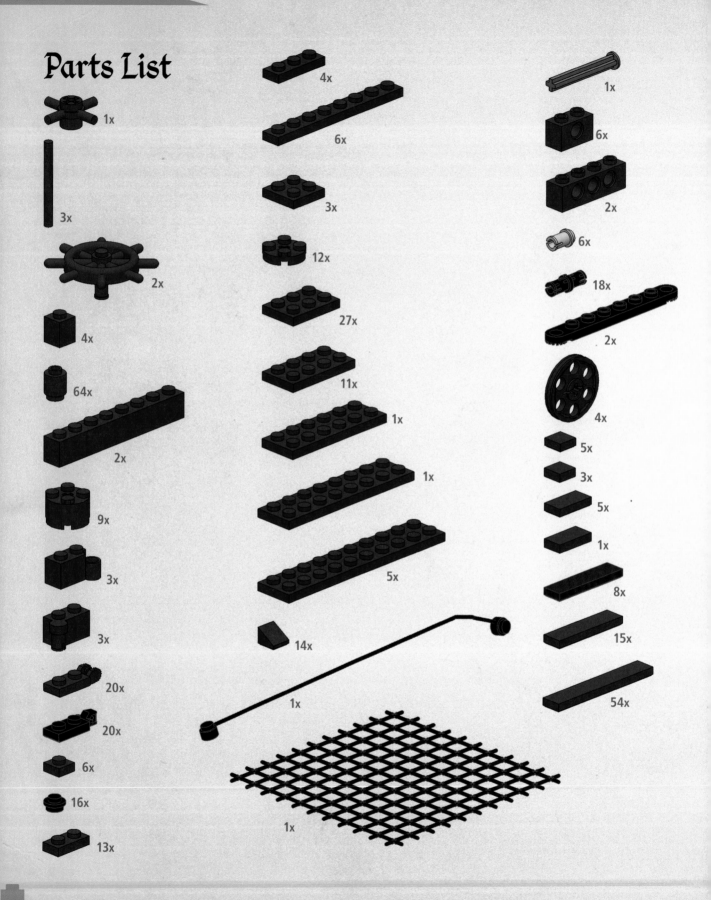

4x

6x

3x

12x

27x

11x

1x

1x

5x

14x

1x

1x

1x

3x

64x

2x

9x

3x

3x

20x

20x

6x

16x

13x

1x

6x

2x

6x

18x

2x

4x

5x

3x

5x

1x

8x

15x

54x

Quantity	Color	Element	Element Name
1	Reddish Brown	48723	Bar 1L Quadruple with Axlehole Hub
3	Reddish Brown	30374	Bar 4L Light Sabre Blade
2	Reddish Brown	4790	Boat Ship Wheel
4	Reddish Brown	3005	Brick 1 x 1
64	Reddish Brown	3062b	Brick 1 x 1 Round with Hollow Stud
2	Reddish Brown	3008	Brick 1 x 8
9	Reddish Brown	3941	Brick 2 x 2 Round
3	Reddish Brown	3831	Hinge Brick 1 x 4 Base
3	Reddish Brown	3830	Hinge Brick 1 x 4 Top
20	Reddish Brown	44302	Hinge Plate 1 x 2 Locking with Dual Finger on End Vertical
20	Black	44301	Hinge Plate 1 x 2 Locking with Single Finger on End Vertical
6	Reddish Brown	3024	Plate 1 x 1
16	Black	4073	Plate 1 x 1 Round
13	Reddish Brown	3023	Plate 1 x 2
4	Reddish Brown	3623	Plate 1 x 3
6	Reddish Brown	3460	Plate 1 x 8
3	Reddish Brown	3022	Plate 2 x 2
12	Reddish Brown	4032a	Plate 2 x 2 Round with Axlehole Type 1
27	Reddish Brown	3021	Plate 2 x 3
11	Reddish Brown	3020	Plate 2 x 4
1	Reddish Brown	3795	Plate 2 x 6
1	Reddish Brown	3034	Plate 2 x 8
5	Reddish Brown	3832	Plate 2 x 10
14	Reddish Brown	54200	Slope Brick 31 1 x 1 x 2/3
1	Black	x127c41	String 41L with End Studs
1	Black		
1	Dark Bluish Gray	87083	Technic Axle 4 with Stop
6	Reddish Brown	3700	Technic Brick 1 x 2 with Hole
2	Reddish Brown	3701	Technic Brick 1 x 4 with Holes
6	Light Bluish Gray	4274	Technic Pin 1/2
18	Black	2780	Technic Pin with Friction and Slots
2	Black	4442	Technic Plate 1 x 8 with Holes
4	Reddish Brown	4185	Technic Wedge Belt Wheel
5	Reddish Brown	3070b	Tile 1 x 1 with Groove
3	Reddish Brown	3070a	Tile 1 x 1 without Groove
5	Reddish Brown	3069b	Tile 1 x 2 with Groove
1	Reddish Brown	3069a	Tile 1 x 2 without Groove
8	Dark Brown	2431	Tile 1 x 4 with Groove
15	Reddish Brown	2431	Tile 1 x 4 with Groove
54	Reddish Brown	6636	Tile 1 x 6

This is what many mediaeval scenes look like these days. Just have a long quiet look: there's so much to learn about the age of chivalry.